HEADSCARF POLITICS IN TURKEY

PREVIOUS PUBLICATIONS

Siyasetin Oyunu [The Game of Politics] (2008)
Ortunun Altinda Kalanlar [Hidden Under the Veil] (2008)
Bati'da Musluman Olmak [To Be Muslim in the West] (2008)
Dunyanin Guzel Insanlari [Beautiful People of the Earth] (2008)
Basortusuz Demokrasi [Scarfless Democracy] (2004, trans. to: Arabic and Persian)

HEADSCARF POLITICS IN TURKEY

A POSTCOLONIAL READING

Merve Kavakci

Foreword by John L. Esposito
and
Afterword by Lord Eric Avebury

palgrave
macmillan

HEADSCARF POLITICS IN TURKEY

First published in hardcover in 2010 by PALGRAVE MACMILLAN® in the United States—a division of St. Martin's Press LLC, 175 Fifth Avenue, New York, NY 10010.

Where this book is distributed in the UK, Europe and the rest of the world, this is by Palgrave Macmillan, a division of Macmillan Publishers Limited, registered in England, company number 785998, of Houndmills, Basingstoke, Hampshire RG21 6XS.

Palgrave Macmillan is the global academic imprint of the above companies and has companies and representatives throughout the world.

ISBN: 978–1–137–48473–4

The Library of Congress has cataloged the hardcover edition as follows:

Kavakçi, Merve.
Headscarf politics in Turkey : a postcolonial reading / Merve Kavakci ; foreword by John L. Esposito and afterword by Lord Eric Avebury.
p. cm.
ISBN 978–0–230–10665–9 (hardback)
1. Hijab (Islamic clothing)—Turkey. 2. Hijab (Islamic clothing)—Law and legislation—Turkey. 3. Muslim women—Clothing—Turkey. 4. Islam and politics—Turkey. I. Title.

HQ1726.7.K38 2010
305.48'894350090511—dc22 2010013863

A catalogue record of the book is available from the British Library.

Design by Newgen Knowledge Works (P) Ltd., Chennai, India.

First PALGRAVE MACMILLAN paperback edition: November 2014

10 9 8 7 6 5 4 3 2 1

To her;
who cared,
fed,
smiled,
and left;
My grandma.

CONTENTS

FIGURES

ACKNOWLEDGMENTS

I am grateful to Dr. Mervat Hatem, Dr. Jane Flax, Dr. John Cotman, and Dr. Sulayman Nyang for their support, guidance, and encouragement during my research. I am indebted to Dr. Nyang for sharing his invaluable insights and helping me find my niche in Washington, D.C. to pursue my academic aspirations. In fact, one day in late Spring 2004, during a meeting at his office, the very first seeds of this process were inadvertently planted that eventually led to the production of this book. Dr. Flax and Dr. Cotman, both beacons of their field, walked me through the worlds of political theory and comparative political analysis respectively, guiding me through the plethora of knowledge on a wide range of issues from rights dilemmas to challenges of nation-state building. In this process, last but not least, I am grateful to Dr. Mervat Hatem, who was my immediate advisor. She was my teacher, my mentor, my senior colleague, and my guide who walked with me every step of the way that led to this day. Without her assistance I could not have produced this book. I also thank Dr. Zahid Bukhari for providing his constructive critique at the end of my research.

I am thankful to Dr. John Esposito for writing the foreword for this work, my first book in English. To have received his support, as a luminary in many of the areas covered here, is an invaluable contribution. I am grateful to Lord Eric Avebury for writing the afterword. His contribution as someone who is known for his commitment to empowerment of the disenfranchised, the minorities, and women all around the world is indispensible. I am thankful to Ambassador Swanee Hunt, an academic and ex-politician like myself, for her support throughout the years. She encouraged me, a former student of hers, to continue to stand up for what I believed in and always to remember that nothing is impossible. I am elated that she spared the time to read the manuscript and shared her thoughts in a blurb. To Dr. Noam Chomsky, a legend in the world of academia and more so in the empirical world of human rights and civil liberties, as a former teaching fellow of his, I pay my heartfelt appreciation for offering his comments in the blurb. I cannot take his contribution for granted. I am thankful to Dr. Ümit Cizre for her support through her constructive comments. To have received her endorsment is a great honor in of itself. I also thank Richard Peres for his assistance in the editing process of the manuscript and the creation of the index.

In addition to the strength I received in the academic world through the contributions of the aforementioned luminaries, I am also surrounded by a familial support group that deserves recognition and to share the fruits of my endeavor. I am indebted to my parents—my mother who is my role model and my father who has always been there for me, listened to my naggings, and responded with a glimpse of hope and a smile. As usual Ravza, was instrumental to ensure that the deadlines were met without respite during the publication preparation process. Elif, shared most of my motherhood responsibilities and managed the background. I am grateful for their sisterhood support. My special thanks belong to my daughters, the light of my life, Fatima and Mariam, for being who they are and for being mature and patient enough to support their mom on this strenuous road. Without them, I would not be where I am.

Alhamdulillahi Rabb- al-Alemin (praise be to the Owner of the universe) for situating me at the right institution, among the right people, and increasing my knowledge.

MERVE KAVAKCI
February 28, 2010,
Washington, D.C.

FOREWORD

John L. Esposito

The veil, or hijab, has been a symbol of faith and freedom for many women, but also a symbol of oppression and gender inequality as well as the object of politics and power. In recent years, the emergence of Islamic political and social movements, sometimes indiscriminately conflated under the term "Islamic fundamentalism," has led two secular countries as diverse as France and Turkey to demonstrate the anti-religious character of their unique brand of secularism and the extent to which many establishment elites' almost paranoid fear of Islam is driven by their "secular fundamentalism." The net result has been their shared perception of the hijab as a dangerous political symbol, which has led to its banning in certain government contexts.

An appreciation of Turkey today requires an understanding of the emergence of modern Turkey and the place of Islam in Atatürk's policies. The post-independence period witnessed the emergence of modern Muslim states whose pattern of development was heavily influenced by and indebted to Western secular paradigms or models. Saudi Arabia and Turkey reflected the two polar positions. Saudi Arabia was established as a self-proclaimed Islamic state based upon the *Shari'ah* (Islamic law). At the opposite end of the spectrum, Atatürk (Mustafa Kamal) created a secular Turkish republic. The vestiges of the Ottoman Empire—the caliph/sultan and its institutions, the *Shari'ah*, Islamic institutions, and schools—were replaced by European-inspired political, legal, and educational systems.

Turkey provided the secular paradigm for those who viewed with alarm the resurgence of Islam in Muslim politics and society. Whatever seemed to be happening in other parts of the world, pundits agreed that Turkish secularism was immune from the "threat" of political Islam. Indeed, with the breakup of the Soviet Union, many, fearing the Islamic influences of Iran, Saudi Arabia, or Pakistan and the dangers of Islamic activism in the newly independent Central Asian states, advocated the Turkish secular model, sometimes referred to as "Muslim secularism" or "secular Islam."

Two factors seemed to preclude Turkey's being swept up by the Islamic wave that seemed to be moving across much of the Middle East and broader Muslim world: (1) the revered memory and legacy of Atatürk (1881–1938) with its strong secular (laic) tradition and institutions and (2) the self-proclaimed role of the army as the "guardian of the secular republic," defenders of the secular ideology and stability of the state. To the astonishment of many in Turkey and in the West, in 1996, secular Turkey had its first Islamist prime minister, Dr. Necmeddin Erbakan. More than 28 cities had elected Islamist mayors in elections in which the Welfare (Refah) Party, an Islamic party, garnered up to 21 percent of the vote. By 1997, Erbakan had been forced out of office by the Turkish military, the so-called defenders of Atatürk's legacy and its secular state. The military and secular political and social establishment's understanding of secularism was and is not simply about separation of church and state but in fact a "secular fundamentalism" that saw religion as a threat, a source of backwardness, and an obstacle to modernization, and feared that Islamists had a hidden agenda to create an Islamic republic. For hardline secularists, the hijab became a symbol of the "Islamist threat," as women wearing forms of Islamic dress became more widespread and visible in major cities and urban areas like Istanbul.

Kemalism's singular definition of modernity had imposed a model of the modern Turkish woman and banned the headscarf in government and educational institutions. Secular elites' fear of Islam was dramatically reflected in their charge that a Muslim government and the loosening of restrictions on wearing the hijab would result in all Turkish women being forced to wear a headscarf. Their concerns glossed over the status quo ban on the headscarf as a violation of human rights: Turkish women who wear the hijab are banned from serving in parliament, from entering or working in government buildings, and from attending university. In a celebrated case, Merve Kavakci, the author of this excellent study who was elected to parliament in 1999, was prevented from taking the parliamentary oath because of her hijab She was subsequently stripped of her Turkish citizenship on the pretext that she had not disclosed her United States citizenship.

In 2001, key leaders of the former Welfare Party established the Justice and Development Party (*AKP*). Though its founders, Recep Tayyip Erdoğan (prime minister) and Abdullah Gül (foreign minister and now president of Turkey), were key figures in the Islamic Welfare Party and its successor, the Virtue Party, the *AKP* chose to create a more reformist and inclusive pluralistic (non-Islamic) party that was Turkish, Muslim, and Western in orientation, with a strong emphasis on economic development and social conservatism. The *AKP* is a moderate party that advocates a liberal market economy and Turkey's membership in the European Union. Its history and performance demonstrate that the realities of politics can lead former Islamists to learn from experience, broaden their vision, adapt to multiple constituencies, and govern effectively.

The *AKP* won a landslide victory in the 2002 elections. Of the eighteen political parties that competed for seats in the parliament, only two obtained 10 percent of the nationwide vote in order to seat representatives in the assembly. The *AKP* won 34.26 percent of the popular vote and 363 of the 550 seats in parliament, while the long-established Republican People's Party won only 19.4 percent of the votes. In July 2007, PM Erdoğan was reelected with a stunning victory in which the *AKP* took 47 percent of the vote. The *AKP*'s electoral victories in Turkey are especially remarkable in that it won a parliamentary majority in a Muslim country long regarded as a symbol of secularism in the Middle East.

The *AKP*-led government has proven more successful than its predecessors internationally, working with Europe on Turkey's admission to the EU and other shared concerns involving the United States and Muslim countries, while still upholding Turkey's independence. Domestically, fears expressed by the military and secular opposition that *AKP* would create an "Islamically oriented" or Islamist government have proven unfounded. The *AKP* leadership has reaffirmed its commitment to Turkish secularism. However, their notion of secularism—separation of state and institutional religion—contrasts strongly with hard-line secularists' anti-religious approach.

An even more glaring example occurred when the *AKP* came to power. The wives of the prime minister and of the majority of cabinet and parliament members were unable to attend an annual reception given by the "secular-oriented" president of Turkey because they wore headscarves. Moreover, the prime minister's daughters could not attend university in Turkey because of their headscarves; instead, they studied in the United States.

Women's dress remains a contentious issue in Turkey, symbolizing an alternative moral/social order that many Muslim women seek within modern secular Turkish society. The choice is not seen so much as one between Islam and modernity or Islam and secularism as it is an effort to define an alternative Islamically informed model for being a modern Turkish woman, to build an Islamic way of life within a secular order. Many Islamically oriented women embody their own brand of "feminism," wishing to liberate women from the constraints of patriarchal society and an excessive dependence on Western cultural norms and to redefine the role of women so as to combine their central role in the family with the right to education, employment, and political activism. Because the status and role of Muslim women remains not merely a religious question but a significant political and social issue, Merve Kavakci's *Headscarf Politics in Turkey*, which combines both her impressive scholarship and draws on her personal experience, is essential reading.

ABBREVIATIONS OF POLITICAL PARTIES IN THE STUDY

ANAP	Motherland Party
AKP	Justice and Development Party
AP	Justice Party
CHP	Republican People's Party
DP	Democrat Party
DSP	Democratic Left Party
DYP	True Path Party
FP	Virtue Party
MHP	Nationalist Movement Party
MNP	National Order Party
MSP	National Salvation Party
RP	Welfare Party
SHP	Social Democratic Populist Party
SP	Felicity Party

CHRONOLOGY OF SIGNIFICANT EVENTS

1876	First constitutional period
1908	Second constitutional period (Constitutional Revolution)
1912	First Balkan War
1913	Second Balkan War
1914	World War I
1918	Outset of *Milli Mücadele* (National Struggle—War of Independence)
April 23, 1920	Opening of Turkish Grand National Assembly
1922	Revocation of sultanate
October 29, 1923	Establishment of the Turkish Republic
1924	Revocation of caliphate
	Reform in education
	Closure of religious educational institutions
1925	Passage of Hat Law
	Acceptance of Christian calendar
	Passage of Swiss civil code
	Acceptance of Latin alphabet
	"Islam" removed from the constitution
1930	Women granted the right to elect and be elected in local elections
1934	Women granted the right to elect and be elected in general elections
1937	Secularism adopted officially
1938	Death of Atatürk
1946	Passage to multi-party system
1960	Military coup
1980	Military coup
1981	Banning of the headscarf for public servants and university students
1997	Post-modern coup

CHAPTER 1

INTRODUCTION

This book is the product of a long journey. It is a journey that has been shared by thousands, if not millions, since 1981. It is my own journey as well, the one that took me as a junior politician, a software engineer, a political activist and transformed me into a social scientist, an academic with a critical eye. It is a journey that changed me from one who talks (a prevalent trait of politicians independent of their national and cultural origins) and often propagates, to one who observes, writes, and produces knowledge through objective analytical thinking.

At the core of this book is the research I have conducted for my doctoral dissertation. The aspiration behind the production of this multifaceted work, however, was not strictly attributable to academic fervor. First, it was academically savvy to explore an area of research that contributes to the existing literature of Middle East political science, women's studies, and Turkish studies by probing what can be described as a nascent and recently developing phenomenon of headscarved women. Headscarved women are now a key part of both the global and national discourses. In the global context, women with headscarves are intrinsic to the debate that is known as the discourse of Islam and democracy's compatibility. Women of Islam—their rights, their dress, their place in the public realm—are an indispensable part of that debate. At the national level, they are part of the local political discourse with respect to the concepts of nationalism, citizenship, empowerment, and development, from France, Denmark, Norway, and Germany, to Tunisia, Egypt, Iran, Malaysia, Turkey, and so on. This is to say, Muslim women are part of a lively current debate across the globe. There is an audience that is curious to know who these women are, what they do, and how they are represented. Although women of the Orient have long been of interest to the peoples of the Occident (with endless material produced about them), these women were invariably presented through the monotonal voice of the Orientalist from a position of outside authority. Here the reader will hear, for a change, the insiders' voices from within the Orient, the voices of the contemporary Turkish women who cover willingly and, yes, decisively. Therefore, as Professor Mervat Hatem, a luminary in her field, termed it when she effervescently reacted to my potential dissertation research topic, I want to share this "gold nugget!" with you: the paradox of Turkey's role-model status and its treatment of headscarved women.

Scholarship aside, I also had a moral responsibility that came with the weight put on my shoulders because of who I am, as one of the aforementioned thousands, if not millions of women with headscarves who paved my path toward this work with their limitless courage. Their journey is mine; and mine is theirs. We are all very different and yet very much the same, sharing an uncanny similar trajectory of experiences in fate.

I have also taken part in some of the most widely followed cases regarding women with headscarves and their quest for religious freedom. The most apt way to describe my place in the headscarf debate is to confess that I come from a family whose experiences have shaped my life through this debate. I witnessed my mother, an academic, pay a severe price for wearing a headscarf. My father, also an academic, suffered because he defended the rights of women with headscarves. What my mother experienced as a member of the faculty, a lecturer at the department of German literature of the School of Arts and Sciences at Atatürk University in Erzurum in the early 1980s, repeated itself later. This time I replaced my mother as the protagonist, trying to find a way to reconcile my beliefs with my studies at the Medical School of Ankara University where I was a student. Right there and then, my parents, to the chagrin and awe of all their friends and family, took a bold step and left Turkey for the United States to provide educational opportunity for their daughters without having to compromise religious obligations—for many at that time, this was an unfathomable step. Little did they know that years later I would follow in their footsteps for the very same reason.

My direct involvement in the headscarf debate dates to a later time in my life though. My experience became identified as the *Kavakci Affair* in Turkey's political history. Many academics all over the world studied, presented, and wrote about it. After my successful election by the first district in Istanbul, I entered the Turkish parliament to be sworn in on May 2, 1999. I was jeered for forty-five minutes, accused by the president, the prime minister, and the military of Turkey of being a threat to the secular state, prevented from taking my oath of office, attacked by the press, stripped of my Turkish citizenship, and forced to leave my country after the closure of the party and ensuing ban on my political activities for five years by the constitutional court.

The vicissitude became a defining moment in my life, bringing me to a crossroad between my past profession and the present one. I decided to take the incident as inspiration to engage in the world of academia and probe the theoretical basis of Turkey's treatment of women with headscarves and how its concern with legitimization produced and reproduced the denial of citizenship rights and basic universal human rights of a sizable group of Turkish women on the basis of dress.

Freshly out of political life, ruminating over what happened, how, and why, I stepped into the academic arena for the first time. Until then, I had worn my politician hat (or rather the headscarf!), but from that moment on I took it off and replaced it with an "academician headscarf." With the guidance of beacons in their fields such as Mervat Hatem, the president of Middle East Studies Association, Jane Flax, John Cotman, and Sulayman Nyang, I shed the rhetoric and partisanship that mired my critical thinking to embrace academic rigor and analytical tools to explicate certain political behavior.

The objective of this work is to provide the reader with a general history of the politics of dress in the Turkish Republic and the small role that I played in that history. Although the reader might expect me to be polemical and subjective, my account is neither partisan nor one-sided. On the contrary, I bend over backwards to understand all arguments shaping the complexities of this particular history. I do that by remaining at equal distance to both the secular and the religious, offering a critical assessment of both for having failed the headscarved women. I probe the similarities and the differences between the two and the proximity in their behavior toward this particular group of women.

What this book, unlike others produced in the same field, does is to offer the reader an exclusive insider's view of the emotional weight put on the headscarved women who were coerced to make life-altering decisions for themselves and for others surrounding them. My "front row experience" uniquely allows me to explore the intricacies of Islamist politics and its political and life-changing implications for today's modern Muslim women. I play a dual role of author and protagonist, as I shaped some of the history of this issue. I am both a woman with a headscarf and an academic who studies women with headscarves. I have maintained factual correctness in this discussion, but this does not necessarily stretch into emotional correctness, for I continue to hold my particular position. This book does not only include political analysis but it conveys the personal toll and the impact of politics in quotidian terms. That is exactly the value-added characteristic of this book compared to the existing literature. No other work can cover the issue in this way.

Western and Turkish secular intellectuals treat Turkey as an example for the Muslim world because of its commitment to modernization. They particularly laud secularism as the underlying reason for the creation of a "westernized" (and therefore "modernized") Turkey. They point to the Turkish model of separation of state and religion rendering Turkey a role model for other states in the region with Muslim populations. This book questions the role-model status of Turkey with respect to the advancement of female agency in the secular context with a specific reference to its treatment of women with headscarves, who are called *başörtülü kadınlar.* Central to this project is a rigorous exploration of the system of representation produced by the state that puts women with headscarves against modern Turkish women who do not cover their heads. The evaluation of this historical construction and its deconstruction is one of the important goals of this study. By achieving that, the work poses a critical challenge to the ubiquitous argument that Turkey has kept its promise to Turkish women in general by granting them empowerment through its modernization project. Intrinsic to this process is the examination of secularism, not as the guarantor of religious expression but rather as a means of sequestering religion by questioning the definition of the secular character of the state, which is instrumental in denying the citizenship rights of *başörtülü kadınlar.* The treatment of these women by the state shows the internalization of Orientalist ideals that contradict the goal of the Turkish Republic's progressive aspirations with respect to women.

The Pride of the Republic: *Laiklik*

Secularism, which is known to Turks as *laiklik*, lies at the center of modern Turkey's state edifice. One of the most recent salient manifestations of *laiklik* is the ban on women's headscarves in the public sphere, which was introduced in 1981. The republic's promise to Turkish women is to empower them through the modernization project it has espoused and to equip them with the values of the "civilized" and "modernized" world. Women were put in the center of this national project. In other words, women's social, political, and economic liberation became the yardstick of the success of Turkish modernization. Yet as *başörtülü kadınlar* became more visible in the public realm starting in the early 1980s, the Turkish Republic began to perceive them as defying the modernization process. The state banned the headscarf at government facilities and universities. This left many observant Muslim women at a crossroad. They could either cave in to the ban and become objects and beneficiaries of modernization offered by the Turkish Republic, or hold on to their beliefs, which would be used to deny them inclusion, and pay a price for their resistance.

The republican system of representations devalues the religious Turkish women (*başörtülü kadınlar*, who, in order to meet the ideals of the Turkish Republic, needed to be liberated in the 1920s) and privileges the "modern" Turkish women whom the republic intended to be its full citizens. The oppositional binary created between these two groupings of women poses a serious obstacle in the Turkish Republic's attempt to implement its progressive female agenda and attests to the inconsistencies of the Turkish modernization project.

Alternative Readings of Turkish Modernization

Turkish women were made instrumental in the reinvention of the national identity. Efforts to improve women's status were used as a means to cultivate Turkish nationalism and adopt Western notions of equality and secularism.[1] Women were granted full citizenship rights along with men through the replacement of the Islamic civil code with the Swiss secular code.

These reforms were lauded by the students of the region and those in the West as "yet to be matched for Muslims anywhere."[2] Modern Turkey was believed to have what neighboring states did not have.[3] Therefore for the better part of the twentieth century, the Turkish experiment was held as a model for Islamic societies in the study of Middle East women's studies. Recently, critics have emerged arguing that the Turkish Republic has fallen short of its promises to its female constituency, but the critics blamed it on incomplete modernization.

In this book, I employ alternative theoretical explanations for the problems facing religious women in the secular Turkish Republic by employing Orientalism, postcolonialism, and paradox of rights. Orientalism is used to delineate the construction of opposing systems of representation of the religious Turkish women who wear headscarves as an "other" to the "modern" Turkish women. Postcolonialism is employed to critique and deconstruct those systems of representation typically associated with the colonial condition. World War I and the threat of occupation contributed to a mindset associated with the threat and reaction to it. Finally, the language of rights discourse is used to explain the state's response to the treatment of *başörtülü kadınlar*.

As Orientalism points to the distinction between the Orient and the Occident, which is reified into a hierarchy rendering the latter hegemonic, the "positional superiority" puts the "Westerner in a whole series of possible relationships with the Orient without ever losing him the relative upper hand."[4] The Turkish Republic's approach to *başörtülü kadınlar* embraces an Orientalist's attitude to these women in a similar way. The former represents the superiority of the European ideals while the latter represents the non-European, unenlightened face of the Orient represented by an Islamic society.

Of particular relevance in this context is the Western perception of the Oriental women. Contemporary discourse, including that of the Turks', on veiled or headscarved women stresses the need to liberate them from this symbol of oppression. It is important to point out here that the Occident, from the outset, failed to see women of Islam for who they are and—as in the case of everything else pertinent to the Orient—created its own "Orientalized" Muslim woman. These constructions were less based on the reality that Muslim women presented than their presumed ahistorical relation to their Western counterparts. This is not to deny the fact that Muslim women faced challenges in the past and continue to face challenges today. The category "Oriental woman" presents that group in an ahistorical and undifferentiated way. It does not discuss the changing specificities of the societies within which they live. For instance, some of the challenges that Muslim women face are cultural and some are developmental. Some are due to the parochial and patriarchal interpretation of the divine scripture by scholars. Some Muslim women face more challenges than others. Some are more empowered than others. Some are more liberated than others. Nonetheless, in the eyes of the Orientalist there is an unchanging, homogeneous Muslim woman. She is a constant and, in Said's terms, is awaiting rescue by her Orientalist saviors. In the same way, the unchanging, homogeneous group of *başörtülü kadınlar*, represented as in dire need of liberation, is waiting to be rescued by the Turkish Republic from the trappings of their religion.

The treatment of these women by the Turkish Republic is also well explicated by the prism of postcolonialism. Postcolonialism sees the political, social, and cultural practices that the Orient today suffers from as, to an extent, the result of the preservation of the colonial heritage via the power of its system of representation by contemporary neo-colonizers within. At independence, Western presuppositions are bequeathed to and embraced by a native group who makes up the new intelligentsia.[5] This leads to not only the survival but occasionally the thriving of colonial traditions in postcolonial states in internalized and externalized forms.

The Turkish Republic represents an interesting example of this conjuncture. Turks, as the descendents of the Ottoman Empire, did not experience colonization in their past. Their passage from the empire to the republic involved a resistance against the British, French, Greeks, and Italians who attempted to partition and colonize the country following World War I. The defiance against potential colonial forces and the transformation into republicanism occurred in tandem. The context was delineated as a religious Islamic war against the West. Nonetheless the emerging republic, under the leadership of an intelligentsia that was both an admirer of the West and instrumental in founding the new Turkish state, adopted a westernization project whose underlying premise was the superiority of the West and its values. Thus while the Turks never lived under colonial conditions, the leaders of the Turkish Republic intellectually embraced an attitude of westernization that was colonial-like in their relationship with the majority of the population.

Postcolonial theory, which is often employed to explicate the predicaments of internally colonized cultures and groups within the developed world such as that of the African Americans, the Scottish, and the Irish,[6] is extended to address the question of *başörtülü kadınlar* in Turkey who are forcefully westernized by the Turkish Republic as part of the national desire to be developed.

The theory sheds light on the "epistemic, ideological, and political authority of Western and elite knowledge"[7] coercively used in the construction of Turkish female identity to preserve Western ideals' domination over those emanating from the Islamic Turkish culture. It examines how knowledge about *başörtülü kadınlar* is produced through the modernizing efforts of the Turkish Republic and how the republic creates and subsequently validates its own insecurities in its dealings with *başörtülü kadınlar*. The republic's uncompromising stance on *başörtülü kadınlar* entails their marginalization. Knowledge produced by the state concerning these women is incorporated in policies that ensure their devaluation, which is then presented as a consequence of their religiosity. This is disseminated throughout the society, becoming quasi-legitimized as it is reproduced time and again until it is firmly consolidated. At the end, the republic's control over the system of representation of *başörtülü kadınlar* makes them products of a state power.

This power is an example of, in Foucault's terms, "impersonal force," which operates on these women transforming themselves into somebody other than who they are: women striving to go about their daily businesses in a modern society while adhering to their religious convictions. Refusing to see *başörtülü kadınlar* in the way they construct themselves and divorcing them from their identities in the public eye enables the republic to transform them through a re-forming process. Afterward through the process of categorization under various rubrics of representation such as reactionaries, intruders, political opportunists, brainwashed, subordinates, peace-breakers, and the like, *başörtülü kadınlar* become ready for academic and political consumption as the objects of inquiry. They would by then be processed in the state machinery reflecting the implications of, in Frantz Fanon's term, "de-cerebralization" demonstrated by the distance between how *başörtülü kadınlar* see themselves and the image they are coerced to carry in the public realm.[8] As the objects of study, these women are to be followed to the university gates with cameras in hand only to be recorded while having to take off their scarves or put on their wigs in celebration of the secular Turkish Republic's victory to westernize them. Their suffering is generally overlooked and only highlighted by a few media outlets.

Young's view of Orientalist–Oriental divide resonates with a similar divide one sees between the Turkish intelligentsia, who are proponents of the headscarf ban, and *başörtülü kadınlar.*

> When western people look at the non-western world, what they see is often more a mirror image of themselves and their own assumptions than the reality of what is really there, or of how people outside the west actually feel and perceive themselves.[9]

The arguments of the Turkish elite vis-à-vis the plight of *başörtülü kadınlar* would invariably be predicated upon their own circumscribed personal experiences, thoughts, and convictions. In political circles and intellectual discussions, the intelligentsia would very often start by stating what has become a cliché: "My grandmother also wears a scarf, but ..." or "I am a Muslim too, but ..." to legitimize the treatment of *başörtülü kadınlar.* The place that the headscarf assumes in their lives as their grandmother's headscarf limits their ability to see it as a right for other women who are not necessarily "grandmothers." The elite can only concede to or tolerate the headscarf within the specified familiar contexts (i.e., the scarf of a grandmother who is expected to be a homemaker or a female farmer and the maid—both of whom represent the lower social and economic classes of the society). Parochial perception and conservative thinking are characteristics of this mindset. At other occasions, the argument to justify the ban would be predicated upon the Western take on the symbolism of the headscarf representing the binary of male domination–female subjugation. That is to say that no woman would cover herself as a result of her free will. There must be some other impetus that pushes her to cover and that can only be the fear of the larger society, male relatives, etc. who want to see her covered.

Başörtülü kadınlar are rendered homogenized members of a large political collectivity by the republic that represents them as an aggregate of women with the same qualities, therefore they can be dealt with at once without having to pay attention to their particularities. With this typology, the republic strives to achieve two goals. First, the republic seeks to manipulate the social phenomenon of *başörtülü kadınlar* in order to control knowledge about the republic as well as the women themselves. Second, the republic wields *başörtülü kadınlar* to advance its own agenda and strengthen its position. It finds legitimacy for its own status as an entity that fights against the backwardness, abjection, tardiness, and darkness of what it considers to be a non-enlightened past within and outside of its own boundaries. Through the politicization of the headscarf, the Turkish Republic finds its own validation.

The Turkish Republic invariably expresses callousness toward the sufferings of *başörtülü kadınlar.* They deserve the denial of their human rights and civil liberties because the state, similar to an Orientalist, knows what is best for these deplorable and helpless women who need to be rescued from their backwardness. In response to this savior state, they are expected to hail their secular creator,[10] the Turkish Republic, and its founding father, Atatürk. The fact that these women are only visible through their scarves and that none of their other attributes receive recognition by the Turkish Republic—that is, the republic is unable to get past their appearance—resonates with the Orientalist approach. Denied access to public space, Oriental women cannot escape the fences placed around them.[11]

Finally, the question concerning the treatment of *başörtülü kadınlar* can be illuminated by the paradox intrinsic to the language of rights. Rights constitute a discourse:

> ... of enduring universality rather than provisionality or partiality. Thus, while the measure of political efficacy requires a high degree of historical and social specificity; rights operate as a political discourse of the general, the generic, and universal.[12]

By appealing only to the general and the universal, the state comes under attack for becoming the "primary threat to citizens' rights."[13] *Başörtülü kadınlar* who are not permitted into the public realm lament that some of their universal and citizenship rights are revoked as a consequence of the headscarf ban. The state, on the other hand, argues that it only promises citizenship rights to collectivities without any attention to their particularities. Hence it, in fact, does not promise to meet any individualistic demand based on differences of its subjects. In the eyes of the state, the citizens are abstracted from their affiliations defined by family, social, economic, political status, and culture.[14] They are treated as disembodied entities rendered the same. As the state sees its subjects as the same, it rejects recognizing their particularities that render them different. This paradoxical situation leads to the exclusion of those who insist to stand out with their differences.

The discussion becomes paradoxical at another level based on the conceptualization of the individual. The state, on one hand, recognizes its subjects as abstract prototypes based on the very definition of "citizen," however, on the other hand, it refers to the uniqueness of human beings that stems from the differences that distinguish them from others.[15] This way, it finds itself in the quandary of treating its subjects as human aggregates with specific traits deserving inalienable rights despite their differences or as abstract entities that have the same needs.[16] The paradox presented here refers to the tyranny of dualism.[17] On one hand, the rights of *başörtülü kadınlar* are perceived to be abridged because they do not fit the abstraction, hence their difference is perceived as a threat. On the other hand, the state fails to concur that it ever promised them these particular rights, but argues that it gave women, as a collectivity, their rights.

In response, *başörtülü kadınlar* refer to the concept of equality and argue that their treatment is antithetical to the principle of equal citizenship rights. Nevertheless this does not provide a solution either since, for the state, equality is predicated upon human sameness, which these women lack.[18] They lose their claim to the public realm as their differences are treated as their private matters.[19] As *başörtülü kadınlar*, they must fit in the rubric of the same in order to be treated the same in the public realm. In other words, they can choose between being treated as equal, which requires them to be the same as other citizens, or they can choose to be different, which means that they will not be treated by the same standards.[20]

Furthermore, the abstraction process strips *başörtülü kadınlar* from their particular identities and reshapes them, creating a new subjectivity for them before it deals with their claim. Hence the abstraction process neither represents who *başörtülü kadınlar* are nor represents their exact needs. By granting the abstract individual rights in the way that it understands, the state appears to have solved the problem of rights without really meeting the needs of the actual citizens. This leads to a continuation of the state's control over them. Their subordination becomes ensconced further through this manipulative process. As a result, *başörtülü kadınlar* with their rights claims in hand must first not target "to discover what [they] are, but to refuse what [they] are."[21] That is to say that they must challenge their subjectivity constituted by the rights claim they use in their interaction with the state. That subjectivity does not represent who *başörtülü kadınlar* are, thus it would not serve their goal of gaining what they call their "right." On the contrary, it makes *başörtülü kadınlar* become trapped in the power relations that they are striving to escape from. They lose their authenticity by contributing to their own production by the state, that is, state-made *başörtülü kadınlar.* This prevents *başörtülü kadınlar* from being active in the ban's discourse, leading them to stay as passive recipients of power equations.

The possibility of a demand for redress also complicates the discourse on the rights claims. If the state caves in to the demands of *başörtülü kadınlar,* chances are good that other groups—such as those with different religious or ethnic identities, including Christians, Alevis, and Kurds—would demand rights for their particularities as well. Hence, the state becomes paranoid about citizens who identify themselves with their differences. By taking action against those individuals who are insistent on their particularities through attacks, denigrations, and prevarications, the state contributes to the misrepresentation of these women. Rather than opening up society, the rights discourse may lead to a reduction of liberties and emancipations.[22]

Following this theoretical introduction of the subject matter, I want to turn to the content of different chapters that will develop these themes and arguments. Chapter 2 will examine the role *başörtülü kadınlar* played in the national struggle for independence and Turkish women's centrality to the nationalist modernization project. It will define who *başörtülü kadınlar* are and delineate how the republican discussions developed the representation of *başörtülü kadınlar* and modern Turkish women as binary oppositional categories. It will conclude with a discussion on the critique, recently raised, of the process of modernization with respect to women's advancement. Chapter 3 will turn to the politics of religion in the new republic. It will provide the reader with an in-depth analysis of the gradual changes in policies of each government and each government's contribution to the politics of religion and dress. This chapter will also explore the trajectory that produced the headscarf ban and the subsequent shifts seen in the ban's discourse. It will analyze coping and resistance mechanisms employed by *başörtülü kadınlar* to overcome the ban. Chapter 4 will zero in on the social and political implications of the headscarf ban that was introduced in 1981. It will examine the curtailment of educational rights of women, the development of persuasion chambers through which students were coerced to uncover by their professors, and the expanded public debate of the headscarf ban, including the role that the written and visual media played in the devaluation of the *başörtülü kadınlar* and the economic restrictions imposed upon them. As part of this discussion, the concepts of "white" versus "black" Turks, where the former represents modernist proponents of the headscarf ban and the latter symbolizes the traditional, religious people of the Turkish Republic, will be studied. This binary opposition represents the power relations between the two camps and how Orientalism has become internalized in the discussion of *başörtülü kadınlar*. Chapter 5 will focus on how the ban forced some of the women with headscarves to leave Turkey for educational and professional purposes. This chapter will also discuss the disappointments faced by *başörtülü kadınlar* in the religious community within which they have emerged. It will offer a critique of the Islamist governments and how they have abandoned these women in their broader fight against secular fundamentalism. The current government's approach to the headscarf ban, its attempts to lift it partially, and the considerable resistance it faced in this process will be discussed. The chapter will conclude with the changes in the international community since the recognition of the ban in the international arena as a human/civil rights issue. Chapter 6 will be the conclusion in which a discussion on various conjectural scenarios involving the future of *başörtülü kadınlar* will take place.

CHAPTER 2

WOMEN IN NATION-BUILDING

The Role of *Başörtülü Kadınlar* in the National Struggle

Women were wielded as opposing symbolisms during and after the Independence War. During the war, women's bodies and attire were utilized as the symbols of Islam against the Western, non-Muslim, imperialist invasion. The war was carried out in the name of ousting the Europeans from the Muslim territories, therefore, it was perceived by the Turks as a religious war. Starting with the establishment of the republic, however, women's appearance was turned into the symbol of a secular, westernized way of life, bereft of Islam.

During this early period, Turkish women were mostly *başörtülü kadınlar* from different social strata. They made distinct contributions to the victory gained at the War of Independence. This was a war fought by both sexes. Women took an active part in the fight against the colonial invaders. Prominent women, such as Halide Edip, Nakiye Elgün, Fatma Aliye, and Münevver Saime, played significant roles in the dissemination of nationalist sentiment through their public speeches, which galvanized the nation to protect their land. The Anatolian Women's Association for Patriotic Defense established its branches in ten major cities.[1] The Women Workers' Brigade was established by the Fourth Army. The Islamic Association for the Employment of Ottoman Women helped in the recruiting process of women. The Ottoman Ministry of Trade enacted mandatory employment for women. Peasant women played a particularly crucial role in the *Milli Mücadele,* fighting alongside men. Their role would be celebrated in the narrative of war and victory.[2]

Women's involvement in the struggle for independence brought with it the feminization of the popular struggle.[3] The territories that the Turkish people were defending assumed feminine characteristics. This was the "motherland," a land fraught with mothers who needed to be protected from the non-Muslim enemy. This was a war that needed to be won not simply for the practical purpose of warding off the enemy but for the preservation of the Muslim people's honor. The struggles of Turkish women against the harassments of the European enemy, such as pulling off their veils or attempting to attack them, were used in the war narrative and considered signs of valor by the nation. They were construed as symbols of the larger struggle, a struggle against the violation of the Turkish *Anavatan* (i.e., the motherland). The founding father Mustafa Kemal Atatürk acknowledged Turkish women's role in the victory.

> The Anatolian woman has her part in these sublime acts of self-sacrifice and must be remembered with gratitude, by each one of us. Nowhere in the world has there been a more intensive effort than the one made by the Anatolian peasant women. Woman was the source of vital dynamism: who ploughed the fields? She did. Who sowed the grain? She. Who turned into a woodcutter and wielded the axe? She. Who kept the fires of home burning? She. Who, notwithstanding rain or wind, heat or cold, carried the ammunition to the front? She did, again and again. The Anatolian woman is divine in her devotion. Let us therefore honor this courageous and self-sacrificing woman. It is for us to pledge ourselves to accept women as our partners in all our social work, to live with her, to make her our companion in the scientific, moral, social and economic realm. I believe that this is the road to follow.[4]

Among the heroines entrenched in the collective Turkish memory were Nezahat Hanım, Nene Hatun, and Kara Fatma, who demonstrated extraordinary valor against the occupying forces on the frontlines. Nezahat Hanım was called the Joan of Arc of the Turks.[5] They were granted the *İstiklal Madalyası* (Independence Medal) alongside men.[6] Hence *başörtülü kadınlar* were the ones who fought against the enemy. They paid their dues to the society. They sacrificed their lives in the war against the Europeans in the name of preserving their Islamic lifestyle, which was symbolized by their *tesettür* (i.e., Islamic dress code). Decades later, the fact that other *başörtülü kadınlar* would be treated as internal enemies or perceived as a threat would create a cruel irony.

Women at the Center of the Nationalist Modernization Project

With the establishment of the Turkish Republic in 1923, Turks turned toward Europe to start the project of becoming westernized. The new regime was predicated upon Turkish exceptionalism compounded by its total embrace of the modernization project constituted by an intransigent form of westernizing process. Entrenched in the sense of exceptionalism, the first prong of nationalism, was the belief in Turks' innate superiority as a people,[7] which served both as a cause and effect for the nationalism project of the republic. Belief in the supremacy became the cohesiveness necessary for the emergence of nationalism first, and part of the state ideology later. Within this context, Turks were presumed to carry a distinct noble blood. Exceptionalism was wielded to distance Turks from the rest of the Muslim world, rendering it a unique Muslim-yet-secular country. Furthermore, it justified modern Turkey's condescending stance vis-à-vis the peoples that comprised the rest of the *Ummah* (i.e., the global Muslim community). The uncontested commitment to westernization—the second prong of nationalism—provided the sense of urgency to catch up with the developed West. This invigorated the legitimacy of the basis of the first prong, that is to say that Turkey was distinct from other Muslim states due to its adamant and immediate embrace of the westernization project. Therefore its niche was not among the Muslim world but rather in the "civilized" West; over time, this led to the emergence and entrenchment of a sense of inferiority with respect to the West. As a result, Turkish national identity came to accommodate both inferiority and superiority complexities contemporaneously within its construction. In its own eyes, it was invariably better than the Arab Middle East but never as good as the European West.

Westernization was incorporated in the process of nation-building as part of a historical continuum. The fact that the Turks' march toward the West was traced back to their pre-Islamic history dating back to Central Asia was used to normalize the westernization project as much as possible at a time when the nation was experiencing a transition from fighting "against" the West to "becoming" the West. Atatürk was clear in directing the nation:

> The success that we have won until today has done no more than open a road for us, towards progress and civilization. It has not yet brought us to progress and civilization. The duty that falls on us and on our grandsons is to advance, unhesitatingly, on this road.[8]

Renowned thinker Ziya Gökalp referred to the significance of this transformation in order to:

> uncover the Turkish culture which has remained in the people, on the one hand, and to graft Western civilization in its entirety and with all its living forms on to the national culture, on the other.[9]

The ideals reified in the transformation process would later constitute the ideology of Kemalism.

> In Turkey, the hegemony of Kemalism is preserved in a variety of legal, constitutional, practical-political, and sociocultural ways, covering nearly entire gamut of social and political life. Among the most notable cultural forms are the ways in which the personality of Mustafa Kemal Ataturk occupies a preeminent presence in all sites of human social relations in Turkey. Kemalism is sustained by the promotion of Kemal as the "Eternal Chief," "the Grand Leader," and the "Father of us all."[10]

Solidarity was indispensable for the republic. Pluralism, due to the proverbial reason of avoiding divisions, was not part of the Kemalist ideology. Sameness, the antithesis of pluralism, was the inclusionary basis of the national identity. Through education, the republic put a concerted effort into creating an almost "all alike" citizenry. There was a single authoritative account of the common good and it was not open to contestation. And that account was by no means reflective of the nation as a whole. It was a reflection of the ruling elite, the intelligentsia.

In Kemalist ideology, the welfare of the republic was prioritized over the welfare of its subjects. The underlying premise used to justify such prioritization was that for Turks not to fall again into their previous situation on the verge of foreign domination, they had to protect the newly established system. Hence individual liberties could be abridged, a new history could be imposed, language restrictions could be applied, a particular dress code could be foisted, cultural and religious differences could be undermined, and the like.

The first consequence of the transformation was detaching the nation from the Islamic culture of the past and replacing it with the symbols of the modern and Western nation.[11] Within that context, the reemergence of the headscarf would later pose a problem. The crux of the westernization process was the secularization of Turkish society. *Laiklik* is "not a neutral paradigm," but "state's preferred self-representation," a "state ideology" and a "hegemonic public discourse."[12] It was adopted by the Turkish context from French *laicité* and was utilized in the rearrangement of religion's place in public life, which in turn led to the rearrangement of social classes that so far existed. The process involved a militant discourse.[13] While religion would be pushed into the confines of the private realm, the upper social classes, invariably assuming the center and economically well advantaged, would brag about their break from the trappings of religion. *Laiklik* is closer to the

French secularism than the concept of separation of church and state in the Anglo-Saxon context.[14]

Atatürk worked his way through two parallel channels to introduce the changes of secularization in various facets of life. The process involved political, economic, and social change both at the institutional and individual levels. Atatürk submitted that the war was behind them but now it was time to struggle "to achieve Western civilization."[15] Now they had to establish the institutions and the legal infrastructure that would accommodate the westernization project and work on creating an immediate and conspicuous Western appearance that would eventually entail a Western outlook from the inside out. These changes constitute the Turkish revolution. It came in the form of reforms that were instrumental in eliciting the shift from "traditional" to "modern" in the political realm. The aim was "liberating Turks from the various social, cultural, economic and psychological constraints of the Ottoman Islamic system and world view."[16] In Weberian terms at the institutional level the authority shifted from a "traditional" religious source to a "legal" source. Here the traditional authority stood for an "established belief in the sanctity of immemorial traditions and the legitimacy of those exercising authority under them" while the legal authority stood for a "belief in the legality of enacted rules and the right of those elevated to authority under such rules to issue commands."[17]

Women were employed both as actors and symbols in the process of introducing the changes and preserving these changes in the nation-building process,[18] for the main salient stumbling block between Western and Islamic worlds was believed to be in the realm of women. The systems of representation of religious women and modern Turkish women are "powerful signifiers" in the main discourses of nationalism and modernity.[19] In order to break any connection with the past, the new Turkish women had to be westernized both legally and socially and had to think of themselves as the proud emblem of a westernized Turkey. But this was easier said than done.

> Even though the war of independence proved that women could successfully assume so-called men's tasks, it did not radically alter entrenched customs and roles. Women who fought for their country and earned their living did not demand the legitimacy, let alone the extension, of their newly-acquired roles.[20]

In other words, women preferred to return to the status quo. As a result, a large segment of women did not find the revolutionary reforms to resonate with them.[21]

The contrary was true with the elite stratum, contributing to a growing chasm and an ensuing resentment among various groups over the years.

> By the time the nation-state was established, the resistance between the center and the provinces of the country had turned into a power struggle for the control of the institutional structures of the state. This struggle was between the periphery, unified under the domain of religion, and the state espousing modernity, nationalism and centrality. (Özbudun, 1976)[22]

The ruling elite were content with the changes, including the elite women who were satisfied with the rights granted to them. This class, however, did not mix and mingle with the people of the periphery—the elite took pride in their detachment from the rest of the society. To them, a large portion of the Turkish population was made of Orientals, incapable of becoming modernized.[23] This pejorative account of the Oriental local Turks would dominate the country for decades, symbolizing the sharp divide between the Kemalist minority elite and the rest of the country. It would also give legitimization to the encroachment of the Kemalist elite on the the Oreientals' life in the name of protecting the Turkish revolution. It also justified the efforts of the Kemalists, in the name of republican ideals, to block any attempts of change on the part of the rest of the country that might threaten the political and social status of the former in the society. Thus if a new idea or ideal stemming from the social, political, or economic needs of society, which might offer a nuanced critique of the principles of the republican revolution, was brought into the public debate for consideration, it would be discarded regardless of its value. The issue of protecting the Turkish revolution would also be raised by the state in the headscarf discourse as a pretext to justify the ban.

The second channel Atatürk utilized in implementing his project of social change was the introduction of immediate changes in the appearance of women and men as symbols of westernization. The Hat Law, which mandated Turkish men to wear hats in lieu of the Islamic *fez,* was introduced within this context. The law is still in effect.

> He wanted it as part of "civilized dress", the common dress of civilized people, banishing distinctions of culture. He was convinced that all civilized people should have the same way of life, that culture and civilization were synonymous.[24]

Atatürk also restricted the wearing of *sarık* (i.e., the headgear of the Ottoman sultans and Ottoman religious authorities) in 1934. He argued that *sarık* could only be worn by people who had the liability and only during their work hours.[25] For the most part, Turkish men succumbed to the pressure of the modernization project and renounced Islamic attire, including *fez,* at the outset. Dissidents who stood against the regime were immediately punished. Most of them paid the price at the *İstiklal Mahkemeleri* (i.e., the Independence Courts), which were the inquisitional tribunals established in 1920 to prosecute dissidents of treason. The courts were scattered around the country, in cities of different regions.[26] They were primarily utilized for repressing dissent of those who resisted the westernizing social reforms, including the Hat Law. This law was significant for it was the source of the most serious dissidence among the entirety of reforms.[27] The hat was the marker of the non-Muslim, and Islam required Muslims to be dressed in a way that distinguished them from people of other denominations.[28] İskilipli Atıf Hoca was one of the people who rejected wearing a hat as mandated by the law. He was executed. A woman named Şalcı Bacı, who was described as defenseless because she had nothing to do with the dissent movement, was executed for spite, even though women were not mandated to dress in a certain manner.[29]

Unlike men, most women resisted and did not give up on their *tesettür* very quickly. As noted, they were not mandated to dress in a certain way by law. Women were only encouraged to dress in Western styles with the hope that they would finally drop their *tesettür* and join public life in the same way that men did—with a secular appearance. Atatürk was often surrounded by women who had modern looks, fashionably dressed in Western clothes. He did not put out an explicit view that would clarify his stance on the issue of *tesettür* in general. He presented a nebulous position replete with discrepancies in the same way that he did with respect to religion. In some of his speeches he hailed Islam, while in others he implicitly reproached it. He stated that "our politics we [felt], let alone be antithetical to religion, was deficient and insufficient from the perspective of religion" and that the "Turkish nation [had to] be more religious."[30] On the other hand, he argued that if the Turkish people knew the Turkish meaning of what they have been reading in their prayers (since prayers are performed in Arabic), they would have been disgusted by it.[31]

Atatürk organized occasions where men and women could comport themselves in the same manner as westerners—environments where they could mingle, consume alcohol, and enjoy the company of the opposite sex. At one such reception in the early republican years, where there were only three women (the wives of Atatürk's three friends) attending a function, one of the women lamented and asked Atatürk if they were the only three "sacrificial lambs" of the reforms.[32] During another function in celebration of the establishment of the republic in its early years, Atatürk noticed that women were not dancing. He said: "My friends, I cannot imagine any woman in the world who would refuse a Turkish officer's invitation to dance. I now order you: spread out through the dance hall! Forward! March! Dance!"[33] Such symbolic steps would send the message to the rest of the world that the Turkish Republic was on its way to becoming a Western state even if it was through coercion, which sometimes came in the form of a command.

> [A]ttempts to liberate women were more than restrictions against a mode of dress, further education or establishing legal rights. These attempts were the fight between one mode of social and global consciousness and another for the ways in which individuals, classes and the symbolic order of the society were going to be constructed.[34]

Hence, there was no compromise on Atatürk's part. He employed his militarist power without respite when it was needed. He was against *tesettür* of women, but at the same time was sagacious enough not to push the limits of the Turkish people. Therefore he gave subliminal messages through his speeches.

His wife, Latife Hanım, was a prime example of how Atatürk wanted to see Turkish women modernize. When Atatürk married Latife Hanım she was in full *çarşaf* [*char-shaph*] (i.e., a one-piece, one-color outfit that covered the woman from head to toe) in the public realm. During their marriage, Latife Hanım generally wore a headscarf with a skirt or pants. Later in their marriage, she took her headscarf off completely. The transformation she went through was the kind of transformation the republic wanted to see in its female citizens. Proud of his wife, Atatürk would travel across the country pointing to her as a role model.

> Nonetheless, the elements of state patriarchy were present in Kemal Atatürk's family life as well. Latife Hanım was a well-educated and ambitious woman who wanted to become a parliamentarian. She was an active member of the women's movement fighting for emancipation. Kemal Atatürk, however, was against the idea that his wife would be in politics. When Latife Hanım confronted him once on this matter, he said that he was not against women being in politics, but that he would want to be comforted at home and that only his lovely wife could provide him with that comfort.[35]

The tension depicted in this dialogue between Latife Hanım and Atatürk points to the way and extent to which the Turkish Republic decided to emancipate Turkish women. While they were granted equal citizenship rights and encouraged to take their respective places in the public space next to men, women were reminded that their primary responsibility was in the realm of the household.

The history of the early 1920s attests to a prevalent westernization of appearance among the Istanbul elite. By 1924, women started appearing in dancing salons.[36] Beaches and sport clubs were at the disposal of middle- and upper-class women.[37] Women of the elite class—wives of economically upper-class men—were the markers in the transformation of women's clothing: they first took off their *çarşaf* and kept their *başörtüsü* [*bush-ortoosue*, *baş* = head, *örtü (sü)* = cover] (i.e., the headscarf) or they wore *türbans* that were similar to the French *bonnet*. Some also circumvented the gradual transition from *çarşaf* to *türban* and started with the *şapka* (i.e., hat, derived from *chapeau* in French) after they took off their *çarşaf* or *başörtüsü*. In this transition, wives of military members and federal employees were trailblazers.[38] Sauntering on the streets with their *türbans*, hats, or their uncovered hair, they were to be taken as models to be emulated by the women of the periphery.

Women who decided not to compromise on their *tesettür* in any way chose to contribute to the nation-building by rearing the future citizens of the nation and becoming homemakers. They continued living where they used to live prior to the War of Independence, generally at the periphery. Here, without seeking formal education, they turned to informal sources of knowledge such as the wise men and women of the village or the town who taught religion. Most of these women worked at the farms as unpaid family labor workers to keep their families going. Some who were more prone to the modernization project and were amenable to working outside of the private realm became the low-income blue-collar workers at factories. They had little or no formal education. Some of the young girls who were to adopt *tesettür* in the future pursued education up until the end of the fifth grade, where they would complete the elementary school before they adopted the *tesettür*. Some, on the other hand, reconciled their religious convictions and the state's pressure to modernize their appearance by taking off their *tesettür* at the educational institutions and putting it back on afterward. Some who were economically more privileged also chose to be educated at an all-girls school, such as the private Catholic schools in the urban areas. Furthermore, once the *İmam Hatip* schools, which were state-funded schools that taught religion, opened their doors to girls, they became the most appealing institutions for young women in *tesettür*. Higher education was not at all common for these women up until the mid-1970s. Prior to that, most of them were satisfied with a high school diploma. Some girls chose to go to vocational schools that trained them as nurses and teachers. Teaching at all-girl schools and elementary schools, where they did not have to worry about their *tesettür,* became popular for these women. Albeit few, some pursued higher education in fields such as law, medicine, and engineering.

Başörtülü Kadınlar as a Protean: Adaptability and Novelty of *Tesettür*

In the Turkish context, the phrase "Muslim women" is a loaded and much-shunned term. The state refers to its female subjects as the "Turkish" women under the unifying force of Turkishness rather than as "Muslim" women. The reason for that is that from the regime's perspective, 99 percent of the Turkish population is composed of Muslims, and Islam is assumed to be the religion of almost every member of that population. Hence under the Turkishness that women are identified with, their religious identity as Muslims comes as an uncontested subfield of their identity. Nonetheless, different groups and classes have different takes on Islam, such as how Islam is constituted, what it mandates, and the implications of these mandates on women. Many disagree, for instance, on where Islam should be in quotidian terms. There are contested issues that come with questions such as: to what extent can Islam be determined in the public realm or even within the private realm? Can Islam have a public representation or must it be confined to the realms of the private? What are the criteria employed in the demarcation of the private and the public?

The most ostensible manifestation of the contention over Islam's space in the public realm is seen in the issue of wearing the headscarf. The state treats *başörtülü kadınlar* as a large collectivity with specific homogeneous traits. It fails to recognize the diversity among them. This makes it possible for the state to confine *başörtülü kadınlar* in stereotypes that they cannot break away from. It also serves the purpose of dealing with them all at once through the ban. Yet *başörtülü kadınlar* are not a homogeneous group—they are a heterogeneous aggregate with varying traits. In Turkey, *başörtülü kadınlar* comprise 63.5 percent of the female population.[39] They make up two groups of women, some of whom are perceived as a "threat" to the secular regime while others are not. The nonthreatening group includes the homemakers and the rural-area women. They are not homogeneous within themselves. These women wear traditional headscarves and coverings and they are not perceived as a threat to the state so long as they remain within the confines of the private realm or "not-so-public" public realms. The latter here refers to the public realm where they perform low-income and low-status jobs as maids, janitors, labor workers, and the like. Hence they are at the economic margin of Turkish society.

These women generally wear their headscarves tied under their chin with a knot. They also might wear more traditional coverings marked by geographic regions. They wear their headscarves for a variety of reasons. Some wear them because they are part and parcel of their local culture. Some wear them because of peer pressure, including from male family members. Some wear them consciously because the practice is a mandate from the Creator. Their formal education varies mostly between elementary and middle education. Their primary function is to contribute to society as homemakers or through low-income occupations. This book does not focus on this group of women with headscarves since they are not generally considered threats to the state.

The second group of *başörtülü kadınlar* who are seen as threatening will be our focus. These women are identified by the state as *türbanlı kadınlar* (the women with *türbans*) and, using their own terminology, *başörtüsü mağdurları* (i.e., victims of the headscarf ban). They are the women who wear their headscarves due to religious consciousness, who demand a legitimate presence in the public space but are denied to have that space. They distinguish themselves as consciously covered women, unlike the women of the rural areas. They are not a homogeneous group either. Many of them are the children of immigrants from the rural areas.[40] Some of them belong to the lower middle class, middle class, or upper middle class. Some are the by-products of the 1980s' economic liberalization policies. That is to say that economic changes of the 1980s gave way to the emergence of a new urbanizing middle class in Turkey composed of mixed types of families from different parts of the country. Either they moved with their families to larger cities where their daughters had more access to better education or they sent their daughters to urban areas to study. Some, on the other hand, are products of the emerging conservative elite at the aftermath of the rise of political Islam and governments such as that of *Refah Partisi, RP* (the Welfare Party), *Fazilet Partisi, FP* (the Virtue Party), and *Adalet ve Kalkınma Partisi, AKP* (the Justice and Development Party). Yet their political views, formal class, and educational and religious backgrounds vary.

They also differ as to the underlying reasons behind their adoption of *tesettür* [*taa-sat-toor*] (i.e., covering). A 2006 *TESEV* study is revealing: 71.5 percent of the women who are in *tesettür* argue that they cover because it is a mandate in Islam; 7.6 percent refer to the peer pressure and state that they cover because everybody around them covers; 3.9 percent argued that *tesettür* is an inextricable part of their identity; only 3.7 percent see *tesettür* as a prerequisite for honor. Political reason is only mentioned by 0.4 percent, which means that politics is the underlying reason behind *tesettür* for very few *başörtülü kadınlar.* Nonetheless the state invariably argues that all *başörtülü kadınlar* cover because it is a political symbol. When the question "why do they cover?" is addressed to women who do not have *tesettür*, or to men whose wives do not have *tesettür*, 8.7 percent argue that the women choose *tesettür* due to political reasons, despite the fact that almost none of the women who cover concur with that. That is to say that women in *tesettür* do not cover as a political symbol, but the state and a small minority argue that they do. Of the women who were asked if they would uncover if other women around them or in their family would uncover, 94.1 percent respond "no."[41] This would indicate that no direct relationship between lack of peer pressure and uncovering exists.

Another study conducted by Tarhan Erdem for *Milliyet* shows that 46.5 percent of the women in *tesettür* would vote for *AKP*, which has Islamist roots, for a second term.[42] In other words, more than 50 percent of women who have *tesettür* do not have the same political inclinations, hence they do not represent a politically homogeneous group. Their demography also depicts that they have differing educational and professional backgrounds. They also do not belong to a certain age group. Thus it is fallacious to treat *başörtülü kadınlar* as a distinct homogeneous group with a specific identity.

The state refers to them as *türbanlı kadınlar* [*toorban-le ka-den-laar*] (i.e., women with *türbans*), ignoring their reference to themselves as *başörtülü kadınlar* or *başörtüsü mağdurları* (i.e., victims of the headscarf ban), depending on the context. Hence there is a contestation at the level of representation over how they should be identified and who should do the identifying. Despite the fact that they see themselves as *başörtülü kadınlar*, this does not deter the state from dubbing them *türbanlı kadınlar.* From the perspective of the state, these women wear their headscarves as a political symbol as opposed to as a religious obligation, as argued by the women themselves.[43] The state sees this as a purposeful anti-secular act, plotted by men and played out by women, while women argue that this is a matter of freedom of conscience. The concept of *türban* was introduced by the state in the mid-1980s. Then the head of *Yüksek Öğretim Kurulu, YÖK* (Higher Education Council), Ihsan Doğramacı suggested that girls could wear *türban* in the classroom. It was a reconciliatory interim solution for the *başörtülü kadınlar.* Here *türban* referred to a "modernized" form of a small headscarf that would cover the head and the neck as mandated by Islam, but at the same time not present a "backward" (whatever this might mean) appearance from the perspective of a westernized secular world that would connect the Turkish women to the past. However no specificities of the *türban* were provided by the *YÖK*. Thus no one knew exactly what a *türban* had to look like. *Başörtülü kadınlar* used their creativity to transform their scarves in order to make them more amenable and acceptable to the state. This was their take on *türban*. Yet they still called what they wore a *başörtüsü*. By the time the state realized how the *türban* was being worn, it was prepared to insist on the ban. *Türban* did not retreat from the public discourse but was reloaded by the state with a new meaning, this time a negative one unlike the old meaning of a reconciliatory form of *tesettür*. That is to say that *türban* became unacceptable to the proponents of the ban.[44] Since then it has been wielded by the state as a term that refers to a kind of headscarf that would be considered a "threat" to the secular regime.

The term *türbanlı kadınlar* came to acquire connotations among which are having a hidden political agenda, destructive demeanor, and inappropriate resistance. *Başörtülü kadınlar* have never identified themselves with the term *türbanlı kadınlar*. When they were asked, they responded that they were *başörtülü kadınlar*, but the state categorized them as *türbanlı kadınlar* over the years to the point that it became part and parcel of the state's discourse on the ban. The elitist intellectuals who studied these women with diligence, similar to an Orientalist, also referred to them as *türbanlı kadınlar*. Up until the mid-1990s, these *başörtülü kadınlar* lacked the resources to organize and speak for themselves. Therefore, all power holders who had a voice foisted on them the categorization/representation of *türbanlı kadınlar* until the women themselves were strong enough to raise alternative voices and identified themselves as *başörtüsü mağdurları*. Organizations established by these women or organizations that are fervently against the ban include *AKDER, MAZLUMDER, ÖZGÜRDER, Sakarya Platformu, HUDER, Başörtüsüne Özgürlük Girişim Grubu,* as well as some prominent intellectuals who come from liberal schools of thought such as Mustafa Erdoğan, Nazlı Ilıcak, Kürşat Bumin, and Gülay Göktürk, all of whom embraced the term/category *başörtülü kadınlar*. Meanwhile, dissemination of the knowledge produced by the state and its supporters led the term *türbanlı kadınlar* to become so entrenched in the popular culture that even some of the *başörtülü kadınlar* succumbed to it and today they do not correct those who refer to them as *türbanlı kadınlar*.

The usage of the terms *başörtülü kadınlar* versus *türbanlı kadınlar* generally reveals the user's stance with respect to women who cover. For instance, newspapers that were critical of the female MP who was elected despite her headscarf described her as "Kavakci who entered the parliament with her *türban*,"[45] while the news agencies who were supportive of her actions would state "Kavakci who entered the parliament with her *başörtüsü*."[46] On the same note, the surveys conducted by *AKDER*, which is an organization established by the *başörtülü kadınlar* who have been impacted by the ban,[47] never refer to the women in the study as *türbanlı kadınlar*, while *TESEV* on the other hand, a widely respected organization, refers to these women as *türbanlı kadınlar*. By dubbing the *başörtülü kadınlar* who demand a place in public sphere *türbanlı kadınlar*, the state undermines women's power to represent themselves, coerces them to fit into the state's construction, and distracts attention from the historical specificity of the present moment that would connect the headscarf of what it dubs *türbanlı kadınlar* to the headscarf of other *başörtülü kadınlar* who are not perceived as a threat. Furthermore, it makes a distinction between the women who cover today and the women who covered in the past, for instance, the women who fought in the Independence War. In other words, by creating a category such as *türbanlı kadınlar*, the state engenders a discontinuity on the headscarf enterprise and differentiates between the headscarf of one group versus the other. As a result of foisting the term "*türbanlı*" on *başörtülü kadınlar*, the state is driving a dichotomous wedge between the subtle insinuation of "good" *başörtülü kadınlar* (i.e., women with headscarves who do not pose a threat to the regime and abide by its rules) and the "reprehensible" *türbanlı kadınlar* (i.e., women with headscarves who pose a serious threat to the security of the regime and defy the will of the state to modernize). Through this naming process, the state creates a system that seeks to reassert its control and reproduce punishment for these women everyday and everywhere. The discussion of these binary oppositional representations is the epitome of the representational power struggle that the postcolonial critique focuses on between two actors—the *başörtülü kadınlar* and the state—regarding who has the right to speak and who has the power to shape the reality and acceptable forms of resistance. One salient trait of *türbanlı kadınlar* that distinguishes them from *başörtülü kadınlar* in the eyes of the state is the pin they use under their chin to fix their headscarves. I refer to this as the "pin factor," which is fundamental in the state's perception of the threat caused by a woman's headscarf. A safety pin that brings the two ends of a headscarf together makes it not slide back, and thus stays put without revealing any piece of a woman's hair. This purports to the level of religiosity and adamancy of the woman. In other words, a woman who consciously adopts the headscarf as a reflection of her commitment to Islam would probably not compromise on her *tesettür* therefore she would take the necessary measures to keep her headscarf covering the entirety of her hair and ensuring that it stays put. If there is no usage of a pin, then the headscarf tied under the chin with a nod is very likely to slide back, revealing some hair in the front. This would more likely be the covering of a woman of the periphery who is less conscious about her *tesettür* thus merely wearing it for cultural/traditional or social reasons rather than out of religious obligation. Women who fall into this group therefore would not be perceived as a threat since they are more compromising, with the presumption that they are comparably less religious and more obedient to the state's will to modernize their appearance. In short, the *sine qua non* of the making of *türban* involves a pin. Pin on the headscarf is a requirement that needs to be met in order to categorize a group of women as *türbanlı kadınlar.*

With this demarcation of systems of representation of *başörtülü kadınlar* and *türbanlı kadınlar*, the logical argument that follows would be that the universities were closed to *türbanlı kadınlar* but not to *başörtülü kadınlar*, since the latter is not perceived as a threat. However, that was not the case.[48] In other words, the ban in the minds of its proponents would also include *başörtülü kadınlar,* even though they were not a menace to the state. That is to say that *başörtülü kadınlar* who had the state's approval would lose that approval the moment they stepped onto the university premises for they would now be perceived not as *başörtülü kadınlar* anymore, but as *türbanlı kadınlar* even if they did not have the pin! This meant only one thing that was crucial to the discussion of the ban: the most important characteristic of *türbanlı kadınlar* that differentiated them from *başörtülü kadınlar* was not their demographics or how they tied their scarves but only their demand to be in the public sphere. In other words, for the *başörtülü kadınlar* to remain as *başörtülü kadınlar* in the eyes of the regime, they needed only to stay within the confines of the private realm.

This brings our discussion back to one of the underlying premises used in the creation of modern Turkey. The state anticipated *başörtülü kadınlar* to stay as they were wherever they were as a measure for the success of its nationalist project and as representatives of the past, failure, Islam, and backwardness in contrast to modern Turkish women created by the state. By stepping into the public realm, especially at the universities, *başörtülü kadınlar* undermined the state's role as the prime modernizer and its creation of modern Turkish women who were a source of its pride and prestige. Here the state's projections with respect to *başörtülü kadınlar* were miscalculated for two reasons: they were anticipated either to internalize the modernization project and become secular in time (in other words, transform into modern Turkish women) or they were to offer a contrast to the empowerment of modern Turkish women. Instead, *başörtülü kadınlar* came into the public arena representing a distinct successful synthesis of the old and the new as religious modern women demanding full citizenship rights.

Başörtüsü mağdurları is also a term used heavily by *başörtülü kadınlar* within their circles. *Mağdur* [*magh-door*] means "victim" in Turkish. The phrase was coined over time, by the women who saw themselves as being victimized by the ban. It emerged as a result of a discursive process of women's professional identification: their response to a question such as "what do you do for a living?" would be "I am a *başörtüsü mağduru* attorney" or "I am a *başörtüsü mağduru* doctor," which refers to the fact that the person is not able to practice law or medicine. Not surprisingly, neither the state nor the proponents of the ban recognize the term *başörtüsü mağdurları*. This is an insider term commonly used within the communities of *başörtülü kadınlar*. As the state attempted to efface *başörtülü kadınlar* from the public sphere, these women displayed their resistance through the acknowledgment of this unifying term of victimization as a life-forming experience. Victimization provided a sense of cohesion needed to keep this group of women together at an ideological level. That is to say that by identifying themselves as *başörtüsü mağdurları*, these women put forth a fight against the state's efforts to ostracize them in society. Although they were not permitted into universities and public offices, they were not acquiescing to leave the public sphere all together. They transformed their identities from professionals to "victimized" professionals. At the end of the day, they were able to remain as part of the public arena through the usage of the term *başörtüsü mağdurları*. This was the new front of their war against abridgment of their citizenship rights.

The continued usage of the term *başörtüsü mağdurları* by the women themselves was also a response to the coining of the term *türbanlı kadınlar*. Here we see *başörtülü kadınlar*'s development of new categories as part of their vocal resistance against the state. In short, "behind the façade of behavioral conformity imposed by elites" there are acts of resistance and the naming process is emblematic of that, providing an arena where these forms can be analyzed.[49]

While some *başörtülü kadınlar* embraced the term *başörtüsü mağdurları*, others who are proponents of the headscarf ban refer to the *başörtülü kadınlar* by various terms in addition to *türbanlı kadınlar*, depending on their amenability and tolerance to Islam and this group. *İmam Hatipli*, the one who goes to religious state schools, the *İmam Hatip* schools (note the homogenization process: all who wear headscarves are assumed to have a religious education, to be students of religious schools), and derogatory terms such as *sıkmabaş* (tightened head), *gerici* (reactionary), or *kara fatma* (cockroach) are some examples.

The Systems of Representation of *Başörtülü Kadınlar* and Modern Turkish Women

In their probe of the Muslim world, women of Islam have long been a subject of inquiry for Western social scientists. Some of the accounts of Muslim women by scholars of the West have been questionable for the peoples of the region. In most writings, Orientalist assumptions influence Muslim women's representation. Women of the Muslim world are not seen for who they are, but rather as "something" they are made into. Objectification in the hands of the Orientalist craftsman is clearer in the representation of Muslim women. They are reduced to objects that appeal to the carnal pleasures of the male Orientalist. Another area that raises a critique on the part of the Orient itself is the hard line demarcations employed by Western academics in delineating social, political, and cultural boundaries of Muslim women's lives. The Orientalist is criticized for theorizing the "other"; the way he utilizes homogenization, generalization, abstraction, and reification. As a result, in every facet of life, Muslim women's representation appears to be antithetical to that of Western women. Western women are presented as emancipated, independent of religious constrictions, and thus in control and in charge.[50] That is to say that Muslim women are assumed to be religious, subjugated, oppressed, and enslaved and therefore not in control of their own lives.

The systems of representation employed by the republic to delineate *başörtülü kadınlar* in Turkey internalized a similar trajectory. The regime needed to create symbols as "expressions of feeling, or actions intended" to represent the distance from the past.[51] Women, their lives and bodies, became symbols of *laiklik*.[52] Women were defined by their bodies in ways that men were not.[53] This was a clear implication, in Hatem's term, of the "gender difference" espoused by the regime.[54] Based on this symbolic representation, the image of Turkish women whom the republic intended to create was demarcated sharply from the image of the Turkish women who did not change or resisted change. The former was considered to be "westernized" and "modernized" in appearance and in lifestyle while the latter was "not westernized" and "not modernized." Therefore the former was perceived as the success story and the protégé of the republic while the latter represented its failure. The former was the future of Turkey while the latter was the past. The former was the secular "modern" elite (or elite wannabe) Turkish women who became secular not only in their appearance but in their lifestyle as well, while the latter was the traditional Muslim women of the rural area who had *tesettür* and remained observant Muslims. There was no room in these systems of representation for "modern" *başörtülü kadınlar. Tesettür* was an indicator of religiosity, thus non-modernity, at the outset of the republic. It was a symbol of the past to be forgotten, or to be reminded to pay tribute to the republic's blessings.

The stark dichotomous categories crystallized over time. The process of secularization led to the creation of social divisions among the women of Turkey throughout the country based on how much they embraced and benefited from this process. The symbolic codes of "secular-modern" and "non-secular–non-modern" representations served as indicators of social status.

At this point it would be helpful to provide the reader with an overview on the theological basis of Muslim woman's covering. *Tesettür* is a mandate for women of Islam in the same way that it was originally a mandate for Jewish and Christian women. There are two verses in Qur'an, the Holy Book of Muslims, about *tesettür*. One of the verses declares:

> And say to the believing women that they should lower their gaze and guard their modesty; that they should not display their beauty and ornaments except what (must ordinarily) appear thereof; that they should draw their veils over their bosoms and not display their beauty except to their husbands, their fathers, their husband's fathers, their sons, their husbands' sons, their brothers or their brothers' sons, or their sisters' sons, or their women, or the slaves whom their right hands possess, or male servants free of physical needs, or small children who have no sense of the shame of sex; and that they should not strike their feet in order to draw attention to their hidden ornaments. And O ye Believers! turn ye all together towards Allah, that ye may attain Bliss.[55]

The other verse states:

> O Prophet! Tell thy wives and daughters, and the believing women, that they should cast their outer garments over their persons (when abroad): that is most convenient, that they should be known (as such) and not molested. And Allah is Oft-Forgiving, Most Merciful.[56]

Tesettür is germane to religious faith as a force in one's life reflected in gendered attire and a gendered ideal of modesty. Hence Muslim women adopt *tesettür* as a sign of faith and a means of modesty. Moreover *tesettür* elicits recognition. It sends the outer world an untold subliminal message of a code of conduct about the women who adopt it. It signals the society that these women abide by a certain moral code that prevents them from consuming alcohol, committing adultery, giving or taking interest, using drugs, etc. It is also a means of protection for Muslim women. It conceals women's physical being from possible attacks and the gaze of the opposite sex. In that context, it is also seen as a means of liberation by a sizable number of women in *tesettür*. That is to say that the women in *tesettür* feel confident that not their appearance but their other qualities will garner attention and entail them to be valued by others.

In Turkey *tesettür* served also as a "historically situated signifier."[57] It was a symbol of Turkish honor during the War of Independence. The nation was defined as a woman whose honor was to be defended. *Anadolu* (i.e., Anatolia) literally meant "replete with mothers," hence the mother and the land thereof were to be defended. During the war there were infamous confrontations between Turkish women and the European forces where the *peçe* [*pae-chae*] (i.e., the veil that covers the face) of the women were stripped off their faces and their *çarşaf* were torn. Such incidents fueled Turkish nationalist sentiments and served as an impetus for further struggle against the enemy forces in the name of Islam. That is to say that *tesettür* of Turkish women was nationalized as part and parcel of the independence movement, a symbol of Turkish honor before the establishment of the republic. After the War of Independence ended, however, *tesettür* was rendered a symbol of Islam that was seen as among the main reasons for the backwardness of the society and therefore needed to be removed. But this rendering was done through a tacit and gradual process. *Tesettür* was not made into a clear target, unlike other symbols of Islam such as the caliphate and the sultanate.

The most common kind of *tesettür* at the time was *çarşaf*. *Çarsaf* was mostly accompanied by *peçe*. The first *çarşaf* in Istanbul was seen in 1850.[58] Before then, *tesettür* came in the format of traditional *başörtüsü* made of cotton or wool depending on the climate of the region. According to the nationalist narrative, the Turks first learned about *tesettür* when they adopted Islam in the ninth century.[59] Turkish women used different styles of *başörtüsü* as *tesettür* to meet the religious requirement of covering. That is to say that *başörtüsü* was part of the Turkish culture and history for centuries. Between the mid-nineteenth century and the demise of the Ottoman Empire, women wore *çarşaf* as a form of *tesettür*. Underneath their *çarşaf*, women still wore their *başörtüsü*. The first mention of *türban*, a rather "modern" covering, came before the establishment of the republic during the last periods of the Ottoman reign, at a time when discussions of modernization were taking place. It was introduced to the Turkish women by Russian immigrants and not long after that it became prevalent in Istanbul.[60] *Türban* served as a transitional mediator between the headscarf and the hat in the early years. It was more like the shape of a French bonnet, which covered the hair and ears but not the neck.

As early as the 1870s, reforms encouraged the women's movement to bring women's rights issues to the table. Within this discourse, *tesettür* of women was an incendiary element. Most of the discussions and articles on *tesettür* at the beginning were about *peçe,* (i.e., the covering of the face). Fatma Aliye Hanım, in her debate with Şeyhül Islam Mustafa Sabri Efendi, who was the last religious authority of the Ottoman Empire, argued that *tesettür* could be maintained by loose clothing and a headscarf rather than with *çarşaf* and *peçe.*[61] Among the men who promoted removal of *tesettür* altogether as an ideal or a current mode of dress were Abdullah Cevdet as well as Selahattin Asım. Rasime Hanım criticized the Ottoman government's interference over women's *tesettür.* Some others opined that with the educational advancement of women, *tesettür* imperative would disappear. A women's magazine called *Kadinlar Dünyası* played an important role in the discussion of *tesettür*: It introduced modernized new styles of *çarşaf* and called for the removal of *peçe.*[62] Halide Edip, under the influence of Turkism, promoted introduction of new lines of clothing that would connect the Turks back to their roots in the Middle Ages and at the same time be in accordance with Islamic imperatives.[63]

Later Atatürk referred to an "acceptable" form of *tesettür* that would not prevent women from existing in public space. He did not come across as being against *tesettür* per se, but he opposed the *peçe.* Nonetheless he did not define how that acceptable *tesettür* should look. The regime took Turkish women's incremental "de-*tesettür*ization" project into its agenda during İnönü's presidency in the late 1930s, as will be discussed later. It was then that the seeds of the bifurcation of dress into Western versus Islamic were put conspicuously.

While at some of his public addresses Atatürk promoted women's public representation with *tesettür,* at other times he addressed the issue of *tesettür* in an indirect ambivalent way as part of the reason for Turkey's backwardness. He stated that *tesettür* "must not be in a way that would cut her off of her life and her existence. It must be in a shape that is simple, yet not against morality."[64] He said that *tesettür* was "appropriate both for life and virtue."[65] On the other hand, women around him generally appeared with no *tesettür.* He criticized then the Afghani King Emanullah Khan for openly coercing women (via a law) to dress in Western ways. He advised a famous Turkish singer to cover her hair on stage.[66] Once he pointed out that women in cities were dressing in two extremes—that is, either too westernized or too conservative—both of which were not acceptable for him.[67] At another speech he argued: "the civilized people of civilized Turkey who argue that they are civilized must show, through their appearance head to toe, that they are civilized and progressive" and he went on to criticize women's *peçe*.[68] Hence *peçe* was a target for Atatürk, but not the concept of *tesettür*, *çarşaf*, or *başörtüsü*.

By the mid-1930s, some replaced their *çarşaf* and *peçe* with suits, long coats, and silk *başörtüsü*.[69] Women who were hesitant to give up on their *çarşaf* but at the same time were afraid not to do so would wear a loose coat with the same color *başörtüsü* so that its function would be similar to that of *çarşaf* as if it were one piece. It is important to reemphasize at this point in the discussion that *başörtüsü* was part of the Turkish cultural tapestry for a long time. It was either used as an inner *tesettür* under *çarşaf*, as expressed earlier, or within the household to depict more piousness. By the removal of *çarşaf* from the public scene, *başörtüsü* was moved from the private sphere of the household to the public arena as the outer *tesettür*. *Başörtüsü* was generally tied under the chin before it was replaced with *türban* and finally with the hat.[70]

Under President Ismet İnönü, who succeeded Atatürk, women's *tesettür* was disparaged by the regime and *çarşaf* was banned in most cities.[71] The dichotomous divisions that would grow over the years and bring the Turkish people into the twenty-first century with a clash between Kemalists and the religious Muslims, including *başörtülü kadınlar*, were put in place mostly under İnönü's rule. The Republican People's Party's persistent campaign against women's *tesettür* contributed to the greater divide between the periphery and the urban elite. İnönü promoted "cleanliness of the heart" in lieu of religious action. The argument, similar to that of Christianity and Judaism that went through enlightenment, was that in order to be religious the only prerequisite was cleanliness of the heart, not *tesettür*.[72] Adnan Menderes's rule between 1950 and 1960 as the prime minister brought positive changes for the religious Muslims. Ending the autocratic rule of İnönü, people were content to have a leader who was not only a democrat in name but in character as well. They were ready to reclaim Islam. Albeit not a religious man, Menderes was politically astute to appeal to Islamic values and therefore "gain the allegiance of the rural religious leaders."[73] He responded to the needs of the larger Turkish community, not just the elite. He turned *ezan* [*adh-an*] (i.e., the call to prayer) back to Arabic as soon as he came to power. People wept on the streets when they heard, after eighteen years, the Arabic call to the five-daily prayer. Menderes opened public schools that would provide religious education, the *İmam Hatip* schools, winning the hearts of the religious. On the other hand, his policies garnered the bile of the military that led to the 1960 coup d'etat.[74] His cabinet was charged with a variety of criminal activities, among which were misuse of public funds, abridgement of the constitution, and treason.[75] As a result, Menderes was executed.

It was at this time that no tolerance was elicited toward symbols of Islam in public life, including *başörtüsü*. This was also the time when the greatest discrepancy between the elite and the conservative religious Muslims occurred. The military's role at the time, as the intruder on civil governance, was significant in fueling this growing chasm between the ruling elite and the rural areas. Religious people were finally regaining their confidence under Menderes reign, sending their children to *İmam Hatip* schools and encouraging them to take part in the public arena. The Kemalist elite and the middle-class modernized bourgeoisie were not content with that. The spaces they so far assumed alone now had to be shared with people whom they considered backward and rural. The need to distance themselves from the religious kicked in within this context.

Systems of representation of modernized Turkish women and women who had *tesettür* became more entrenched in the popular culture at this time. The clash between two opposing groups brought with them a fight against *çarşaf* campaigns.[76] While the ideological clashes that explicate the quandary of *başörtülü kadınlar* were present in late Ottoman and early republican history, the problems that led to today's headscarf ban find their active roots in recent history of the late 1960s. Only a handful of *başörtülü kadınlar* began challenging the traditional roles imposed on them by the state and for the first time they left their private spaces and moved into the public arena as professionals. These women were members of the bourgeoisie and upper middle class who already had an education and careers before they adopted *tesettür*. They were not necessarily in compliance with the traits attributed to them as *başörtülü kadınlar* by the widely accepted systems of representation. They were perceived to be in defiance of these systems of representation of *başörtülü kadınlar*.

They were received in awe and anger by the Kemalists. The system of representation of *başörtülü kadınlar* at the time implied that they were uneducated, subjugated, controlled, imprisoned at home, disgruntled, impoverished, and needy as opposed to women who did not wear headscarves who were automatically rendered secular, educated, free, content, and affluent, and hence in control of their lives as it was assumed in the case of "Western" women. For the purification of the latter, the former needed to be denigrated and despised.[77] The westernized modern women needed the old category of *başörtülü kadınlar* in order to develop a self and establish an identity. Accordingly, the empowerment of the former was contingent upon the disparagement of the latter. The qualifications of the modern Turkish women were not self-evident per se, and modern Turkish women did not necessarily carry in them the entirety of all the good traits. Nevertheless they were perceived as perfections at the end of a comparison with the *başörtülü kadınlar.* Therefore the characteristic attributes of the modern Turkish women needed to be distinguished from and contrasted against the attributes of the *başörtülü kadınlar.* That is to say that the system of representation of modern Turkish women presented these women as possessing all worldly goods, not necessarily because this was true, but simply because the system of representation of *başörtülü kadınlar* was presenting a deplorable plight to be compared against. Evidence that will be provided in the next section clearly depicts that modern Turkish women were not so "modern" or emancipated after all. The state created its own imaginary communities of modern Turkish women and imaginary communities of *başörtülü kadınlar* not necessarily based on the reality on the ground.

These oppositional systems of representation of the two groups of women were kept intact through written and visual media. The movies of the early republican period invariably depicted *başörtülü kadınlar,* or women in *çarşaf,* as ignorant, simple minded, witch-like, old, scary, pessimistic, handicapped, ugly, and problem makers. The transformation of the country girl who came to the big city was invariably symbolized by a scene where she, in her headscarf, would be crying while the secular, westernized and affluent girls and boys would belittle her. In the following scene, invariably, the country girl would appear as westernized as the others, in a miniskirt and without her headscarf ready to take the revenge of her tormentors before she falls in love with the wealthy handsome boy and lives happily ever after. In the mid-1960s, the headscarf represented backwardness and miniskirts represented progressiveness in the modernization discourse.[78] *Başörtülü kadınlar* were represented as incompetent and mentally challenged. A student's published testimony included her encounter with one of her professors who would stop his lecture, turn to his student with the headscarf, and say:

> You are not listening to what I am saying. Even if you did, you can not even understand one fourth of what I am saying. What is that?! You are all covered up and wrapped! You look like a turtle in that![79]

Assailments and public humiliation were ubiquitous and were utilized as part of the deterrence strategy. A professor compared his students who were *başörtülü kadınlar* with Christian nuns and said: "In the early ages of Islam, prostitutes used to dress like you," before he threatened to flunk them in his course if they did not take off their headscarves.[80] A physician yelled at his dialysis patient: "You all are sick, dirty reactionaries, get out of here!" while another admitted that he would not treat *başörtülü kadınlar.*[81]

Despite all challenges, *başörtülü kadınlar* remained in the public sphere. Under this relentless social pressure, their profile changed over time as to create their own fashion, wearing trendy clothes, driving sport utility vehicles, exercising at health clubs, going out to movies at night, attending concerts, smoking, etc. Nevertheless, the system of representation of *başörtülü kadınlar* did not experience any positive change.

The Kemalist regime did not budge on its intransigent stance on the headscarf. In the 1980s and 1990s, the regime repositioned itself for the purpose of a more effective assault on *başörtülü kadınlar.* In the re-conceptualization of *başörtülü kadınlar,* the state added the "threat" factor to increase the cogency of its arguments used in legitimizing its stance. The headscarf is perceived as a representative of fundamentalism that threatens the Turkish state's security. Therefore from the perspective of the state *başörtülü kadınlar* are conspirators implanted in society by alien powers. They serve Islamic extremists. Their threat agency is rendered based on their "access to social resources."[82] These women turn to informal educational venues such as arts, language, literature, and information technology in lieu of a formal state education. It is important to note here that formal education in Turkey covers both public and private education. The state controls education provided by all institutions, hence the headscarf ban is not only observed at public institutions but at private ones as well. Here it becomes clear that the Turkish Republic falls into a more intransigent category compared to France in its commitment to *laiklik.* Unlike France, which permits religious symbols such as the headscarf at private educational institutions and at all universities, the Turkish state applies the ban at all educational institutions including the privately funded ones from primary to higher education. This means that the state closes all doors of education to *başörtülü kadınlar.* Under no circumstances can they receive formal education.

As a result, *başörtülü kadınlar* join nongovernmental organizations or political parties to utilize their energy. This way, they become visible agents in the society refusing to be confined within the realm of the household. Symbolically, from the perspective of the state, they are constant reminders of Islam's alleged backwardness, female's subjugation under patriarchal male dominance, and the failure of the modernization project. They should not be feared but only deplored. Yet they are still perceived as a threat.

Threat only comes with power. The system of representation of *başörtülü kadınlar* included a power discourse as well. They were perceived as powerful agents of social and political movements, capable of allegedly changing the republican regime to a theocracy. This entailed an oxymoron. The state contradicted itself by arguing on the one hand that these women were backward—subjugated hence powerless—and on the other hand that they posed a threat to the republic. As a security state, the Turkish Republic believed that it "[had to] root out the enemy within. There [was] always the danger that among us [were] agents who [had] an interest in disturbing our peace.[83] *Başörtülü kadınlar* were these agents.

Başörtülü kadınlar were never perceived as autonomous. They were even expected to learn how to dress from others. During the early years of the republic, the elite (i.e., the military members and the government employees) were given the responsibility of teaching the nation how to change in order to become more westernized. In the same manner, after eighty years of republicanism, *başörtülü kadınlar* were supposed to learn how to wear their headscarves from the powers that be—the only acceptable way of wearing it being the traditional way, that is, tied under the chin—and ultimately they would only be permitted to wear headscarves within the confines of the household.[84] Their public status was reflected in a state-sponsored summer camp that had a sign at its entrance that read: "*Başörtülü Kadınlar* and domestic animals are not permitted in."[85]

Başörtülü kadınlar were seen as lost, hence they needed assistance from modern Turkish women. In the 1990s, notorious "persuasion rooms" became part of the discourse. These rooms were utilized at universities to talk *başörtülü kadınlar* out of their decision to wear headscarves. Today the public space that is also the state-controlled space remains closed to the professional *başörtülü kadınlar*. This feeds into the growing dichotomy between *başörtülü kadınlar* and modern Turkish women. The treatment of *başörtülü kadınlar* and the reflexive of control that kicks in suggest commonalities with authoritative systems in essence.

> [T]he physical appearance of women is made to assume such a great and decisive importance in [the] society, and the other aspects of her personality are subordinated almost to the point of extinction.[86]

Gender does not serve as a common denominator among women of Turkey today. For *başörtülü kadınlar* there exists, in Maxine Molyneux's terms, "a conditionality of women's unity" from the perspective of secular Turkish women.[87] This conditionality stresses secularity. The former are not secular and thus are discredited from the support of the latter. The latter feels threatened by the former. In order for the secular woman to grant importance to herself and vindicate her own presence, she must provide the most salient and persistent opposition to the *başörtülü kadınlar*.[88] In short, a system of representations similar to the system of representations employed by the Orientalists to delineate Western and Muslim women was nationalized by the Turkish regime's treatment of modern Turkish women and *başörtülü kadınlar*.

Meanwhile, systems of representation of women did not go through a bifurcation of femininity through dress in Turkey. Women's femininity was not transformed depending on the way women appeared and assumed roles in public life. Although the bifurcation of dress into binary oppositions of Western and Islamic implied changes in the women's gender roles both inside and outside, in the Turkish case the primary roles of women as mothers and wives did not change as a result of education and public work. All that changed was that more women who had access to education could work outside the home. But the maternal duty of women remained the priority for all women. Rural-area women always worked alongside their husbands at the same time that they were wives and mothers. Hence, even though women who were westernized and women who did not westernize were not polar opposites, the changes that the early republic hailed did not challenge the Islamic assumptions of the primacy of the roles of motherhood. In other words, no matter how the women dressed, they were first mothers and wives and then public agents as professionals. Women's education was geared to teach them not only how to read and write and become professionals, but also how to be good wives and mothers, to help with the education of their children and the health of the family.

A Critique of Turkish Modernization with Respect to Women

Despite much praise of the Turkish Republic's support for modernization and its role-model status, there are questions raised about its success in recent decades. Turkish modernization was more involved with a westernized appearance than the content of modernity.[89] Elements such as universal values of human rights, rule of law, democratization, and free market economy that altogether make the fulcrum of Western modernity have not made strides as anticipated.

With respect to the modernization question of Turkish women, the republic finds a hyperbolic pride in the advances modernization brought to Turkish women disregarding the seeds of the process implanted during the last two centuries of the Ottoman reign.[90] It justifies the modernization of women with reference to the detachment from the past. It also assumes homogeneity in the receiving end of the process with the assumption that Turkish women enjoy the citizenship rights modernization bestowed upon them.

> While the state encouraged increasing the involvement by a group of elite women in public life, it sent a different message to an increasingly large number of "other" women who were expected to contribute to the

> modernization process by becoming housewives by bringing "order" and "rationality" to the private realm by going to "evening girls art schools" (akşam kız sanat okulları) where they learned to cook, sew, run a household as a "modern" housewife. In short, Kemalist principles of gender equality produced a group of elite women who had the opportunity to receive education and practice their professions, while the majority lived in smaller towns and villages, mostly unaffected by these changes.[91]

While modernization and westernization were invariably interchangeable in the Turkish context, Turkish women's modernization had clear distinctions from that of Western women. The new Turkish state was a "republic of brothers" with men as the main beneficiaries.[92]

> While women were encouraged to enter and participate in the public sphere of life, they were restricted by some moral and behavioral codes that were meant to preserve the "respectability" and "honor" of their families.[93]

The family patriarchal system of the Ottoman period was also substituted by the state patriarchy of the modern republic.[94] Here we witness the common grounds shared by modern secular and religious political discourses vis-à-vis the plight of women.[95] In the political arena, women are kept under the shadow of male counterparts. The regime argues that it is good for them to be modernized through a process of modernization exacted by the state.[96] They must be satisfied with what the state provides them and not ask for more. If they dare to ask then they will find the state thwarting their path. One historical example is seen in women's political activism during the early republican years. Churning in the spirit of equality, republican women established their own political party, namely the Women's People's Party. It was abolished in 1923. Subsequently, they founded the Women's League of Turkey. It was disbanded by Atatürk with the pretext that its objectives were met and hence "there was no further justification for its continued existence."[97]

On the matter of motherhood, a similar trajectory is followed allowing secular and religious discourses to dovetail. In the new republic, this was stressed to be the most important duty for women through which they would contribute to the national progression by rearing the future generations of Turkey. Atatürk stressed the indispensability of this duty:

> History shows the great virtues shown by our mothers and grandmothers. One of these has been to raise sons of whom the race can be proud. Those whose glory spread across Asia and as far as the limits of the world had been trained by highly virtuous mothers who taught them courage

> and truthfulness. I will not cease to repeat it, women's most important duty, apart from her social responsibilities, is to be a good mother. As one progresses in time, as civilization advances with giant steps, it is imperative that mothers be enabled to raise their children according to the needs of the century.[98]

Women's continued dependency on men was also assured by the state by rendering the husband the legal head of household.[99] This remained in effect until 1999.

While the republic promoted the continuation of the patriarchy for a large segment of Turkish women, it also promoted the "othering" of the very same women. In other words, it espoused Orientalist assumptions in its treatment of women who were not conducive to the modernization project. The republic perceives women who do not fall under the category of "modern" Turkish women as victims of traditions, religion, and domestic violence at the same time that it promotes the very fundamentals that might lead to such sufferings. This victimization position provides the necessary pretext for the state's encroachment. There is a parallelism between the colonial powers legitimizing their prolonged domination in foreign lands and the republic's meddlesome attitude in this context. In this respect, the Turkish Republic's goal is to "salvage" women from their misery and victimization. The Orientalist bias does not ask women what they need or what they want or *if* they want. The state renders itself omnipotent. It claims the right to know what its female citizens want, or rather what they should want. Hence women are not left to themselves to decide what is good, but rather are inculcated to adopt certain sets of behavior, dress, and the like in the same manner that "no Oriental can know himself the way an Orientalist can."[100]

Generalizability as an attribute of Orientalist ideology is present in the republic's work on women as well. Under the larger rubrics it constructs to define women as modern, anti-modern, religious, or rural area women, it again adheres to the homogeneity principle. According to these categorizations, *başörtülü kadınlar,* regardless of their economic, social, political, ethnic, or religious differences, are treated as having the same attributes of Muslim women in the eyes of the Orientalist and they are dehumanized and backward, as Edward Said articulates it, waiting to be salvaged. They are undervalued. *Başörtülü kadınlar* are easily reduced to human flatness, which explicates the state's callousness to their sufferings. In Said's terms, they are backward Muslims before they are women; therefore their sufferings can be overlooked.

CHAPTER 3

POLITICS OF RELIGION (1938–2000s)

The Changing Discourse on Religion

Başörtülü kadınlar, or in state's terms the *türbanlı kadınlar* who became increasingly visible in the urban areas starting in the 1980s, were an uncalculated result of the westernization project the republic espoused.[1] The state's projection at the outset of the republic was that the elite-led modernization would pick up its pace, in time percolating into the rural areas and the economically challenged lower classes of the Turkish society. Through coercion and appeasement, resistance to change would be undermined and women at the periphery would be influenced by the elite women in the urbanized areas, learning from them the benefits of westernized life and how to adapt to new ways in their daily lives. Nonetheless, the state's predictions would be proven wrong. The elite, both men and women, remained confined to their cocoons, growing apart from the rest of society. The process of forced modernization contributed to the separation of communities, creating two Turkeys: "modern" Turkey and "*öteki*"(the other Turkey). They lived and dressed differently. The former was made up of the Kemalist urbanized elite and its replicated versions in the upper middle or middle classes while the latter comprised the rest. *Başörtülü kadınlar* claiming their space in the public sphere emerged from the latter. In this section, I will discuss how the different Turkish governments that rose to power between 1938 and the 1980s contributed to the policies concerning religion and how these affected the rise of *başörtülü kadınlar* and their banning from public realm. This historical process was influenced both by internal and external factors.

The İnönü Years

After Atatürk's death and throughout his twelve-year presidency that lasted until 1950, İnönü followed in Atatürk's footsteps to internalize the reforms and eliminate defiance. As the head of the *Cumhuriyetçi Halk Partisi, CHP* (the Republican People's Party) that was established by Atatürk, he saw himself as personally responsible for protecting the reforms. He alerted the notorious *İstiklal Mahkemeleri* (i.e., the Independence Courts) to the rising oppositional voices that accused Atatürk and his friends of acting in a manner antithetical to Islam.[2] He warned them that he would not hesitate to quell the opposition through these notorious judicial bodies where, in the early years of the republic, people were imprisoned and executed without any substantial evidence for resisting the reforms.[3] He knew Atatürk's aspiration to distance Turkish society from religion's public representation. Therefore İnönü augmented the following laws concerning religion:

> Law 4055 of June 2, 1941 brought heavier penalties for wearing the *fez*, using the Arabic script and the call to the prayer in Arabic. Some changes were made in the penal code (Article 526) with respect to Law 4055. Thus the prison sentence was increased from 1 month to 3 months. Likewise, Law 5438 dated June 10, 1949 was conceived as supplementary to Law 677 of 1925; jail terms, fines, or exile was to be the penalties for those who established religious orders, became the head or a member thereof, or rented their property to dervish gatherings, etc.[4]

Articles 141, 142, and 163 of the penal codes banned any association with ideals that would be antithetical to republicanism with a possible imprisonment for seven years.[5] He warned against religion's rise, which would stand in the way of progress.[6] İnönü's restrictive policies were not circumscribed to issues concerning Islam and Muslims alone. In 1942, the government passed the infamous Capital Tax Law, which mandated that non-Muslims would pay ten times higher taxes than Muslims.[7] Resistance was punished with deportation.[8] In 1949, however, the government reversed its anti-religion policy and introduced religious education to elementary schools to combat the rise of communism. It required, however, that the content be entirely in Turkish.[9]

Tesettür was among the targets of İnönü's government. There was a futile attempt to ban the veil.[10] Campaigns against *çarşaf,* in which Kemalist women played an important role, stayed in the public eye. This was a war waged by women against women. The mass media was utilized in the publicity process to taint women who wore *çarşaf* by alleging that "those women who hid themselves behind that black *çarşaf* were involved in [deceptions, fraud, prevarications, etc.]."[11]

By the late 1940s, most of the religious scholars of the late Ottoman period and the early republican years were executed, sequestered, exiled, or had passed away from natural causes. There was no religious authority left to guide the society at ritual matters such as funerals, religious holidays, etc. To fill this gap, İnönü introduced short-term religious courses. These courses would become the seeds of the long-controversial *İmam Hatip* schools of the later Menderes period. At the same time, the School of Theology was established at Ankara University.[12] The results were mixed.

> [T]he record of a generation of bureaucratic despotism could not be washed away with a few concessions; on the contrary, the concessions only served to arouse the suspicions of the people, making them doubt the sincerity of the Republicans, so long identified with unremitting and militant secularism.[13]

Yet İnönü went along with these concessions, hoping that these would also help his *CHP* in the elections as a token of political gain against a rising opposition. The transition from a one-party system to a multiparty system in 1946 would bring about change in future governmental policies. The country had been ruled by *CHP* for twenty-three years by then.

> The interventionist policy of İnönü was especially resented by some villagers, smaller tradesmen, craftsmen, and some officials. The men of religion and the traditionalists had not forgotten certain grievances they had against the [*CHP*], which had followed a policy of secularism that they strongly opposed.[14]

The nation was searching for an alternative. Meanwhile they developed their own systems of resistance.

> After about 25 years of excessive secularism, the people wanted to return to traditional values that had played a major role in the daily life in earlier times. Religious belief among the people at large had never ceased to exist. It is only the expression of religion in public that was affected. Moreover, illegal religious instruction and traditions had continued in certain places.[15]

In fact, people who were insistent on acquiring religious education did so by risking their personal security. Many had pursued their studies by remaining under the radar to avoid any undue attention. They resorted to simple tricks. For instance, children had to hide religious material under their shirts on the way to their teachers and when they were questioned by the gendarme about where they were going, they would say that they were going to a friend's house to play. Others would meet before dawn to disguise their religious education.

The Advent of the Multi-Party System: An Eclectic Definition of Religion

In 1950, *DP, Demokrat Parti*'s win under Menderes opened the public space to the *öteki* by adopting a more flexible tone toward secularism.

> It is well-accepted fact that the *DP* government directly or indirectly encouraged private initiatives favoring religion such as the building of mosques and the setting up of centers of religious instruction by private funds or communal donations, the increase in the number of pilgrims going to Mecca and that of people who visited the tombs and shrines of holy men and a more widespread observance of the fasting during Ramadhan.[16]

Under this came the changing of *ezan* to Arabic and opening of the first religious state-sponsored schools, the *İmam Hatip* schools. These schools became the educational institutions for children of rural-area dwellers and practicing Muslims who had concerns about the secularizing state policies. These schools would later become the center of the Islamist–Kemalist strife, accused of aiding and abetting reactionaryism. Despite such claims, they are not in contradiction with modernization. Their curricula cover the same sciences as in public schools, in addition to religious education. Hence they provide access to both religious and positive science. In 1956, an optional course on religion was added to the curriculum for first and second grade of state-run middle schools, followed by the opening of the Institute of Islamic Studies in Istanbul in 1959.[17]

During the ten years of *DP* government led by Menderes, the *tesettür* debates continued to be about annihilation of *çarşaf*. *İmam Hatip* schools were only available to boys since these schools were originally intended to train imams (i.e., the religious leaders), who could only be male. Girls who wanted to wear headscarves had to choose between the option of taking it off or quitting school. That is the reason behind many families' decision not to send their daughters to school at some point during this period. Kemalist women continued to be at the frontlines of the anti-*çarşaf* war as a sine qua non for modernization.[18] Female parliamentarians of *CHP* argued that *çarşaf* was embarrassing and belittling them in the eyes of the other nations.[19]

Military's Self-Prescribed Role as the Protector of the Secular Republic

The efforts to increase religion's public representation were sufficient for a perturbed military that saw itself as the protector of Kemalism to take action against the Menderes government.

> In 1958 *Ulus* [a national newspaper] had headlined Ataturk's remarks, made in an exasperated moment after a riot by religious reactionaries in Bursa in 1937, to the effect that the youth of Turkey must be prepared to take direct action to protect his reforms, even if it led to clashes with the authorities.[20]

Menderes was forced out of office and executed by the leaders of a coup d'etat. The *Milli Birlik Komitesi* (Committee of National Unity), a military group, rose to power under the leadership of General Cemal Gürsel, who was made both the president and the prime minister. People were fearful that the new administration would retreat from the expansions provided to the religious realm by the previous government. To their surprise, Islam assumed a more national and progressive image to promote change in the society. Acknowledging that Islam can be a source of inspiration to galvanize masses and that it was still an important part of Turkish people's lives, President Gürsel reminded people that it was religion that ordered them to be hardworking and perfectionist.[21] The Gürsel government, however, was not friendly to the *çarşaf*. Modern Turkish women were to modernize the women of *öteki*. They were encouraged to share their coats with women with *çarşaf* who were not able to buy coats because they lacked the money.[22]

Altering Political Actors: From Demirel to Erbakan

The next actor that emerged in the political field was *Adalet Partisi, AP* (the Justice Party), between 1965 and 1971. Prime Minister Süleyman Demirel allowed graduates of *İmam Hatip* schools to have access to higher education.[23] He was recognized as a man of the people. He was not a practicing religious Muslim per se but wielded Islam in his politics. He often referred to his religious family background.[24] He later changed his political colors, becoming an agent of Kemalism in the 1990s.

A significant development within the body of *AP* involved another member, Necmeddin Erbakan, who left the party in the late 1960s to establish *Milli Nizam Partisi, MNP* (the National Order Party), becoming the first leader of political Islam in the republic. He would later establish *Milli Selamet Partisi, MSP* (National Salvation Party) in 1973, the successor of *MNP*, and the *Refah Partisi, RP* (Welfare Party) in 1987 in tandem when the predecessor of each party was shut down by military interventions. Erbakan was against Turkey's close relationship with the West.

> [T]he European, by making us copy him blindly and without any understanding, trapped us in this monkey's cage and, as a result, forced us to

> abandon our personality and nobility. That is to say, he was successful in this because he used agents recruited from within, who felt disgusted with themselves bringing to his knees the Turk who for centuries could not be defeated by the crusades and the external blows.[25]

He was cognizant of the fact that the Orientalist assumptions were promoted by the local representatives of the Orientalist tradition. This entailed disunity among the people, dividing them into various opposing camps in social and political life. Erbakan did not believe in the superiority of the West, hence he challenged the very premise that the republic was predicated upon. This would put his movement under close surveillance by the protector agencies of the state. *MNP* stood for the religious constituents and saw lack of religiosity as the reason for all social ills. Not content with the manifestation of Turkish secularism, Erbakan argued that *laiklik* should not mean that the state can pry into religion.[26]

Paralleling the organization of politically minded Turkish groups, the 1960s saw the rise of a few *başörtülü kadınlar* as professionals. Şule Yüksel Şenler was "Turkey's Malcolm X" of the time.[27] She was a prominent writer who promoted *tesettür* through her newspaper column and lectures around the country. She appealed to the women of the elite, trying to transform them into *başörtülü kadınlar,* and was imprisoned for that.[28] Another author who served time in prison was Emine Şenlikoğlu. Other writers from *başörtülü kadınlar* included Bakiye Ersoy, Mümine Güneş, and Zeynep Münteha Polat.[29] Gülhan Kavakci (my mother) was another professional woman who was the only headscarved teacher in Istanbul's first established *İmam Hatip* school for boys.[30] Years later, her name would be included in the court documents of the closure case of *Fazilet Partisi, FP* (the Virtue Party; i.e., the successor of *RP*) as "the mother who has been dismissed from public service for not taking off her *türban*."[31] During her term at *İmam Hatip,* the school produced future political leaders. Among them were Prime Minister Erdoğan, the mayor of Istanbul Kadir Topbaş and many others who currently hold high-ranking public offices throughout the country. Hümeyra Öktem, a senior member of *başörtülü kadınlar* and a physician, and Meliha Yalçıntaş and Aynur Mısıroğlu, who are lawyers, were among those who assumed professional positions. By the late 1960s, in most places *çarşaf* was supplanted by a long coat and *başörtüsü* as a consequence of the pressure from the regime. This period spurred a debate on various issues pertinent to religion, from *başörtülü kadınlar* and *çarşaf,* to teachers of the Holy Qur'an and men with beards as evidences of *irtica* that is reactionaryism (backwardness) in the media.[32] This was a transitional period in the history of *tesettür.* The debate shifted during these years from *çarşaf* to *başörtüsü,* leading *çarşaf* to marginalize women. The first direct connection between *başörtüsü* and *irtica* was made by the *CHP* then.[33] In 1975, the state gave girls access to *İmam Hatip* schools.[34] This is an example of the Janus-faced stance of the state. On one hand, the state was encouraging women to get rid of their *tesettür*, on the other hand it was accommodating the female children of religious people to pursue education in these institutions. This period coincided with the general wave of rising Islamism in the larger Middle Eastern region. *Başörtülü kadınlar* became visible at various universities, some of whom were graduates of *İmam Hatip* schools while others adopted the headscarf after they started their higher education.

On March 12, 1971, a memorandum resulted in the banning of *MNP*. Once again the military cast its shadow over civil administration, beginning a long record of disparagement, harassment, and animosity against *başörtülü kadınlar* in public spaces.[35] The first publicized headscarf incident came in 1968, with Hatice Babacan, a student of Ankara University School of Islamic Studies, as the target. One of her professors claimed that he had not seen any student with a headscarf until then, and he would not accept seeing one from then on. Another professor stated that Babacan was wearing a headscarf for other reasons despite the fact that Babacan repeatedly stated that she was wearing it due to her religious convictions. The dean made it clear that Babacan was being manipulated by outside forces; that is, she was paid for wearing the headscarf as an agent of other nations and that she had a hidden agenda.[36]

A year before Babacan entered the university, Nesibe Bulaycı was coerced to take her headscarf off.[37] Also in 1968, a group of students who visited the tomb of *Rumi*, the Sufi poet, in Konya were taken into police custody due to their long coats and big white scarves. They were released after investigation.[38] In 1972, Emine Aykenar was disbarred from the Ankara Bar Association because "a religious cover could not be compatible with civilized dress and professional outfit."[39] The president of the bar association defended the disbarment decision by arguing that if they did not efface them from the bar, then "*başörtülü* [*kadınlar*] would fill up every corner."[40] The fear of dissemination of these women across professional lines was used to justify the harassments. Incidents in Konya, Malatya, Urfa, Isparta, and Emirdağ ensued in the years to come, in which students with headscarves were harassed at schools and their headscarves were torn.[41] During the school year 1977–1978, the school administration of Izmit *İmam Hatip* school brought a case against 215 students with headscarves.[42] In 1979, *başörtülü kadınlar*, along with bearded men, were not permitted to take the university central exam.[43]

The anti-*tesettür* campaign, led by the university administrations, school principals, and women's organizations, directly targeted the headscarf through claims that Islam does not mandate any punishment for the lack of *tesettür* and that in Turkey women of the cities never covered themselves like the *köylü kadınları* (i.e., peasant women, used as a pejorative term).[44] In the eyes of the regime, women of the periphery, the *köylü kadınlar,* were ignorant and backward. Religiosity was to remain within the confines of the villages and small towns without disseminating to the urban areas. The headscarf—a symbol of Islam, the Ottoman period, *köylü kadınlar,* and all pejorative traits attributed to them—was not supposed to invade the public arena, which, until then, was only occupied by the ruling elite and modernized bourgeoisie. Additionally anti-*başörtüsü* claims at this time presumed *tesettür*'s incompatibility with modernization.

The 1973 elections gave way to the birth of *MSP,* the successor of *MNP. CHP* and *MSP* established a coalition in which Bülent Ecevit and Erbakan assumed the positions of prime minister and deputy prime minister, respectively. For the first half of his political life, Ecevit, who was a journalist with a high school diploma, was a socialist. He was recognized as "populist Ecevit" by his supporters. Nonetheless, he would go through a transformation similar to Demirel and become a champion of Kemalism in the 1990s.

Under pressure from the *MSP,* the Ecevit–Erbakan coalition government of 1974 made optional religious education compulsory under moral education.[45] *MSP* predicated itself upon defending a religious view of the world, a call for swifter industrialization, and a redistributive populist economic and social ethic.[46] *MSP* tabled various resolutions that were rejected by *CHP.* MSP argued that the state should not be involved in manufacturing alcoholic beverages and that Friday should be the day of rest in lieu of Sunday.[47] The government was ephemeral. It dissolved after eleven months due to disagreements between the two parties in 1974.

Demirel became prime minister in 1975. Under pressure from *MSP* in the coalition, he agreed to give graduates of *İmam Hatip* schools access to higher education.[48]

During that period, political violence plagued the country on an ever-increasing scale. Not only did some students in institutions of higher education take part in the violence but also teenagers in secondary schools, as well as workers, unemployed youth, and ethnic separatists. Even though the main contention was between the right and the left, there was also internecine settling of accounts within the left and right.[49]

With the rising violence, the military under General Kenan Evren's command intervened on September 12, 1980. The coup "followed a six-year-long carnage of terror which had resulted in the deaths of more than 5,000 individuals throughout the country."[50]

Although Islamists were not at the center of the conflict as much as rightists and leftists were, the Jerusalem Night organized by *MSP* in Konya in support of the Palestinian people was among the reasons behind the military's meddling.[51] Years later, in 1997, a similar night with the same name, ironically, was organized by the successor *RP* and would be used as the pretext for another coup, leading to the march of military tanks on the streets of a town where the night was originally organized.

The Genealogy of the Ban

The next section will trace the changing administrative definitions/articulations of the ban by various governments in power and how *başörtülü kadınlar* reacted to each, which in turn contributed to the development of their agency and politicization.

The Evren Years: Turkey Meets the Ban

Evren assumed the presidency and enunciated that a committee comprised of military generals would be the governing body until the next election, which would take place in 1983. He imprisoned many and executed hundreds, in particular young people. Twenty-five years later, he would refer to the chilling criteria they used in their decision-making process at the time: "We said let us hang one from the right, one from the left."[52] To his critics, he responded, "what should we do? Not hang'em but feed'em?"[53] The leading figures in the political parties, including Erbakan, Demirel, and Ecevit, were imprisoned and banned from politics for ten years. Their parties were dissolved. The Evren government introduced an amended new constitution in 1982, which added further restrictions on freedom of expression. He refused the demands of academicians and religious activists to provide a clear definition of *laiklik* in the constitution.

Evren saw himself as the master of all knowledge, in particular religion. He would frequently opine on matters of religion, lecturing the public on what Islam does and does not mandate. He would bring his own interpretation in these public elucidations, arguing that Kemalism and Islam were compatible with one another. This was "Evren's Islam."[54] Until then, *laiklik* could be construed as a relationship where, in line with Joseph Nye's use of the term, hard power was used for the state to get what it wanted. Evren's approach was different. Under his command, the state not only continued with its interventionist policies through hard power, but also engaged in a more intellectual plan that could be described as Nye's "soft power." The former worked by eliminating religion's role in the public arena to an extent, while the latter aimed at changing the hearts and minds of the people. "Hard power" was effective in the short term while "soft power" was efficacious in the long term. Such a shift in approach could have stemmed from the fact that, despite all efforts, religion was a growing force.

> He employed Islam to promote his secular ideas and policies as well as to expand the social base of the military government. Evren believed that there is an enlightened Islam that is open to change and secularism. He used religious arguments for raising national consciousness, social responsibility, and health concerns, promoting birth control and social cohesion of the Turkish society to overcome its ethnic and ideological divisions. He underlined the rational nature of Islam to promote modernity and stressed religion's role as a unifying agent or social cement.[55]

In that spirit, in order to keep people's perception of Islam under control, the government introduced compulsory religious education to children between fourth and eleventh grade.

> Courses on religion and ethics were not confined to schools. In the spring of 1982, the Ministry of Justice began to provide courses on religion and ethics to more than 80,000 prisoners in jails all over Turkey.[56]

By the 1980s, not only had the number of young *başörtülü kadınlar* in the public sphere increased but the reaction to them increased as well. The fact that *İmam Hatip* schools accepted young *başörtülü kadınlar* as students encouraged families to send their daughters to school. The opening of society in post-1950 Turkey gave hope to religious Muslims who were concerned about their exclusion from politics. The religious peoples' activism in politics like that of Erbakan raised the confidence of these disenfranchised masses. As a result, they began to get involved in the emerging civil society. These developments contributed to the popularity of Islamic tendencies, including the adoption of the headscarf. Nonetheless, the denial of access to classrooms became very common in state universities throughout the country. At this time there were no private universities. By the late 1980s, private universities had been established, but they continued to deny entrance to *başörtülü kadınlar.*

The 1980s witnessed increased attempts to outlaw *başörtüsü* from the public realm.[57] In 1980, female parliamentarians who saw a group of *başörtülü kadınlar* attending the plenary session of the parliament as guest observers from the balcony protested them: "How did these women come into the Turkish Grand National Assembly that Atatürk established? Immediately throw them out."[58]

The military coup of 1980 was a turning point in the plight of *başörtülü kadınlar*. The Evren government "created *Yüksek Öğretim Kurumu, YÖK* (i.e., the Higher Education Council) with the goal of purging left-leaning professors and centralizing the curriculum and administration of the universities."[59] In Turkish history, Evren would be remembered as the person who introduced the headscarf ban. His unique interpretation of Islam included comments on *tesettür* as well. In a speech, he argued that "in the past there were no combs and hairdresser, therefore they used to cover!"[60] This argument was reminiscent of another argument used in the 1970s by elementary school teachers in explaining why *çarşaf* was banned. To pinpoint the dangers of wearing *çarşaf*, the teacher would refer to it as unhealthy, arguing that *çarşaf* was made so loose hence one would easily get sick from the cold air that could come in from under it. Along the same lines, children were taught that the reason behind Atatürk's alphabet reform was that Arabic letters were very difficult to learn while it was easy to learn the Latin alphabet.

General Evren banned the wearing of headscarves for students in 1981 through a decree of the National Security Council. Evren opined: "We will not let *başörtüsü* into the university. We are adamant about that. No one should insist on it. There is no such thing in the religion, anyway."[61] The administrative provision read: "Staff and students at the higher educational institutions must be in plain attire that is compatible with Atatürk's reforms and principles" and that "including foreign citizens residing here, all female and male students' outfits, shirts and shoes will be clean, preened up and plain; head will be uncovered and it will not be covered inside the institution."[62] In addition to *YÖK*'s provision that banned the headscarf, Evren introduced a second ban for government officials in 1982 through a provision to Article 657 of the Federal Employees Law.[63]

Although the ban existed for these two groups of women, the implementation was left to the discretion of universities, presidents, deans, and the faculty. At some universities the ban was harshly enforced while at others it was not applied as strongly.[64] Meanwhile *başörtülü kadınlar* learned to adapt to the exigencies. They transferred between universities. Some even changed their majors depending on the leniency of departments with respect to the headscarf. Some chose to freeze their education for a year or two while others submitted to the new rules and took off their headscarves. Some wore wigs on top of their headscarves. Some resorted to hats to cover up the headscarf underneath. Some managed by taking external examinations without having to come to school. Some simply turned to *Anadolu Üniversitesi Açık Öğretim*, the only online university in Turkey, as a solution.

Over time their experiences, their challenges, and their solutions became part of the history of representation of *başörtülü kadınlar.* They created their own vernacular. The fact that they represented themselves as *başörtüsü mağdurları* became a social phenomenon. This identification of victimization enabled them to share their experiences, learn from each other's encounters, cope and heal together, and fight toward a solution. The wall where they took off their headscarves before entering the school premises came to be known as *türban duvarı,* or the *türban* wall.[65] Public humiliation became part of the process. At times, news reporters, with camcorders in hand, waited at the gates to shoot dramatic footage of young *başörtülü kadınlar* in tears transforming themselves into "modern" Turkish women. Young *başörtülü kadınlar* at *İmam Hatip* schools faced the same predicament. In 1980, *Diyanet,* the Religious Affairs Directorate, opined that *İmam Hatip* students had to be permitted to cover because it was a religious mandate, however girls were only permitted to cover during Qur'an classes where they read the scripture.[66]

The Özal Years: Vacillation in between Lifting the Ban and Not

Evren decreed a new election in 1983. With all political party leaders in prison, Turgut Özal, who established the *Anavatan Partisi,, ANAP* (the Motherland Party), came to power garnering centralist, rightist, and Islamist votes. The Turkish republic entered a new era at this time. This marked the beginning of an active civil society.

> The post-1980 era in Turkey was a turning point, because the state-induced modernizing movement (Westernization), which had started in the mid-nineteenth century and had become institutionalized during the 1920–1980 period, virtually came to an end as the leading political paradigm. With the relative autonomization of economic activities, political groups, and cultural identities, an autonomous societal sphere began to develop, and the focus increasingly shifted from the state to society; consequently the modernizing elites began to lose their power to transform the society from above and were increasingly replaced by more representative elites. Paradoxically, the latter were mostly technocrats who belonged to the center-right political parties.[67]

These technocrats would be forced to share the public sphere with the rising religious conservative entrepreneurs in 1990s, leading to a power struggle between the two. The former then would transform itself into a Kemalist front to dismantle the latter. The leftist and Kemalists were represented by *Sosyal Demokrat Halkci Parti, SHP* (the Social Democratic Populist Party), a left-wing party with Kemalist inclinations under the leadership of Erdal İnönü, the son of İsmet İnönü. Özal's main challenge was the lack of separation of powers in the state and bureaucratic machinery. To be in office did not necessarily mean to be in power. Nonetheless, he came to be known as the man who opened Turkey to the free market economy in the 1980s. One might assume that Turkey's capitalist market was borne of liberalism, but it was actually statism that gave way to capitalism in Turkey.[68]

Özal served as prime minister from 1983–1989. He believed in people's right to exercise religious freedom. Therefore he wanted to relax the strict code of *laiklik*. He strove to advance awareness about Islam during his term.

> [He] encouraged religious indoctrination of the youth through state subsidies to religious schools [i.e., İmam Hatip], pious societies and mosques. Among the achievements of his epoch one can cite the building of 15,000 mosques. Carrying further the accommodation of Islam started by the military, during his power, he allowed the building of mosques on university campuses, encouraged the opening of more than 2,000 [Qur'anic courses], and increased the share of public money going to the directorate of religious affairs.[69]

YÖK passed another provision (upon Özal's demand) in 1984 to lift the headscarf ban. According to this new decree, *başörtüsü* were strictly banned from university premises, however wearing "*türban* in a modern way" was acceptable.[70] Here, Özal's role was somewhat successful in his attempt to integrate *başörtülü kadınlar* to public life. Students would be able to pursue their education while wearing *türban*. Nonetheless, as expressed earlier, it was not clear what *türban* was and how it was supposed to provide an acceptable alternative. The general public view was that it was supposed to be more modern looking than the *başörtüsü* in order to avoid the wrath of the Kemalists, maybe somewhat similar to that of the French bonnet. Hence everyone was entitled to his/her opinion as to what *türban* was. Unfortunately Özal's personal achievement concerning the ban would face a backlash from the judiciary system only months after *YÖK*'s decree. Until then, some of the universities required that women wear *türban* rather than *başörtüsü*, while others let *başörtülü kadınlar* in as they were. Nonetheless some others, including Ankara University Medical School, Hacettepe University Medical School, and Erzurum Atatürk University, did not budge. The doors were closed to *başörtülü kadınlar* no matter how they covered their head. This was the period when sundry transfers took place in order to avoid the ban. Many of the students moved around the country, changing their schools and/or their majors in order to not have to deal with the ban. This process, in a strange way, contributed to the empowerment of these *başörtülü kadınlar.* This was the period when most of them learned to be independent, take risks, and leave the nurturing, protected family environment and move to other cities on their own. "Cities" would later become "countries," in the late 1990s, as *başörtülü kadınlar* had to leave Turkey to pursue education in other places, mostly in Europe and the United States. During this time, they started igniting internal changes in their own religious communities and distinguishing themselves from the rest. This coincides with the time that *başörtülü kadınlar* started creating a well-rounded agency.

The *türban,* whatever it was supposed to be, did not supplant *başörtüsü.* There were four reasons behind that. First, the fact that *türban* lacked a clear description led to confusion and prevented it from becoming entrenched in the political culture. One had to know what it was before deciding to adopt it or discard it. Second, the fact that some of the universities did not condone the *türban* led to its loss of appeal among *başörtülü kadınlar. Türban* became part of the problem rather than the solution, from their perspective. Similarly, the Kemalists, who administered the universities, perceived that *türban* was the same as *başörtüsü* and therefore an impediment toward the Western appearance of the modern Turkish women, hence it was not acceptable either. Third, given the fact that it was a small bonnet, it did not meet the criteria of an Islamic *tesettür* that would be required to not only cover the hair but also loosely fall down upon the neck toward the chest. Thus women continued to wear headscarves in a more tucked-in fashion if their school administrations allowed *türban.* In reality it was not the case that the universities did not accept *başörtüsü* but accepted *türban.* They either condoned or banned them both. Therefore in the case of the former, *başörtülü kadınlar* continued to wear *başörtüsü* to the classroom. Fourth, after a short period of truce through *türban, YÖK* would alter its decision and ban *türban* as well. This is when the state would reload the concept of "*türban*" with its new and negative meaning, introducing the threat factor.

Despite these difficulties, the number of *başörtülü kadınlar* did not decline over time. On the contrary, students as young as thirteen years of age joined the *başörtülü kadınlar* group. This new generation of *başörtülü kadınlar* contributed to the differentiation process of what they wore from what their mothers and elders traditionally wore. This led to the further demarcation of *başörtüsü* and *türban.* As expressed before, the former referred to the kind of covering that was limited by tradition, passed on from one generation to the next, and used without questioning its meaning, while the latter referred to the kind of covering that symbolized women's transformation from the traditional realm to the more modern public realm, reflecting women's choice and, more importantly, an Islamic stance and identity.[71] The fact that the implementation of the ban was not strictly enforced at all universities gave *başörtülü kadınlar* more flexibility as to what to wear and how to wear it. Either they espoused different styles of wearing their headscarves depending on the demands of the public or educational institutions or they did not need to make any changes and simply continued to wear their headscarves as before. Hence the word "*türban*" was an enigma, but at the same time it was becoming more widely used. The old *türban,* which was originally intended to be a means of reconciliation, was now transformed into something new: the covering of the women who wanted to assert themselves into the public arena through education and career.

The state, with no intention to meet such demands from *başörtülü kadınlar,* would now use the term to distinguish this particular group of women from *başörtülü kadınlar* at the periphery. Through this sagacious step, the state would insinuate that it was not against *başörtüsü,* per se, but its exploitation by women who had other agendas such as to integrate themselves into public sphere. This was not only necessary in order to refute the claims that the regime was an enemy of Islam but also to frame this new generation of *başörtülü kadınlar* with negative attributes in order to more easily defeat them. If the state could introduce some suspicion in the hearts of the public about these women and their agendas, then it could more easily justify its actions against them.

Due to various factors—such as the general political atmosphere, occurrence of incendiary incidents pertinent to Islam, international Realpolitik, including the fact that the neighboring Islamic Republic of Iran has been perceived as a threat by the Turkish regime that might Islamize Turkey via a spillover effect—the ban was harshly put into effect. At times of political turmoil, the universities would reactivate the ban and force students to take their scarves off. While some would submit, others would halt their education and defer a semester or two. After stability was restored, some of the universities would loosen up the restrictions again. This led to daily negotiations between *başörtülü kadınlar* and the universities.

The next binding legal action came in 1984 from *Danıştay* (the Council of State), which served as the appeals court in a case brought by student Hatice Akbulut that produced a decree and set precedence for other cases involving *başörtülü kadınlar. Danıştay* decreed against the plaintiff:

> girls with insufficient education were wearing headscarves under the influence of the environment and traditions without having any particular thought in mind. Nevertheless, the girls who have sufficient education not

> to surrender to the public pressure and traditions are known to cover their heads while opposing the secular republican principles in order to express that they are espousing a state system that is predicated upon religion. For these people, headscarf, beyond an innocent habit, is a symbol of a world ideology that is antithetical to woman's liberation and our republic's main principles.[72]

It went on to say that "resistance against taking off her headscarf to the point that she is opposing the secular state's principles" renders rejection of her appeal.

The insinuation hidden in *Danıştay*'s argument was that educated *başörtülü kadınlar* should not be wearing headscarves, and if they did then they had a hidden agenda that challenged the premise that education would bring enlightenment and secularization. These women, as educated members of society, presented a different picture, a picture that the state never intended to create: of women who wanted to reconcile their religious conviction with their citizenship at a personal level. But the state was not able to reconcile their religious appearance with the national identity it bestowed upon itself and upon them. This presented a quandary for the state for the reason that it challenged the very premise that Turkey would be a role model as a secular, progressive state represented by the dress of its women.

In 1985, the debate over the ban took another turn on the number of female students that would be accepted to schools of theology at universities. It provided another means to ostracize *başörtülü kadınlar. YÖK* originally stated that female students would not be accepted to theology departments. However, in reaction to street protests, it agreed to a maximum 6 percent female student admission.[73] This is an example of how the state was working to eliminate *başörtülü kadınlar* from the public arena. On one hand it was banning the headscarf at schools as much as possible, on the other hand it was attempting to assure that not many would choose to study religion, which was an area where *başörtülü kadınlar* could legitimately be present. This was a multilayered war against *başörtülü kadınlar.* A similar method would later be used in 1998 against graduates of *İmam Hatip* schools.

The Özal years witnessed incessant contention between Evren and Özal over *irtica* and *başörtüsü.* By 1986, the political atmosphere reached the climax of *irtica* warnings. The pro–status quo columnists were bombarding the public about how bad things were and how prevalent *irtica* was. Evren summoned the National Security Council and enunciated that *irtica* was a real threat at the end of the meeting. In accordance with Evren's statement, *YÖK* banned *türban* at universities in early 1987 by repealing its earlier provision of 1984 that permitted it.[74] In his written statement, the president of *YÖK*, Ihsan Doğramacı, argued that recently there were *başörtülü kadınlar* at the universities who insisted that what they were wearing was *türban* even though what they wore covered the entirety of their head. This referred to the expectation that *türban* would look more modern, and therefore would leave some of the hair exposed, however none of the *başörtülü kadınlar* made that concession. Doğramacı argued that this was an exploitation of *türban*. He also drew attention to the fact that some of them were wearing the same color and same shape of covering, which was interpreted as a sign of a particular ideology.[75] That was to say that these women represented the same political movement and were automatically rendered a danger to the state. The national government went so far as to suggest that these women were part of an organized illegal group. Here we witness the state's encroachment on women's lives by exerting control over their appearance and its redefinition of *başörtülü kadınlar* by categorizing them as a distinct politicized group's members who dress and behave the same.

Başörtülü kadınlar at the universities and their supporters continued their organized action against the ban. They held protests at parks, circles, and in front of their school gates. Some held starvation protests while others held sit-ins. Meanwhile, Özal was beginning to realize that he might not win this war. If *YÖK* was going along with him, another institution, such as *Danıştay,* was becoming the stumbling block. It was clear that Özal did not see the headscarf as independent from the role of religion and the definition of public arena, which were all under attack. Kemalists' complaint about *irtica* was an effective tool in this fray.

Danıştay continued to decree against *başörtülü kadınlar* in 1987, 1989, 1992, and 2005 in various individual cases. A gradual restriction of the wearing of *başörtüsü* ensued. The decisions showed that the tolerance of *tesettür* had diminished and resulted in the state's further intrusiveness beyond the education system, the workplace, and work hours. The 1987 decision differentiated between *başörtüsü* and *türban,* rendering the former antithetical to *laiklik* but not the latter, based on the way it was used.

> *Başörtüsü* is rendered anti-secular ideological symbol because it fits the head tightly and diligently covers all parts except the face. *Turban* on the other hand does not present such parochial appearance. Hence it is appropriate for the disciplinary committee not to see *başörtüsü* as *türban*.[76]

Lacking a clear definition by the state with respect to how it must look, *türban* was presented at this decree as an acceptable form of *tesettür.* Then what was *türban*? The state remained silent until 1992, when it declared that both *başörtüsü* and *türban* were antithetical to *laiklik*. Similar to this case, the 1989 decision argued that *başörtüsü* was not a contemporary outfit, resulting in a warning for the plaintiff.[77] As a result of an unremitting campaign of persistent parliamentarians who believed in freedom of expression for *başörtülü kadınlar* from Özal's *ANAP* in the Grand National Assembly, *YÖK* revoked the ban in 1988 by adding Article 16 to the Student Discipline Provision, which read "due to religious belief, the neck and the hair can be covered by a cover or *türban*."[78] The Turkish parliament also added the same provision to the law numbered 3511 as Article 16.[79] The opposition party (Social Democrat Populist Party) immediately ignited an anti-*başörtüsü* campaign. The media followed suit. Tension quickly escalated, and Evren vetoed the bill. The reaction to the veto from both the parliamentarians of *ANAP* and people on the street was so strong that Evren had to enunciate through his spokesperson that he was not against *türban,* but he was against the way the provision was worded. After a few changes, Özal sent the bill before Evren for a second time, arguing that this was a human rights issue and that he was going to support it no matter the cost. Evren signed the bill but also took the case to appeal at the constitutional court.[80] The court repealed Article 16 based on the argument that it contradicted Articles 10, 24, and 174 of the Turkish constitution, which dealt with equality before the law, freedom of religion and conscience, and the protection of the revolutionary laws, respectively.

> Even if it was an imperative of religion, no regulation stemming from religion could be valid before the Constitution. Freedoms are circumscribed by the Constitution. Actions that are antithetical to the principle of secularism of the Constitution and the secular educational regulations can not be argued to be rendered democratic rights.[81]

In other words, the constitutional court espoused the view that in a secular state, religion cannot serve as a frame of reference. Accordingly, in 1989, *YÖK* revoked the pertinent article that was passed in 1988.

Başörtülü kadınlar were harassed on campuses, were verbally abused in the classroom by their professors, and disciplinary actions were taken against them. After hearing the recent decree of the constitutional court, a professor at a local university in Ankara confronted his headscarved students in class: "Now we will efface you from this school," while another one challenged a headscarved student: "Are you a student? You can't be a student with this attire. You go and wear your student attire and come back. You are not even a human being with that attire."[82]

Özal assumed the presidency in 1989. At that time, Mesut Yılmaz, a long-term member of *ANAP,* became the leader of the party. The fact that Özal became the president gave hope to *başörtülü kadınlar.* Demirel, who was heading *Dogru Yol Partisi, DYP* (the True Path Party), which was the successor of *AP,* supported *ANAP* on this issue. He argued that whoever wanted to wear a headscarf should wear it, whoever did not want to did not have to wear it and that he was pro-freedom and against all bans.[83] Later, both Demirel and Yılmaz would be instrumental in the post-modern coup d'etat of 1997 and would wage one of the worst wars against religious Muslims in the decade to come. However, at this point they played along with the liberal rhetoric.

As a result of the concerted efforts of *ANAP* and *DYP,* in 1990 the Turkish Grand National Assembly passed law no. 3670 to add Article 17 to law no. 2547 of *YÖK.* Article 17 read "at institutions of higher education outfits are permissible so long as they are not antithetical to the laws enacted."[84] However the opposition went to the constitutional court to repeal Article 17. The court decided that Article 17 was in accordance with the Turkish constitution. This was a victory for *başörtülü kadınlar,* who started enjoying their education and career in the public arena. That is not to suggest that the problem went away but only to suggest that the headscarf issue was solved for a while, until 1993 when the constitutional court brought a new interpretation to Article 17 stating that the permissibility of outfits would not accommodate wearing of the headscarf for religious reasons.[85] In 1992, *Danıştay* concurred that covering the neck and hair with *başörtüsü* and *türban* was antithetical to the Turkish constitution, and hence was exempt from freedom of dress.[86]

Looking at the trajectory of the constitutional debate that followed with respect to freedom of expression (including headscarf-related issues), one would see that it was, invariably, centered around the concept of *laiklik.* Article 2 of the constitution read: "State of Turkey is a republican, nationalist, populist, statist, laic and revolutionist state."[87] *Laiklik* mentioned here is the only foreign word to the Turkish culture. *Laiklik* requires the state to become the sole custodian of religion. Unlike the prevalent Western conceptualization of secularism where both religion and state do not intervene with one another, allowing them to burgeon on their own, *laiklik* in the Turkish context allows for the state's encroachment on religion in the public realm, and even in the private realm to the extent that it sees fit. In its efforts to limit religion's involvement in state affairs, the Turkish Republic ironically becomes excessively involved in matters of religion. Within this context, *Diyanet,* the directorate of religious affairs, serves to oversee religious affairs and education in the name of the state. As a result, while eschewing establishment of a religious state, the republic created a state religion through its involvement in religious affairs as a regulator. That is what *laiklik,* that is, secularism, in the

Turkish context is.[88] *Laiklik*, as it stands as an intricate part of the state and national identity representations, is not up for contestation. Therefore it is treated as a taboo. As the founder of this religion-like secularism, unique to the Turks, Atatürk is attributed a divine-like character by the regime.[89] Following are examples of the poems produced in the early republican period by poets Ömer Bedrettin Uşaklı, Ilhami Bekir, and Yusuf Ziya Ortaç respectively, to celebrate the existence of the Founding Father Atatürk:

> [Lonely like a sun,
> You are our mission God]
>
> *Bir güneş gibi yalnız*
> *Sensin ülkü tanrımız*[90]

and

> [He drew the map of the soil to the flag
> Not Allah, he wrote our destiny]
>
> *Toprağın haritasını çizdi bayrağa*
> *Allah değil, o yazdı alın yazımızı...*[91]

and

> *He creates everything from nothing just like God*[92]

Since 1980, the back-and-forth passages and repeals of the ban only made it a more polarizing and volatile issue. The parliament and the elected did not see eye to eye with the judiciary, the appointed. Most members of the judiciary were Kemalists who were parochial on matters pertinent to the "other." They had strict views about freedom of religion and dress and were not open to negotiation, lacking any empathy. Thus they ignore the needs of the "other."

Article 70 of the 1924 constitution included freedom of conscious as a natural right for all Turks. The constitution of 1961, Article 2 stated that Turkey was a "national democratic, secular and social law state."[93] It also referred to freedom of conscious in Article 19: "Everybody has freedom of conscious, religious belief and conviction." The 1982 constitution included the same article within the content of Article 24. Yet none was construed to include the rights of *başörtülü kadınlar.*

The conflicting decrees one after another divided people into camps and raised frustrations. The state could not foresee the explosion in the number of women demanding public spaces in different ways contemporaneously. Hence it assumed that it could, through a decree or individual cases, clamp down *başörtülü kadınlar* and resolve the problem. This proved not to be the case. Most of the *başörtülü kadınlar* were young middle-class women at the universities whose resistance grew more vocal, challenging the preconceived notions about them. This segment of the middle class that benefited from the republic proved to be a formidable foe.

Başörtülü kadınlar who were parents of university students, representing a different generation, faced the same challenges despite the fact that they were not students. Military grounds were closed to all *başörtülü kadınlar,* not only as military officials but even as relatives of the military men. Most of the *İmam Hatip* schools permitted *başörtülü kadınlar* both as students and as teachers or staff, but some did not. Some took disciplinary action against women who resisted the ban. The situation in the private schools owned by the religious communities varied. Students were not permitted to have *tesettür* on the school premises. The teachers, however, were mostly permitted. The biggest challenge for these schools was the inspection period. During the periodic inspections, *başörtülü kadınlar* among the teachers and the staff would either not come to school on that particular day or take off their headscarves for that day. The inspections, however, often took place at unexpected times, which made it difficult for the teachers to prepare. The bureaucratic inspectors, knowing the Islamic tendencies of the school, would show up unexpectedly, leading *başörtülü kadınlar* to run, for instance, up to the attic and hide. This provisional period for both *İmam Hatip* schools and private schools lasted until the military intervention in 1997, which changed things for the worse for *başörtülü kadınlar.*

Tansu Çiller: Paradoxes of the Republican Women

The sudden death of Özal in 1993 brought Demirel to presidency. He bequeathed *DYP* to his minister of economy, Tansu Çiller, whom he called his daughter.[94] She became the prime minister. Çiller represented the privileged class. She was the success story of the republic, a prototype of what the state had intended to create for the past seventy years. She represented everything that the state expected in a modern Turkish woman. She was westernized in appearance, well educated, and affluent. She was a member of the secular elite, not a representative of the *Anatolian* women. Her rise to power at a time when the state was in a long battle with *başörtülü kadınlar* was meaningful for the state at another level. Although the ban was not internationally publicized then (that is to say that it was not an issue that Turkey had to deal with at the international level), it was still a debilitating factor as far as the morale of the regime was concerned. At a time when the state was striving to come to terms with what went wrong with the creation of modern Turkish women and the rise of *başörtülü kadınlar*, Tansu Çiller emerged as a lifesaving figure for the state and its ideology.

The fact that she came to power at a time when political Islam was very popular under the *RP* flag was meaningful as well. For the outside observers who agonized over Turkey's rising Islamism, she presented the modern alternative for the future of Turkey. In 1990, during a visit to Washington, she criticized Özal for being a *yobaz* (a pejorative term used to describe extremely religious simpleminded people) and alerted the American officials against the rise of *irtica*, Islamic reactionary-ism in Turkey.[95] She was the woman the state took pride in "making." However, Çiller made a mistake, common for leaders, of closing herself off to anyone other than her newly established inner circle within the party, which shielded her from constructive critique. Due to the fact that she was educated in the United States, many conjectured at the outset that she would be an open-minded leader, accommodating differences and promoting pluralism. Her rhetoric and actions were contradictory: "The chief paradox was the irreconcilability between her emphasis on democracy and the excessive conservative and authoritarian policies."[96] While she hailed and praised democratization, she also opposed introducing measures to establish more transparency. Furthermore she would easily change her position on a particular matter. For instance, while she promoted opening up the space for the Kurdish population at the outset of her premiership, later she changed her position and sided with the militarist uncompromising position, clashing with the *PKK* (the Kurdish separatist group that rebels against the Turkish state). On a similar note, the same Çiller who accused Islamists like Erbakan for taking the country back to the dark ages would later not mind cooperating with the Islamists.[97] She also appeared to be in favor of civilian control of the military when she first came to power, but soon after she succumbed willingly to the patronage of the military, to the disappointment of many liberals.[98]

Her political life did not last long compared to many of the politicians in the country. Her party's defeat at the ballot box in the 2002 elections was a consequence of her wrongheaded policies. Çiller angered many for various reasons during her political tenure. She was politically avaricious and economically corrupt. She espoused Machiavellian leadership style.[99] Within the party, as is the case for other political leaders, she had to tackle the opposition who was always poised to facilitate her loss of power. After awhile, she failed to maintain the support of her colleagues.[100] She easily changed her position, even regarding very fundamental issues, in order to maximize her power, which made her seem like a person who lacked principle. She disappointed her constituents for being a Janus-faced politician who did not stick with her ideals or keep her promises. She upset the secularists by establishing a coalition government with Erbakan's *RP* after disparaging *RP* publicly for months, stating that she would not work with the Islamists.

Furthermore, forming a coalition with *RP* was perceived by many as condoning the Islamists. This angered the Kemalists, particularly her female constituents in this stratum. She upset the liberals and democrats for undermining the rights discourse, especially during the coup of 1997. In fact, she was instrumental for this intervention. By threatening Prime Minister Erbakan with ending the coalition government, she made it easier for the military to introduce the coup. Religious people resented her for that. Moreover, during her years as the prime minister, they felt that they were left out, for she did not attend to their needs. Islamists disliked her for disparaging the political Islamic movement. With respect to *başörtülü kadınlar,* Çiller did not make any effort to lift the ban or fight against the ones who harassed *başörtülü kadınlar.* Finally, she disappointed the state as a protégé for modern Turkish women, failing the expectations of a politically astute female leader.

Her prime ministry depicted the opportunities open to women in the Turkish Republic, yet she ended up outside of the political loop at the end of a decade, despite all the vested interest in her as a modern Turkish woman. Çiller took the power she assumed for granted, thinking that she would not be held accountable for her actions. However, the constituents took note of her involvement in corruption schemes and her role in the coup of 1997 and they punished her at the ballot box. But one must also acknowledge that she was not any more corrupt or greedy than some of her male colleagues. Nonetheless, at the end of the day her success and failure were dependent on male patronage and eventually her new role was undermined by the persistence of patriarchal attitudes toward women. In order to find acceptance, Çiller had to present herself in public as the "*ana,*" the peripheral version of "*anne*" (i.e., mother).[101] The state patriarchy promoted all Turkish women, modern or non-modern, to be mothers first. Thus she referred to herself as "*ananiz*" (i.e., your mother) at public addresses in *Anatolia.* This seemed to be an artificial post, for she did not represent "*ana*" imagery. Her appearance, her composure, and her speech were far from the image of "*ana,*" a woman of the periphery, both religious and conservative. The media scrutinized her life in the same way that they did the Islamists, which is to say much more than they examined the lives of any secular male politicians. Her mistakes were amplified and less forgivable than the mistakes of her male colleagues.

The fact that Çiller appointed two women to her cabinet was an important symbolic step for women's political achievements. In a country where ministers would invariably be male, including the Minister of Women's Affairs, Çiller's appointment of two female colleagues as Minister of Internal Affairs and Minister of Women's Affairs was significant. During her term, Turkey worked with the United Nations' Convention on the Elimination of All Forms of Discrimination against Women (CEDAW) to improve women's lives. Nonetheless this was politics as usual. Her cabinet did not pay much more attention to women's issues than any other government. Most of the improvements in women's lives were initiated externally as part of the larger European Union integration program.

During her tenure, the headscarf ban started to resurface. The main reasons behind this were the visibility of political Islam and its conspicuous female members starting with the 1994 municipality elections. Demirel and Çiller did not put the headscarf issue on their agenda. They remained out of the conflict between *başörtülü kadınlar* and *YÖK*. Demirel responded both to the rise of Islamism and *başörtülü kadınlar*, targeting them separately, but Çiller's response to *başörtülü kadınlar* was indirect. She sagaciously managed to remain out of the headscarf discourse without tainting herself for supporting a particular camp. She looked the other way when *başörtülü kadınlar* were harassed.

The Erbakan Years: Political Islam Takes Stage

By 1994, a shift occurred in the focus of the state. Until then, *başörtülü kadınlar* were among a small number of groups that consumed the most attention and energy of the state. At the brink of the looming local elections, the state included in its focus the larger religious Muslim community who were active in the Islamist movement. From that time on, the issue of *başörtülü kadınlar* would be politicized because of its connection to the *RP* movement and thus to *irtica*. The visibility of *başörtülü kadınlar* in elections was among the underlying reasons behind the restrictive actions taken by the state against the religious Muslims in the mid-1990s. *Başörtülü kadınlar* became synonymous with the rise of Islamist politics in Turkey. They were treated as both the cause and the effect of the rise of political Islam. Women indeed played a significant role in the success of the Islamist *RP* Welfare Party in the 1994 municipal elections. Prior to this period, they did not espouse political agency—Islamist politics granted them the agency they lacked. They took on the very public sphere that was denied to them as political agents. In turn, the Islamist political movement increased their saliency. Despite the fact that not all of the *başörtülü kadınlar* claimed membership in the Islamist movement, the state perceived all *başörtülü kadınlar* in the public realm as an inextricable part of the Islamist politics and treated them accordingly.

There were two important reasons behind the rise of *RP* in 1994 elections, one of which was political and the other economic. The following two headlines from the ruling elite's media pinpoint these factors: "The other Turkey wins the election" and "the Black Turks versus the White Turks."[102] The late 1980s and into the 1990s, to varying degrees, gave way to the emergence of the civil society in different parts of Turkey. By the early 1990s, the number of associations reached 70,000.[103] There exist around 3,000 organizations in the form of foundations currently working on a wide range of issues.[104] For the first time in the republican history, organizations, associations, and initiatives that accommodate people outside of the elite class were established in mass numbers. They emerged as a reaction and therefore posed a challenge to the "secular and state-centric model of Turkish modernity."[105] In Istanbul, emblematic of the most urbanized and industrialized cities of the country, there was a significant increase in the number of Islamic organizations in the 1980s.[106] In the political realm, secular and Islamist parties presented a discrepancy in their support of the civil society. The former "did not envision benefiting from it,"[107] unlike the Islamist parties like *MSP* and the ensuing *RP*, which utilized the power in these ready-to-serve groups. They managed to turn inert masses into active political actors. At the same time, with the economic incentives the Özal period provided, small- and medium-scale entrepreneurs emerged in *Anatolia* and came to be known as the "*Anatolian* lions." The development of the free market economy created "opportunities for upward mobility and demands for a better political and economic climate for business."[108] Within this atmosphere, conservative Muslims established "their own labor confederation (Hak-Iş) and business association (MÜSIAD)."[109] They were the economic face of the Islamist movement, an alternative to the conglomerates who were the product of the regime and ruled and reigned in their own right for the last eighty years.

The fact that more than half of the municipalities throughout the country were won by the Islamist party offered a two-fold advantage for the *Anatolian* lions. First, it provided the emotional confidence that religious Muslims generally lacked. Their entrepreneur spirit was as free and valuable as that of the secular elite. Second, considering the fact that partisanship and cronyism were part of the reality of the Turkish politics, to have *RP* in office increased their chances of cooperation in a way that would impact these businesses. Meanwhile the star of Erdoğan's cabinet as the mayor of Istanbul and a possible successor of the leader of the Islamist movement, Erbakan, started to shine.

Disturbed by these developments (i.e., seeing the religious Muslims gain power both economically and politically), the state turned on *başörtülü kadınlar* for vengeance. Their harassment became part of the daily reality. The evening news would frequently air stories about them in a scathing manner. One news anchor delightedly reported how the dean of a school pulled a *başörtülü* student to himself and kissed her on both cheeks when she went up to the stage to receive her degree as the valedictorian. Since Islam restricts physical interaction between males and females, the dean violated the value system of his student by not only engaging in physical interaction with her, but also kissing her on the cheek despite her clear resistance. By 1994, a few television channels owned by religious communities were established. They presented an alternative to the elite-controlled pro-status-quo media. They started reporting on how *başörtülü kadınlar* were victimized in their daily encounters in the public sphere.

The 1995 general elections brought *RP* its second victory. Nonetheless, this alone was not sufficient to form a government. Çiller's *DYP* remained in coalitions first with *CHP* and finally with *ANAP*. Meanwhile the state introduced new vocabularies and new justification methods to be used on the headscarf ban discourse. While secularism remained at the crux of the contention, the discussions shifted toward new concepts, such as the public space, political symbolism, and threat in response to the victory *RP* gained. It was clear that the state was frustrated with religious subjects' visibility in the public arena in a manner that was more active than what it had assumed. Unlike in the past, *başörtülü kadınlar* were not willing to remain in their private sphere and succumb to the Kemalist regime and remain as the underdog in the shadows. Victory in politics boosted the conservative masses' confidence further. The state's frustration immediately reverberated on the treatment of *başörtülü kadınlar* through more restrictions.

Başörtülü kadınlar, in accordance with the rapidly emerging civil society and discourse on democratization, began for the first time to voice that they were denied their basic human rights of education and sustenance. Men in *RP* approached the matter from a more masculine perspective, stating that women's education was necessary for their motherhood.[110] In addition to differences of opinion as to why *başörtülü kadınlar* should be permitted into the public sphere within these religious communities, a shift in the state's rhetoric ensued. The state reasserted the *laiklik* card and introduced the public sphere discussion.

In 1996, Çiller resigned from her prime minister seat due to economic instability resulting from high inflation rates and corruption, agreeing to leave her seat to Mesut Yılmaz who was the head of *ANAP*. *ANAP* and *DYP* established a coalition where Çiller and Yılmaz would take turns as prime ministers. The main goal of this government was to thwart Erbakan's *RP* from coming to power. A negative campaign against *RP* was launched by the state with the active participation of the mass media. Rapacious for power, Yılmaz and Çiller joined in. In this multilayered campaign, everybody contributed at different levels: the bureaucracy, judiciary body, and military insulted the *RP* publicly while the media carried out a campaign based on assaults and denigrations. The media would not just target an ideology or a movement, but made its attacks very personal to diminish the public standing of the political figures. Yılmaz and Çiller enunciated that they would not have anything to do with *RP*. Meanwhile they could not avoid the conflict between each other.

> The political rivalry between Yılmaz and Çiller opened a new window of opportunity for the *RP*. According to the coalition's rotation agreement, Yılmaz became prime minister first, and Çiller was to assume the post in January 1997. However, Yılmaz's main aim was to prevent Çiller from assuming the premiership, and thus he began to search for evidence of corruption allegedly carried out by the Çiller family. Hoping either to remove Çiller as head of the *DYP* or to divide the *DYP*, Yılmaz leaked some of the incriminating documents to *RP*, the main opposition party in the parliament. But *RP* used these documents not to attack Çiller but rather to assault the coalition government.[111]

RP's actions influenced Çiller to end the coalition government. Meanwhile an investigation was underway to probe the allegations. Now *RP* was supposed to assume office as the largest party in the parliament, but only if another party agreed to establish a coalition. No one agreed. Parties at the center, right, and left distanced themselves from *RP* publicly. Every door *RP* knocked on was closed in its face. The motto quickly became "never with *RP*." Çiller's attempt to have Yılmaz enter into another coalition was futile. Finally she acquiesced to establish a coalition with *RP*. This move angered Kemalist groups against Çiller for lending her status for Islamist political gains. Their anger was due to the fact that she was not consistent in her arguments and that she was making a coalition with the "backward" Islamists. From their perspective, Çiller was power hungry and could not resist the temptation of coming to office again, even if it was with the Islamists' support. Çiller was not able to stand tall after this in the eyes of her Kemalist constituents and the establishment.

RP would soon disappoint its constituents as well. The government under Erbakan was established in June 1996. He became the prime minister while Çiller became the deputy prime minister. To the chagrin of its constituents, who expected moral conduct in the name of religion from *RP,* they cleared Çiller on two major corruption accounts in *TEDAŞ* and *TOFAŞ* and the allegations about her personal assets. This had been Çiller's condition for agreeing to form the coalition with Erbakan. This was unacceptable for religious Muslims who were taught to be on the side of the right even if it went against their own self interest, as Islam mandated. Confronting disconcerted constituents, the party argued that such concessions were necessary in the real world of politics. In that world, there was "widespread disenchantment with other parties that were increasingly sinking in a slime of corruption, kleptocracy, interpersonal feuds, and ineffectualness."[112] *RP* decided to take advantage.

On the other hand, this was a long-awaited victory for *RP* supporters, a victory that came after thirty years of earnest hard work. In the immediate aftermath of the negative campaign carried out against *RP,* the people made a choice to support *RP.* This was a clear slap in the face of the Kemalist elite. *RP* rolled up its sleeves without respite:

> The *RP* proposed two solutions for Turkey's underdevelopment: revitalizing cultural bonds in order to ground modernity in authentic Islamic values and industrializing Turkey in order to secure political and economic independence.[113]

Within this system, *başörtülü kadınlar* and modern Turkish women were expected to exist together without one swaying the other. When Erbakan formed the coalition government with Çiller in 1997, he publicly heralded that soon the presidents of the universities would salute the *başörtülü kadınlar.* This angered the Kemalists enormously. They would not permit Erbakan to deliver on this promise. On the contrary, the state would use it as a pretext to stifle *başörtülü kadınlar.* Moreover, Erbakan's words would be construed as posing a threat and would be stated among the reasons for closure of the *RP* by the constitutional court.[114]

Erbakan had two aims: to open up society by expanding freedoms that stifled the practicing Muslims while also Islamizing the regime and challenging the status quo that enabled corrupt schemes to benefit few at the expense of many. *RP* angered the corrupt elite and their military allies who sat on the executive boards of news agencies and private banks, as well as the military-owned enterprises and banks. The effects of shifting the direction of the financial channels were immediate. In the eleven and a half months that *RP* was in office, it saved \$35 billion while it reduced the deficit from \$45 billion to \$22 billion.[115] In 2007, even one of the masterminds behind the coup against the Islamist-led government admitted that the economy was in good shape.[116] Erbakan also believed in the possibility of establishing an Islamic Union similar to the European Union. The D8, which stood for the "developing eight," was established under his leadership as an alternative to what was then the G7 of the West to unite efforts of Iran, Pakistan, Nigeria, Bangladesh, Malaysia, Indonesia, and Turkey.

A Turning Point for the Nation: February 28, 1997

With the fear of losing power both ideologically and economically, the Kemalists turned to the military, "a strong hand in crushing what they [saw] as a threat to the regime's existence."[117] For "authoritarian elites usually have enough power to repress mass demands, as long as they control the military and are willing to use coercion."[118] General Çevik Bir took the lead in what would be described as the post-modern coup d'etat. The Kemalist military saw themselves as the ultimate protectors of the secular state. Since Turkish modernity was under threat in this post-modern era, a military intervention was imperative to preserve modernity. This intervention was post-modern because it was not a sole intervention by the military, but also civilian (media and Kemalist elite) orchestrated.

The intervention was aimed at toppling the *RP* government, but it also signaled the revenge that the "white Turks" would take on the "black Turks" for the 1994 elections. At one point General Bir warned Ilnur Çevik, a columnist who was vacillating between the two camps: "We don't like gray. We are white. The opposite is black. Make up your mind."[119] The enlightened "white" Turks "felt responsible for the republic and wanted to do something against the religious uprising."[120] Similarly, modern Turkish women closed rank against *başörtülü kadınlar.* Kemalist women "started wearing an Atatürk pin" after *RP*'s victory in the 1994 municipality elections. One stated:

> When I am walking on the street, I want to show that there are people who are dedicated to Atatürk's principles. Look, now there are veiled women walking around even in this [upscale] neighborhood. I push my chest forward to show them my pin as I pass them. I have my Atatürk against their veil.[121]

The post-coup period of the Turkish political history was stifling for the masses—men, women, children, religious Muslims, as well as liberals and democrats. The liberal intellectuals who voiced their views publicly against military interventions suffered the consequences. If they were academicians then *YÖK*, which operated not as much as an educational institution but as a political Kemalist institution, opened investigations on them. If they were journalists then they were fired from their news agencies in accordance with the demands of active military officers. The "cozy" relationship between the military, the bureaucracy, and judiciary body and the relationship between the military and a few business tycoons who owned almost 90 percent of the Turkish media (and had their hands in all industries) provided the political economic framework for the coup and its implications.

In 2007, the tenth anniversary of the coup, the Turkish public learned more about what had happened behind closed doors during that critical time. *Batı Çalışma Grubu, BÇG* (the West Working Group) was established by the military to implement its directives. The military took on the duty of the organizer, bringing together journalists, nongovernmental organizations, professional organizations, women's groups, business groups, and most importantly well-read columnists to listen to their briefings. The Islamist media was neither invited nor allowed onto the military bases where these briefings were held. The *BÇG* informed the public about the seriousness of the situation that the country was in, warned against the direction in which it was headed, and ordered them to organize for protest. *BÇG* also ordered them to create virtual chaos and fear among the public with the allegation that the Turkish Republic was turning into Iran or Saudi Arabia in order to galvanize people as defenders of Kemalism.

The secret pressure mechanism, dubbed *andıç* (i.e., a set of commands from the military to civil society), was used to silence liberal journalists who were against the military intervention.[122] The confidential document of an *andıç* was sent to the editors-in-chief or the owners of the news agencies to fire a list of journalists and to fabricate news to raise the tension on the streets to bring about a coup-fertile atmosphere. Kemalist women were instrumental in negative campaigns in the media and in street protests. Political instability would reverberate in the economy without respite, causing the stock market to plummet. The government would not be able to perform but could only react to the allegations and try to appease crowds and stabilize the economy.

Neither the name nor the concept of *andıç* was publicized then. Turkish people only came to know of *andıç* and its role in 2007, when military scandals were divulged. President Demirel was instrumental at every stage of the coup. A man who had presented himself as a man of the people was now a spokesperson for the pro-interventionist camp and a preserver of the status quo. He would remain so until the end of his political career.

Usage of *fişleme*, (i.e., the surveillance and reporting system) became instrumental in the progress of the Kemalists as they prepared to topple the *RP* government. Under the oversight of *BÇG,* this method provided information gathering and reporting in a bottom-up model. Accordingly, *fişleme* would enable the military to be informed about the activities of people who work as state or military officials and bureaucrats in towns and cities throughout the country. *YÖK* also utilized *fişleme* to carry out espionage about the faculty at universities. As a result, the authorities would be informed of any anti-secular activities, such as men wearing the Islamic silver wedding band instead of a gold band, or having a wife with a headscarf, or refraining from alcoholic beverages—all indicators of an Islamic lifestyle.[123]

During this period, a vast number of academics lost their posts or faced investigations. The president of *YÖK,* Kemal Guruz, confirmed "that some rectors [presidents of universities] have been dismissed but [I] decline to disclose the exact number."[124] The ones who dared to publicly criticize the headscarf ban or condone the presence of *başörtülü kadınlar* in the classroom were removed from their posts or discharged from the university.[125] *Fişleme* and its consequences were not limited to religious Muslims but included surveillance of the liberal, democrat intellectuals, and basically anyone who defied the status quo. Two such voices were those of Mustafa Erdoğan and Atilla Yayla, two eminent scholars at different universities. The former faced prosecution and was tried for speaking and writing about issues of democracy and military interventions while the latter faced charges for publicly criticizing Kemalism.[126]

Various incidents led the National Security Council to ask Erbakan to sign eighteen directives under duress on February, 28, 1997. He received enormous criticism from his constituents for signing the document instead of resigning. The NSC meeting declared "Islamic movement to be the number one internal security threat" and "Muslim businesses, the Islamic education system, media, and religious activism as primary threats to the secular nature of the Turkish state."[127] The directives included altering the mandatory primary education system from five to eight years with the intention of blocking religious education and rendering *İmam Hatip* schools ineffective. The implementation of the directives did not take place during *RP* government; they were undertaken by the ensuing government.

The Ecevit Years: The Road to the 2001 Economic Crisis

RP was forced out of office in early June 1997. The head of the National Security Council enunciated that if it was necessary, the coup would last for a thousand years, stressing the determination of the Turkish military in its fight against the Islamists. The mastermind Çevik Bir described this intervention as a social engineering project.[128] The closure of the party by the Chief Justice Ahmet Necdet Sezer, who would become the next president of Turkey after Demirel, was done through a constitutional court decree, followed by the banning of the leader of *RP*, Erbakan, from politics.

Next the Kemalists went after Erdoğan, who was already perceived as the next charismatic leader of the movement. They used a poem with Islamic references that he read in a public address as the pretext and indicted him for instigating hatred. The aim was not only to put him behind bars but to ensure that he was banned from politics. With both Erbakan and Erdoğan out of the picture, Islamists founded the *FP* (Virtue Party), the successor of *RP*, which was closed down by the constitutional court in 1998. The second-ranking senior member of the movement, Recai Kutan, became the head of *FP*.

Başörtülü kadınlar found themselves on a long, difficult road. The implications of the eighteen directives would include an all-out war against them. There was no compromise forthcoming from the state. The ways in which *başörtülü kadınlar* were impacted by the political developments of the time will be discussed later.

Yılmaz's *ANAP* and Ecevit's *Demokratik Sol Parti, DSP* (the Democratic Left Party) became the actual implementers of the coup directives. Ecevit's political trajectory would shift here from a pro-liberties, populist, socialist/leftist ideology to secular Kemalist ideology that did not condone expansion of liberties. The end of Ecevit's political career represented a convergence of the leftist and ultranationalist agendas. He would become an agent of Kemalism during the last years of his life, until he passed away in 2006 after a stroke at a funeral of a Kemalist who was allegedly murdered by a religious Muslim. Ecevit was announced a martyr of *laiklik* by the Kemalists—he would be remembered as a man who lived and died for *laiklik*. Later the Turkish public learned that the man whose funeral Ecevit attended was not murdered by a religious Muslim but by an underground organization of the deep state established by ultranationalist Kemalist military and ex-military officers.

The implementation of the eight-year mandatory education came first. According to this plan, children who completed a five-year primary education would not be able to attend professional schools or *İmam Hatip* schools. They were required to complete the entirety of eight years in one school. In the eyes of the families of religious Muslims this meant that by the time children reached the end of the eighth grade they would already be somewhat old for religious education. Islamic tradition mandates religious education to start as early as four years of age. By seven years of age, children are assumed to commit their five daily prayers. The eight-year mandatory plan was simply a response to the assumption that *İmam Hatip* schools were the "backyard" of the Islamist movement. After all, people like Erdoğan and many of the leading politicians of Islamist politics had been educated at these schools. Nonetheless, proponents of the new regulation did not address the underlying reasons that made these schools so appealing for many.[129] The new regulation was not sufficient to do away with the threat posed by the Islamists and religious Muslims. Under the sway of the military, the government decided to devalue *İmam Hatip* schools and religious education altogether. General Çevik Bir, a member of Turkish General Staff, sent a top-secret letter to *YÖK* commanding the amendment of Law 2547 in order to thwart *İmam Hatip* schools.[130] A three-step approach was pursued. First, through *YÖK,* the government introduced a new provision to the grading system of *OSYM* (University Central Examination), which stated that the scores that graduates of *İmam Hatip* schools receive in the central examination had to be multiplied by 0.3 rather than 1. This new regulation, which is recognized as the "coefficient problem," had dire consequences for the graduates of the *İmam Hatip* schools. Accordingly, thousands of *İmam Hatip* school graduates were penalized despite the fact that they scored exceptionally high in the examination.[131] The new regulation went further to prevent any transfers from *İmam Hatip* schools to regular public schools at the end of the junior year so that parents would not attempt to trick the system and send their children to *İmam Hatip* schools first and then transfer them in the last year of their education to to avoid the consequences of being *İmam Hatip* graduates.

Secondly, the government targeted the Qur'anic courses, which accommodated the process of *hifz* (i.e., the memorization of Qur'an by heart). This is not a requirement in Islam, however it is an encouraged task. There are approximately half a million Muslims around the world who have completed their *hifz.* The memorization process generally started after students completed their fifth-grade education. Now that they had to remain in primary education for eight years, the families who would want their children to memorize the Qur'an would not be able to do so. Finally the government banned the teaching of Qur'an to children under the age of twelve both in public and private arenas.[132] After the age of twelve, children were permitted to learn the Qur'an and other religious information at state-regulated summer courses. This particular ban was specific to Qur'anic education and did not apply to teachings of the Old or New Testament. To render the new regulation effective, *fişleme* methods were used. Based on information gathered, the informants would send reports of any suspicious activity to *BÇG* in Ankara. Children and the adults who taught them Qur'an "illegally" were invariably caught and arraigned.[133] With the fear that their children would be taken into police custody, parents shunned away from Qur'anic education.

In addition to the changes in the educational arena, the military went after Islamic businesses. It dubbed them *Yeşil Sermaye* (i.e., the Green Investment) and divulged lists of their names to the mass media, encouraging the public to take action against them and not to consume their goods. The intent was specifically to target the *Anatolian* lions. The media and the nongovernmental organizations were subjected to the same attacks. To present evidence was not part of the process:

> The military presented no persuasive incriminating evidence on [1000 companies] or on 19 newspapers, 20 television stations, 51 radio stations, 110 magazines, 800 schools, 1200 student houses, and 2500 associations that it claimed were part of the "reactionary sector" or "political Islam." The army said they collectively "aim to set up a state according to Islamic law" and must be stopped.[134]

The following provision to the Turkish Civil Code concerning the qualifications of the parents who would be considered for adoption was also passed:

> From the perspective of social relations to carry the traits that will not fall against the norms and values of the society, to have the attire and the life style of a contemporary appearance with the mentality that will apply Atatürk's rules and reforms in the daily life...[135]

This would mean that people who appeared to be "too religious" or "too conservative" from the perspective of the authorities who deal with the adoption process would be denied access to the process. This would also abridge the "equality before the law" principle, which is the very premise of a constitutional democracy.

The consequences of the directives engendered uproar among the religious Muslims. Thousands gathered periodically to protest the enchainment of *İmam Hatip* students and *başörtülü kadınlar.* Protests led to further restrictions by the state. The regime was ready to crush anyone in its path. Yılmaz and Ecevit made a concerted effort to implement the directives. Facing the opposition of the religious, Yılmaz challenged: "Even if it would cost [his] political life," he would pass the legislation concerning eight-year mandatory education. He was right. This grave act would cost Yılmaz his political life as he declined and almost disappeared in the coming years. His government fell in the wake of corruption scandals of nepotism and cronyism at the end of 1998.

> Yılmaz found himself entangled in a similar manner to Çiller, namely, grave suspicion of silencing investigations or covering state-Mafia organized crime triangle, and personally being involved in corruption.[136]

This triangle included organized illegal activities of the state.

During this period the treatment of *başörtülü kadınlar* was exacerbated. They were fired or investigated at their workplace and harassed on the streets by Kemalists. The next turning point in the headscarf history of Turkey would come with the emergence of *Fazilet Parti*. The *FP* would be a "passive" player in politics so as not to give any pretext to the military to close it down. It would also be ephemeral. Albeit a successor of *RP*, *FP* futilely tried its best to present itself as independent of its predecessor's politics. Still under the shock of the post-modern coup and the closure of *RP*, *FP*'s supporters were demoralized. They lost confidence in the political machinery. With Erbakan banned from politics and Erdoğan in prison, the party's rhetoric transformed from "the old claim that Turkey was not religious enough to the claim that Turkey was not democratic enough."[137] Yet *FP* did not make reference to the enlargement of the democratic operational basis for all groups inclusively, it was only the religious Muslims and their usurped rights that *FP* was concerned about. It "did not question the nonpluralist form of state–society relations, but singled out only the secularist substance of it as a focus of criticism."[138] For instance, the plight of the Kurdish population was not a concern as a democratic right for existence. Homogeneity promoted by the state establishment was subtly praised by the silence depicted by *RP* and the successor *FP* in the face of Kurds' suffering. Here the similarity between the Kemalist and Islamist ideologies divulged, as both saw the democratic machinery as a way to broaden their own claims to their particular rights alone, excluding others' claims from the process. In this context, "political Islam provide[d] the mirror image of Kemalism in terms of its conception of democracy not as a hallow notion, but as a totalizing and restrictive sense."[139]

The 1999 elections changed the landscape of Turkish politics, contributing to the "institutionalization of the politics of fear."[140] One of the markers of this particular period was the "Kavakci Affair."[141] My election, as one of only two *başörtülü kadınlar* elected to the Turkish Grand National Assembly as a parliamentarian, exacerbated the plight of *başörtülü kadınlar*.[142] The other woman, Nesrin Ünal, who was elected on the *Milliyetçi Hareket Partisi, MHP* (Nationalist Movement Party) ticket, took off her headscarf before the oath ceremony and was applauded by the military officers who were present at the Grand National Assembly. I ran on the *FP* ticket. I was the youngest member of 550 parliamentarians, and a software engineer by training. I pursued my higher education in the United States after having to quit my education as a medical school student at Ankara University due to the headscarf ban. During my political campaign, I was invariably asked if I would take off my headscarf to serve as a parliamentarian. I stated that the dress code of the parliamentarians clearly permitted me to serve my constituents with my headscarf. In my attempt to take the oath of office, I was seen "as an index of political Islam penetrating the Westernized secular realm" of the parliament,[143] not as a young educated woman who had the potential to serve her country. In the regime's eyes I was perceived "not as a woman but as a militant" and "even not as a Muslim merely as an ideological symbol."[144]

I was the product of the *RP–FP* women's movement, one of thousands of women who worked for the success of the Islamist political movement. After serving as the head of the foreign affairs department of the women's commission of *RP* and *FP* respectively for seven years, I was nominated by the party in response to the pressures from within and without. The internal pressures came from the female activists of the party. Around 200,000 women volunteered for *RP* to carry it to office in 1997. Women's contributions to its success were recognized nationally and internationally. Even the Kemalists conceded that women were behind the victory for Islamists both in local and general elections in the 1990s. In return, however, women did not receive anything. They did not have representation in higher-ranking positions within the party, let alone the Turkish Grand National Assembly. This created disconcert within the female stratum. Furthermore, Kemalists and feminists rightly castigated *RP* for utilizing women's power to assume office but denying them their representational rights in the parliament or within the party hierarchy. After *RP* was closed down by the constitutional court and *FP* was founded, the leadership of the *FP* decided to include women in the next election as a response to the critiques. This would also help *FP* to prove that it was not the same as *RP* in its treatment of women and that it was embracing modernizing elements of transformation. In the next general election of 1999, three women were elected on the *FP* ticket. I was the only one of the three who wore a headscarf.

On the day of the swear-in ceremony, the *DSP* members protested my entrance to the Turkish Grand National Assembly. Prime Minister Ecevit, "a thoroughly loyal Kemalist,"[145] gave an infamous speech in the midst of applause (a sign of protest in the Turkish culture) and orchestrated the chanting of "Get out!" from the *DSP* rows. *DSP* MPs (150 of them) joined the protest while the rest of parliament watched. Prime Minister Ecevit pointed at me and yelled: "Put this woman in her place!"[146] Meanwhile, on national television, President Demirel labeled me as an "agent provocateur"[147] for wanting to take my oath of office as a newly elected member of parliament with a headscarf (see Figure 3.1).[148]

These protests were sufficient for the *FP* administration to withdraw its support. That day, I was not permitted back in by my party for a second attempt to take the oath. After a few politically correct statements, I was left on my own to deal with the challenges to come. In the midst of the heated controversy, some voiced the possibility of all *FP* members in the parliament turning to *sine-i millet* (the chest of the nation)

Figure 3.1 DSP members jeering at the oath ceremony in the parliament—May, 2 1999. Photo by Anadolu Ajansı.

(i.e., resigning altogether from the parliament posts) as a protest that would render the *DSP-ANAP-MHP* government defunct. The party never considered it. For a *başörtülü kadın* they would not take that risk. I never took the oath. The due process to revoke my parliamentary status was never pursued. My seat was never filled, therefore my constituents lost their representational rights. This was a political blow to the party that undermined its capacity to successfully function. I was denied the privileges (office space, residence, etc.) that were granted to parliamentarians, and only retained my parliamentary immunity. My name and picture were taken out of the parliament's documents; I was erased from the parliament's history. The party also tried to move on, pretending that I did not "happen." Meanwhile, I was stripped of my citizenship and faced a set of charges, including inciting hatred, discriminating against people, insulting the dignity of the state, and attempting to overthrow the regime.

At this point in the discussion, it is noteworthy to draw attention to the regime's double standard with respect to religious Muslim men and religious Muslim women, the *başörtülü kadınlar.* From the perspective of the patriarchal state, male members of *FP* could be tolerated, condoned, and allowed in while I was not. They, alongside other men in the parliament, were abridging the very law that mandated them to wear a hat. Yet the regime did not take any action against that. Furthermore, some of the male parliamentarians from *FP* had a beard, which was also an Islamic symbol. Again the regime did not find that troubling in a secular setting. As a representative of *başörtülü kadınlar* in appearance, my dress was in accordance with the constitutional laws and bylaws of the parliament. Nonetheless this did not matter for the state. Lastly, at the ideological level, if the state perceived an Islamist party pernicious in principle, even though my male counterparts shared the same ideology of the *FP* as me, I was the only one to be ousted from the Grand National Assembly.[149] I was the only one perceived to be threatening the state. The fact that I was educated—and more importantly, educated in the West—and the fact that I was a woman who climbed up the ladder of politics, which is a male-dominated profession, were not construed as progressiveness, thus did not change my status in the eyes of the state. The most "backward" Islamist man was still better than a *başörtülü kadın* in the eyes of the regime, and hence was entitled to be in the parliament.

The closure process for *FP* ensued without respite. The chief prosecutor, in his official opening statement to close down the party, likened the *FP* to a "bad tumor that had metastasized" preventing the operation of the democratic machinery. He argued that the *FP* parliamentarians were "blood-sucking vampires" and that "Merve was there to demolish."[150] The constitutional court closed down the *FP* in 2001 for its anti-secular activities, banning five members from politics for a period of five years. I was one of the banned members, along with Nazlı Ilıcak, who was a secular female parliamentarian who defended my right to wear the headscarf. I took my case to European Court of Human Rights (ECHR) in 2001. In 2007, ECHR found Turkey guilty of violating free elections.[151]

The *DSP-ANAP-MHP* coalition ensured the implementation of the Kemalist directives for the next three years that they remained in office. The more people showed resistance to their restrictive directives, the more intransigent the government became. At this time neither the *İmam Hatip* schools nor the universities were accessible for *başörtülü kadınlar.* Prime Minister Ecevit, in his announcement of the government program, emphasized his government's resolve in dealing with *başörtülü kadınlar,* whom he accused of wielding their scarves as a political symbol.[152] As a result, *başörtülü kadınlar* were put in the spotlight, enduring harassments—physical and verbal abuses in public places such as government offices, university hospitals, courts, and military premises, not as service providers but as mere citizens. The coalition government went so far as to enforce the ban against *başörtülü kadınlar* at some of the summer camps of public servants.[153] President Demirel lashed out at *başörtülü kadınlar* and argued that they should "go to Saudi Arabia!"[154] Saudi Arabia represented the ultimate backwardness in the eyes of the regime. Hence *başörtülü kadınlar,* as much as they were adamant about not compromising on their headscarves, would only fit in the Saudi Arabian society.

Despite the dire consequences of being in *tesettür* during this time, the saliency of *başörtülü kadınlar* in the public arena did not decrease. That is not to suggest that *başörtülü kadınlar* continued to attend classes or their professional work with their headscarves. That is only to suggest that they did not disappear and retire to their private corners as anticipated by the state. On the contrary, they adapted themselves to the new Turkish "reality." They either quit their education or their careers but continued to be *başörtülü kadınlar* in the public arena at varying capacities, or they took off their headscarves in the classroom or workplace but continued to put them on at other times. Hence when one walked on the street, *başörtülü kadınlar* were still part and parcel of the Turkish society. One possible reason behind the resistance to leave the public sphere might have to do with the overall democratization process of Turkey. *Başörtülü kadınlar* presented their religious affiliation, hence their *tesettür,* as a matter of choice and freedom of conscience. The fact that they were educated also provided them with the ability to articulate the matter in terms of democracy and liberation.

The Sezer Years and the AKP

In 2000, Demirel left office and Ahmet Necdet Sezer became the next president.[155] Sezer was a bureaucrat, an enigmatic figure who became president almost by accident.[156] He spent most of his life as a federal employee working for the judiciary body. He was a man of the status quo. *RP* was closed down on his watch when he was the president of the constitutional court. He was a staunch defender of Kemalism,[157] bringing new interpretations to the ban as to what its scope should include. In 2001, the country endured a grave economic crisis, and the government was incapable of stabilizing the economy. Meanwhile, PM Ecevit became incapacitated due to health problems. Within this setting the now-ruling *Adalet ve Kalkınma Partisi, AKP* (the Justice and Development Party) emerged from the remnants of *FP*. Members of *FP* were divided into two camps over internal agendas—the traditionalist camp and the reformist camp.[158] The shadow leader of the traditionalist camp, which became *Saadet Partisi, SP* (the Felicity Party), was Erbakan, who was under house arrest. Recai Kutan became the leader of *SP*. Erbakan and Kutan comprised the senior members of the *FP*. The younger group of *FP*, the reformist camp, became *AKP* under the leadership of politically banned Erdoğan. The reformist camp criticized the traditionalist camp for agitating the Kemalists but then not being brave enough and caving in to military pressure during the series of events that led to the postmodern coup. They argued that the leaders of the party garnered too much negativity from various state institutions that it was necessary to bring in new leadership and start with a clean slate. The traditionalist wing did not agree, which led to the bifurcation and thus to the birth of *SP* and *AKP*. The separation between the traditionalists and the reformists was marked by the closure of *FP*.[159] Most members of parliament from *FP* eventually joined *AKP* after the closure was decreed.

After an economically disastrous three years, the *AKP* came to power in 2002 with a landslide that was interpreted as a backlash against the Kemalist interventions. Although Erdoğan was the head of the *AKP*, due to his political ban Abdullah Gül, the second-ranking member of the party, became the prime minister initially, until Erdoğan could be cleared from his ban. In 2003, he bequeathed the position to Erdoğan. Despite the prevalent view in the international arena that it was an Islamist party, *AKP* identified itself as a party of "Muslim Democrats." Acknowledging the fate of the two predecessors, *AKP* did not address the headscarf issue. On the contrary, Secretary of State Abdullah Gül, a frontliner on the headscarf issue in the past, had his wife withdraw her case concerning headscarf discrimination from the European Court of Human Rights.[160]

In 1998, Ms. Gül was denied registration to Ankara University because she wore a headscarf.[161] Before the ECHR tabled the case, *AKP* came to office with Mr. Gül as the secretary of state. Mr. Gül argued that there was a conflict of interest, therefore his wife decided to withdraw her complaint.[162]

For *AKP*, this was one way of avoiding the bile of the Kemalist military. Ironically, *AKP* also served as the representative of the state in the case I opened (*Kavakci v. Turkey*) before the European Court of Human Rights. The court decreed on the case on *AKP*'s watch as well. That is to say that my former colleagues—now parliamentarians of *AKP*—who shared the parliamentary seats with me on that infamous day in 1999, were now on the other side of the aisle, the aisle then of the *DSP*. The *AKP* government's representative at the court hearing in Strasbourg in 2005 gave a somewhat apologetic, "sloppy," and ambiguous defense on behalf of the state. He defended the position taken against me at the oath ceremony. It was the Islamically inclined *AKP* that was defending the Kemalist regime against a *başörtülü kadın*.

The *AKP* government also did not want to do much on the issue of *İmam Hatip* schools or Qur'anic courses during their first term. On *AKP*'s watch, *İmam Hatip* graduates still had to deal with the challenge of the coefficient problem. At the end of a futile attempt to solve the matter, Sezer vetoed the bill, finding it antithetical to secularism.[163] In its second term in office, *AKP* attempted to remove the coefficient difference between *İmam Hatip* schools and others several times. In each attempt they faced a repealing decree of *Danıştay*. It is still forbidden to teach Qur'an to children under the age of twelve either at home or somewhere else. On *AKP*'s watch, children continue to be dragged to police stations for investigation if they violate this regulation.

During *AKP*'s first term through July 2007, its greatest challenge was being in office but not so much in power. It was not able to infiltrate the judiciary body and *YÖK* to break the vicious circle within which they operated. These institutions preserved their autonomy and worked solely for the Kemalist ideology. President Sezer served as the main opposition to *AKP*. He resorted to veto power on almost all issues. He vetoed regulations that would provide assistance to the poor, regulations that would ameliorate the educational environment for children and any provision or law that would allow *AKP* to shine in the eyes of the people.

In 2005, *Danıştay* (the Council of State) decreed against a female teacher, Aytaç Kılınç. She would uncover her hair as she entered the premise of public school where she taught. She was promoted to be the principal of the school, but the promotion was overturned due to the fact that she was in *tesettür* outside of the school realm. She took her case to

Danıştay, which decreed against her, arguing that Kılınç "was *supposed* to be the best example to the youngsters who receive education in that institution, [but] failed to abide by the binding main principles mentioned in the legal regulations both inside and outside of the public realm including on the way to and from the school."[164]

Currently there are three laws that are pertinent to the dress code, all of which are legislative decisions. The first one is the Hat Law, which was discussed earlier. The second one is the law that bans the wearing of particular outfits. This law was enacted in 1934 to ban the religious/spiritual authorities such as the imams, priests, and rabbis from wearing their religious robes outside of their vocational premises. The third one is the aforementioned Article 657 of Federal Employees Law, which includes a provision on the outfits of workers at public institutions banning the headscarf for female federal employees.

Today the legal basis of the ban is predicated upon the interpretation of the aforementioned Article 17 by the constitutional court. Article 17 grants *başörtülü kadınlar* the freedom to cover. Nonetheless, the court, drawing on its interpretation of Article 16, another provision by the constitutional court, argues that the freedom mentioned in Article 17 cannot be applied to *tesettür.* By opining in this manner, the constitutional court brings a new interpretation to a code that already exists and is agreed upon. The court treats the article as a new code with a new interpretation. This garnered sundry criticism from the legal pundits. They argued that the court's interpretation violated Article 153 of the Turkish constitution, which states that the constitutional court, in its repeal decrees, cannot adjudicate in a way that it will entail a new regulation as if it is a lawmaker. On another note, "the commentaries of the Constitutional Court are not binding."[165] Yet the commentary of the court on Article 17 has been considered binding, banning *başörtülü kadınlar* from universities. Hence it would be correct to argue that actually there is no ban on the headscarf (i.e., the legal basis is a controversial interpretation of a decree of a court), but in practical terms the ban is so much more prevalent that it is applied beyond the jurisdiction of articles that enact the ban. In other words, it covers beyond the borders of federal offices and universities.

Finally, the decisions of the European Court of Human Rights with respect to the headscarf are perceived as consolidating elements to further the ban. Although Turkey is not yet a member of the European Union, it is under the jurisdiction of the ECHR in Strasbourg. After exhausting the national Turkish legal path, cases become eligible to be brought before the ECHR. ECHR's decisions on various individuals from different countries have not varied. The court invariably decreed in favor of states such as Switzerland, Germany, and France, denying *başörtülü kadınlar* the right to work or to education.[166]

The *Leyla Şahin v. Turkey* case of 2005 was not an exception.[167] Şahin applied to the court as a sixth-year medical school student from Cerrahpaşa Medical School of Istanbul University. She completed the first five years of her university education with her headscarf between 1992 and 1997. In 1998, during the last year of her education, the ban was reactivated at her university. She filed her case with the court at that time. Meanwhile, she moved to Austria and completed her medical education without having to take her headscarf off. After a prolonged process, the court decreed against Şahin, arguing that she was supposed to foresee the fact that she would not be able to enter the university with her *türban* based on the interpretation of the constitutional court of the Article 17 of law no. 2547 of *YÖK,* which stated that the permissibility of outfits did not accommodate wearing of the headscarf for religious reasons. The ECHR argued that since the interpretation of the constitutional court predated Şahin's admission to the university, she was supposed to be cognizant of the ban during admission. But more importantly, the ECHR stated that "the interference/violations of fundamental rights concerning headscarf were acceptable" in the democratic system of Turkey as part of the legitimate goal of "protecting the rights and freedoms of others and maintaining public order."[168] That is to say that although everyone is entitled to enjoy universal rights, the right of *başörtülü kadınlar* to have an education could be suspended in order to protect others' freedoms. It is noteworthy to point to the convergence between European and Turkish hostility to Muslim women's right to freedom. Furthermore, Şahin's decision refers to the paradox presented by the rights discourse. On one hand the state grants its citizens universal rights; in this case, the right to education. On the other hand, the state does not extend those rights to people who have particularities such as the headscarf. It fails to recognize the differences. Furthermore, the court argues that these particularities could pose a threat to people with no such particularities. It draws attention to "the impact which wearing such a symbol, which was presented or perceived as a compulsory religious duty, may have on those who chose not to wear it."[169] In other words, *başörtülü kadınlar* like Leyla Şahin could exert psychological or physical pressure on classmates who don't wear headscarves. Therefore the state argues that it must protect the rights of those women who might feel the sway of *başörtülü kadınlar* over them. Ironically, the state takes its stance on the side of the women who do not cover and favors them as opposed to standing neutral to all women, covered or uncovered. The de facto departure point for the rights argument is secular/uncovered appearance from the perspective of the state. Covering, therefore, is perceived as an aberration. As a result, laws protect and favor secular citizens and render legitimate the abridgment of the rights of a non-secular group. The state also undermines the fact that secular groups constitute the majority and therefore cannot feel coerced by the minority.

This argument is widely used in Turkey by the proponents of the ban as well. The ban is legitimized at a psychological level by arguing that *başörtülü kadınlar* may create pressure on women who do not wear headscarves. A similar argument follows suit with respect to assuming potentialities. This view states that if *başörtülü kadınlar* are permitted to wear their headscarves freely then they might, in the future, become powerful enough that they might force other women to wear headscarves through a regime change. Meanwhile, proponents of the ban deny *başörtülü kadınlar*'s present rights. That is to say that based on the fears of one group stemming from a hypothetical context, citizenships rights of another group could be suspended. Another argument used frequently refers to the so-called subliminal message the headscarf sends to women without headscarves, which is "we are Muslim and you are not." This argument also was voiced by President Demirel upon my attempt to take the oath of office in parliament. He argued that I would be insinuating that I was a Muslim and the other female parliamentarians were not because they did not wear headscarves (although I had neither the perception nor the intention of a stance as such).

ECHR adds a source of leverage to Turkish secularism and justifies its stance through the need to protect it.

> In such a context, where the values of pluralism, respect for the rights of others and, in particular, equality before the law of men and women were being taught and applied in practice, it was understandable that the relevant authorities should consider it contrary to such values to allow religious attire, including, as in the case before the Court, the Islamic headscarf, to be worn on university premises.[170]

Since the ECHR decrees along the same lines with the Turkish Republic with respect to the headscarf (albeit not explicit), the court's praise of the Turkish Republic's stance on the headscarf can be seen as indicative of the assertion of Turkey's role-model status. The court's stance is similar to that of an Orientalist in its assertion of gender equality. Here the court brings a tacit critique to Islam from within by questioning the equality rights of *başörtülü kadınlar*. The fact that it condones the restriction of *başörtülü kadınlar*'s rights in the context of "equality before the law of men and women" shows that the ECHR carries the basic Orientalist assumption that a woman with a headscarf cannot be equal to a man, and that she is, under any circumstances, subjugated, dominated, and oppressed by man.

In short, one can argue that the trajectory of the treatment of *başörtülü kadınlar* is not independent of the trajectory of the treatment of the larger religious community. The stifling of *başörtülü kadınlar* was part and parcel of the restrictions imposed on the larger society. The headscarf was among the major mechanisms used by the state in its constrictive policies with respect to religious Muslims. The second one, similar to the headscarf issue, was the aforementioned *İmam Hatip* schools that were perceived as the backyard of the Islamist movement. Prime Minister Erdoğan, a graduate of *İmam Hatip* school and married to a *başörtülü kadın*, faced an uphill battle in his relations with the state.

New Manipulations on the Headscarf Discourse

Public Space

Problematizing *başörtülü kadınlar* outside of the original framework that was assigned to them led to discussion of the public realm as part of the headscarf debate. The proponents of the ban included it in their evaluation of *başörtülü kadınlar*, but the process was not a simple one. The transformation of the *başörtülü kadınlar* led to this process and, in the end, to the introduction of the term "public sphere." In other words, the changes attested to in the *başörtülü kadınlar* over time made it imperative for the state to approach the ban with a new perspective. *Başörtülü kadınlar* in the past had only been present at the periphery. They were assumed to be uneducated and socially, economically, and politically backward. In the urban areas, they represented the marginalized facets of the economically disadvantaged. Hence the state wielded the argument that *tesettür* was the reason for them lagging behind. This argument had clearly lost its appeal by the 1990s, for *başörtülü kadınlar* appeared neither subjugated nor backward. They appeared as progressive as modern Turkish women who did not wear headscarves. The state now had to find some other explanation to convince the masses of the necessity of the ban. Public space came into the discussion within this context.

Başörtülü kadınlar did not disappear as anticipated or relinquish their headscarves. They simply percolated into the society and became more visible in alternative ways. They were not the teachers, or judges, or doctors whom they wanted to become, but they pursued alternative models for public existence. Informal educational venues were instrumental in this process. Specializing in new areas of interest, they learned foreign languages, painting, sewing, information technology, sports, writing, singing, etc. They asserted themselves into Islamist politics, humanitarian help organizations, intellectual activities, education, publications, and the like.[171]

They were not immune to changes imposed on Turkish society by the exigencies of the time. They adopted new habits and traditions within the larger modernizing Turkish society.[172] Pop culture played an important role here, through which *başörtülü kadınlar,* in particular the new generation of young *başörtülü kadınlar,* tried harder to fit in—that is to fit in with a vengeance. For instance, concerts became very popular among the youth, so the young *başörtülü kadınlar* attended concerts. With changes in the economies of the middle class, *başörtülü kadınlar* who could afford to started driving SUVs as they became more popular. Personal care and fitness climbed up the priority list for modern Turkish women, hence for the *başörtülü kadınlar* as well. They attended gym classes, pilates, and the like. Usage of foreign words became prevalent in the pop culture, so the *başörtülü kadınlar* adopted them, too. They wore designer clothes. In short, they asserted themselves into the public sphere through a variety of means to compete for the public space.

In addition to all the qualities modern Turkish women were expected to have, *başörtülü kadınlar* carried another quality—the symbol of religion and virtue, the headscarf. Theoretically speaking this meant that vis-à-vis their appearance, *başörtülü kadınlar* were everything that the modern Turkish women should be and more. This came very unexpectedly. Tülin Bumin calls *başörtülü kadınlar* of today (the same women who are considered by the state to be *türbanlı kadınlar*) "ultramodern." She defines Turkish women in three categories: *başörtülü kadınlar, basi acik* (i.e., women without headscarves), and *türbanlı kadınlar*—traditional, modern, and ultramodern, respectively. Arguing that the *türbanlı kadınlar* are ahead of modern women in the modernity continuum, she stresses that unlike their mothers, young *türbanlı kadınlar* are not the product of religion. Their religious convictions are the product of the individualist choices they make.[173] Bumin's ultramodernity will be discussed in more detail later in this text. The transition, or rather promotion, from backward *başörtülü kadınlar* to ultramodern *türbanlı kadınlar* came with a price as well, which will be addressed later in this book.

The urge of the regime to control the context within which *başörtülü kadınlar* were discussed followed the soaring saliency of *başörtülü kadınlar,* or in the state's term *türbanlı kadınlar,* in the public realm in the late 1990s. The meaning the state gives to the public realm is of utmost importance. When the state's modernization and secularization mission is stressed, "the public is recognized more as the 'state.'"[174] Hence the public realm as a space is supposed to be a territory that belongs to the state. Secondly, the assumption that the public's or the people's will is unchanging and static is clearly problematic.[175] The unexpected introduction of *başörtülü kadınlar* to the public realm, which remains as unchanging in the eyes of the state, created a challenge to the regime. The public sphere that was so far delineated by the state as homogeneous and not dynamic was now under the "invasion," so to speak, of *başörtülü kadınlar,* who were the trailblazers of change.

Since the state had the tradition of using public territory as its own in matters of secularization or modernization, it had no problem bringing the public sphere into the discussion and going further to expand the restrictions on *başörtülü kadınlar* to areas not previously explored. In this process, the state was the major player that determined what and who constituted the public realm. The public realm was defined as "the area where modernization is actualized," which is to say that "the public realm in of itself is seen as a filtration mechanism, as a definition and prohibition" instrument.[176] Now the *başörtülü kadınlar* were facing the argument that the secular public space could not accommodate a religious symbol such as the headscarf. This new approach had severe consequences for women. It changed the social and political demarcations of the permissible areas for *başörtülü kadınlar.* The term "public space/area/sphere/realm" did not have an unequivocal definition as to know where its limits have started and ended. It was a fluid operational realm. From the perspective of President Sezer, it even included his residence:

> The Presidency is the position which represents the Republic. Secularism is the basis of the Republic and the Presidency is a public realm. The Constitutional Court adjudicated that *başörtüsü* can not be worn in the public sphere. So are the decisions of the European Court of Human Rights and the Council of State. The presidential residence where the Republic is represented, and the reception that is hosted by the President are both public spaces and wearing *başörtüsü* can not be permitted.[177]

Sezer used this justification to avoid inviting the prime minister, the speaker of the parliament, cabinet members, and parliamentarians with their headscarved wives to the national holiday celebrations during his term as president between 2000 and 2007. This revelation that drew new limits of the public sphere occurred for the first time during Sezer's presidency. His predecessors had invited *başörtülü kadınlar* with their husbands. The first incident that initiated this new regulation and set precedence about the ban during Sezer's term involved the speaker of the parliament, Bülent Arınç.[178] It signified a turning point in the ban's expansionist history: Mr. Arınç and his wife (who wore a headscarf) were present at the airport to send President Sezer on an international trip. After the trip, Sezer reminded the public that public spaces could not be assumed with a headscarf.[179] Following that incident, he worked diligently to ensure he would not "run into" *başörtülü kadınlar* at welcoming/farewell ceremonies or other social functions. For national celebrations, he chose two sets of invitations for the invitees—one for the invitees whose wives were not *başörtülü kadınlar* (and they were invited as a couple) and the other for the invitees whose wives were *başörtülü kadınlar* (and they were invited alone).[180] From the perspective of President Sezer, there was no distinction between *türbanlı kadınlar* and *başörtülü kadınlar.* He banned them altogether. Sezer's stance had international implications as well. During the 2003 NATO summit in Istanbul, members of international organizations were invited to the presidential residence alone to prevent attendance of *başörtülü kadınlar,* which raised questions from the invitees, some of whom were not from Muslim countries or did not have spouses with headscarves.[181] Afghanistan's President Karzai, who was known to have a wife with a headscarf, namely Dr. Zeynat Karzai, was hosted alone in Sezer's residence. After the dinner, President Karzai responded to a question about his wife's absence: "My wife was not invited, if she was, she would have come."[182]

The reaction of the *AKP* government toward Sezer's new approach to *başörtülü kadınlar* has been a compromising one. They argued in a conciliatory tone that they would not be a party to tension, therefore their wives would not be attending any public event.[183] *AKP,* the successor of the now-defunct *RP* and *FP,* clearly wanted to remain in office and avoid the fate of its predecessors. The constitutional court ruled against both *RP* and *FP* for becoming a center for anti-secular activities, among which was defending the headscarf in the public arena. Thus *AKP* was determined not to let President Sezer, the constitutional court, and the Kemalists use the headscarf issue to attack them and jeopardize their term in office. The concessions made by the government might have warded off any immediate political clash, but they clearly contributed to the expansive construction of the "new" public space and exclusion of *başörtülü kadınlar* from it.

The legal action buttressing the president's view came from *Danıştay* in 2005 when it rejected the demand of female plaintiff Aytaç Kılınç whose case was discussed earlier. Moreover, a decree from *Danıştay* concerning another case came in the same week. The plaintiff was Abdullah Yılmaz, a male teacher whose appointment to serve abroad was first granted after he ranked second in a central examination conducted by the Ministry of Education throughout Turkey, but later was cancelled due to the fact that his wife, who was also a teacher at the same school, wore a headscarf in her personal life. Furthermore his wife would wear a wig on the school premises. The decree stated that the position abroad had a particular importance and specialty. It also made reference to a National Intelligence Report that read: "Yılmaz's wife Ayşe Yılmaz who also taught at the same school came to school wearing a wig and dressed according to *tesettür* in her daily life."[184]

Danıştay's decision deserves a three-layered interpretation. First, a male public servant's career was directly affected based not on his own professional performance but his wife's personal religious convictions, belief, and dress. Secondly, the fact that Yılmaz's wife was not wearing a headscarf at her work premise but rather was compromising and wore a wig did not make a difference from the perspective of the state. She was a *başörtülü kadın*, after all. Lastly, in defiance of separation of powers invested in the state's institutions, *Danıştay,* one of the highest judiciary organs, was overtly collaborating with the intelligence service to pry into the private space of an ordinary citizen and make references to the latter's report without a legal foundation.

This was not the first time *Danıştay* decreed against a man whose wife wore a headscarf. In 1999, a decision was reached against a man whose appointment to a city government post was suspended "due to his wife's *türban* which was known to be a symbol and that he did not attend functions including national holidays and republican ball with his wife," and that "in a secular country, while knowing that *türban* which became the symbol of religious currents might entail wrong messages, he still made his wife wear it."[185] These two decisions implied that the public realm was not only expanding every day but also was expanding to include the privacy of the *başörtülü kadınlar.* Equally important was the fact that the ban was used to discriminate against men. Furthermore, the wording of *Danıştay* suggested that the wife was "forced" to wear a headscarf under her husband's duress. This reading was in accordance with the Orientalist assumption that Muslim women were not free to choose to cover but they were coerced to do so against their free will.

Finally an incident at *Yargitay* (the High Court of Appeals) concerning Hatice Hasdemir Şahin's case set another precedent in the discussion of public space for *başörtülü kadınlar.* Şahin was prevented from testifying before a civil court in Ankara where she appeared as a defendant and was escorted out of the courtroom. The judge "defined the courtroom as public space" where one has to be "in a demeanor, behavior and outfit that is in accordance with the regulations."[186] The minutes of the hearing stated that "During the identity check of the defendants, it was understood that Hatice Hasdemir Şahin had entered the court room her head wrapped up with *türban* and she was taken out of the court room in order for her to uncover her head."[187]

Başörtülü Kadınlar ***and Security***

The 1990s witnessed further politicization of *başörtülü kadınlar* as combatants of political strife under Islamist parties, namely *Refah Partisi RP* and its two successors *Fazilet Partisi FP* and *Adalet ve Kalkınma Partisi AKP. Başörtülü kadınlar* contributed to the social and political project of Islamism at three levels. The first one involved a positive contribution: some of the *başörtülü kadınlar* who were involved in politics became political agents of their parties and carried their party message into households, to the entirety of the nation from periphery to the center. They were the actual implementers of the social projects of Islamist parties. They attended weddings and funerals, distributed food for the homeless, helped the poor, opened educational institutions for the youth, etc. In short, *başörtülü kadınlar* turned political agendas of Islamists into a reality by percolating into the smallest unit of the society, i.e., the family. At the second level *başörtülü kadınlar* contributed to the political project of Islamism as potential constituents. That is to say that Islamist parties saw *başörtülü kadınlar* as a group awaiting the address of their problem, i.e., the lifting of the ban. Hence they were among the target groups that all parties, including the Islamist parties, need support from. Invariably during every election period, the headscarf ban would become part of the election promises for each party for the sake of garnering votes. At another level, *başörtülü kadınlar* had a negative impact over Islamist political agenda—they became an insurmountable problem, a burden for Islamists. On one hand, they were perceived as a contagious ailment that everyone avoided. On the other hand the visibility of *başörtülü kadınlar* prevented them from being ignored and forgotten. Yet the Islamist parties did not bring about changes that would ameliorate the plight of *başörtülü kadınlar.* In other words, like the Kemalists, the Islamists failed the *başörtülü kadınlar.* They preferred staying in power as opposed to challenging the status quo to lift the ban. Political considerations were more important for the Islamists than undertaking groundbreaking changes for *başörtülü kadınlar.* Issues pertinent to other groups, such as the religious and ethnic minorities, were addressed but not the problem of the ban. *Başörtülü kadınlar* were always warded off and told to be patient. The solution was deferred to gradual efforts in the long run, but meanwhile *başörtülü kadınlar* were expected to put their lives on hold. It was condoned to see *başörtülü kadınlar* with shattered lives generation after generation until the day would come and the ban would be lifted.

But then the ones who lost their lives, their youth, and their productive professional years were not to be compensated.

Through their inaction, Islamists were inadvertently strengthening the hand of the Kemalists at two levels. First, the fact that after five years in power the *AKP* government did not move a finger on the matter was a confirmation of the Kemalist assumption that the former failed to value women's rights in Turkish society. Furthermore, *AKP*'s visible distance from the subject gave the Kemalists confidence in themselves and in the war they waged against *başörtülü kadınlar.*

Despite all the negativities involved, the political party platforms became the place of inner reconciliation for *başörtülü kadınlar.* Politics gave them the long-awaited positive recognition they had been deprived of. They did not have to defend themselves against opposing forces or explicate why they were in *tesettür.* Moreover they felt empowered as they glided from the status of *başörtüsü mağdurları* to political activist status. The education that they could not receive at the universities was replaced with the informal education that the political party provided and the professions they could not pursue were supplanted by the political agency that helped them to gain a sense of identity.[188] Political activism also served the practical purposes of making them feel like they belonged to a community and made productive usage of their time.

Political activism of *başörtülü kadınlar* was not positively received by the state and the proponents of the ban. They accused women of using their headscarves as a political symbol.[189] No matter how much the women tried to prove otherwise, they could not make any strides. Those who considered *başörtülü kadınlar* suspect frequently questioned their intentions. Many of the *başörtülü kadınlar* at the universities were asked questions such as: "Tell me, where do you get paid from? Iran? Saudi Arabia?" and accompanied by lamentations such as: "We never had the problem of *türban* before," referring to pre-1980s and adumbrating that this was an artificial development imposed in the aftermath of the rise of political Islam in the region. What the anti-*başörtülü kadınlar* failed to understand, however, was that up until the 1980s, *başörtülü kadınlar* acquiesced to their traditional roles within the confines of the household and were not conscious enough to demand their citizenship rights such as education and freedom of expression. In fact, the emergence of political Islamist views among some of the women who adopted *tesettür* at a later point in their lives was relatively recent. Not all *başörtülü kadınlar,* or, in state's terms, *türbanlı kadınlar,* worked or voted for the same political party (i.e., the Islamist party). To assume otherwise is to undermine and ignore women with headscarves who support and work for *MHP* or *ANAP* or *DYP,* none of which aspires to Islamic ideals, or those who support *CHP,* which is a proponent of the headscarf ban. That is to say that there are sundry women who vote for parties other than those of the Islamists, which attests to the fact that there is no single political ideology among all *başörtülü kadınlar.*

Another response to the ones who pointed to the political symbolism of the headscarf was that it was, in fact, a constitutional right of anyone to use any political symbol. As a matter of fact, the politicians quite often turned to the employment of religious symbols as political symbols. The male party leaders would suddenly appear in the congregational Friday prayers during election time, greeting people after the prayers, for instance. Or they would simply halt their address and wait for the *ezan* to end at public gatherings. Or they would kiss the Holy Book of Qur'an handed to them by constituents in the crowd before they put it to their forehead out of respect, right in front of the cameras in order to show their reverence to religious values. Or they would wear a cap symbolizing the Bolshevik Revolution if they were social democrats. For instance, Ecevit, the leader of the Democratic Leftist Party, rarely took his cap off. Female politicians or wives of female politicians sometimes appeared with a headscarf wrapped around their heads in their visits to the villages to ask for votes.

None of the preceding scenarios was perceived as using Islamic references, signs, and symbols in politics, and none was frowned upon by the state but the headscarves of the *başörtülü kadınlar,* even if the preponderance of their population was not involved in politics. *Başörtülü kadınlar* who were active politicians or political activists defended themselves simply by stating that they were wearing the headscarf for personal religious reasons. The fact that there was, in fact, no legal basis for preventing one from wearing it for a political reason or as a political symbol contrasted with the way the headscarves were used to put *başörtülü kadınlar* on the spot and pressure them to defend their choices.

Another political symbolism was embedded in the comparison of me to Ünal, the other female parliamentarian who also wore a headscarf but took it off before the oath ceremony under pressure.[190] Ironically, I, someone who has been wearing a headscarf for most of her life, was accused of wearing it as a political symbol and for political gain because I did not cave in to the regime,[191] while the other parliamentarian was the one who wore it throughout the election campaign, asking for votes with an image of a conservative religious woman, and then took it off right after her win.

Even if one hypothetically concurred that the headscarf must not be worn as a political symbol, it is difficult to determine the reasons behind each woman's decision to wear the headscarf and who wears it as a political symbol or not.[192] The politicization of the headscarf gave way to the idea of a perceived or real threat *başörtülü kadınlar* posed.

> [T]hreat perception is a social construct. The line individuals and societies draw between the Self and the Other determine[s] whether or not material factors are viewed as important in the threat assessment.[193]

Accordingly, the threat *başörtülü kadınlar* is supposedly inflicting on Turkish women is twofold: at one level, disturbing the secular regime and at another, threatening the modern Turkish women. The fact is that the *başörtülü kadınlar* as we defined in this book remained visible in the Turkish political agenda for thirty years, creating polarizing divisions among women.[194] Despite the fact that they wanted to go about their daily businesses, the challenges they faced due to their headscarves put them right back at the top of the contentious issues list. Their incessant saliency in the public realm as *başörtüsü mağdurları*, their capacity to adapt to the changing environment, their perseverance to remain as part of the "public," enhanced the perception by others that they were a threat. The state saw them as disturbing the peace, troublemakers, foreign agents, theocracy lovers, and the face of failure of the Turkish modernization project.

The threat *başörtülü kadınlar* posed to the modern Turkish women was, on one hand, part of the larger power struggle among women and, on the other hand, was about the fear of pressure.[195] The former was pertinent to the fact that for the past eighty years modern Turkish women were the ones to collect the fruits of the republican regime. Now *başörtülü kadınlar* were simultaneously demanding acceptance and the same benefits on their own terms. This was about sharing of the space and opportunities allocated to women. The latter was about the fear internalized by most of the modern Turkish women. The thrust of the fear involved the possibility of "revenge of the oppressed on whose subordination their identities and positions depend[ed]."[196] The fact that modern Turkish women were the ones who were almost always on the frontlines of the anti-*başörtülü kadınlar* campaign deepened "the unconscious guilty recognition of the determining role of domination in the formation of subjectivities" of *başörtülü kadınlar.*[197] In my case, for instance, it was the female parliamentarians who appeared on the frontlines of the protest against me in the oath ceremony. Hence the modern Turkish women were afraid to be outnumbered and/or displaced by the *başörtülü kadınlar.*

Demonstrations, marches, starvation protests, and sit-ins were the methods *başörtülü kadınlar* used to raise awareness about the issue and demand a solution (see Figures 3.2[198] and 3.3[199]). Hand-in-hand chains gathered hundreds of thousands to make a human chain starting from the eastern border of the country to the west. They conducted "white walks"

Figure 3.2 Students protesting the ban, they hold a picture of a student and a police officer that reads: The ban still continues. Are you hearing? The (D) stands for the subliminal question: Are you sleeping? Photo by Anadolu Ajansı.

of medical doctor *başörtülü kadınlar* in their white physician attires in their on-foot trip from Istanbul Cerrahpaşa Medical School to the parliament in Ankara.[200] Their demand "for abolishing the ban on *türban* at the universities, expressed by sit-ins and hunger strikes in the larger provinces and

Figure 3.3 Student holding a sign: Do not touch my friend. Above, pictures of two women, a Turkish woman with a headscarf and an African American woman from Alabama. Photo by Anadolu Ajansı.

at modern universities, not only annoyed and hurt the pride of Kemalist women but were also interpreted as intrusion on the secular, and Western, achievements of the country."[201] It also served as a challenge to the old representations of the religious women and helped them establish their modernist credentials. Yet the already steep political chasm between *başörtülü kadınlar* and the Kemalist women deepened further and further.

Wigs for "Coping" or Resistance

Some of the *başörtülü kadınlar* who were students at universities or who were professionals or who needed access to public space as mothers and wives of university students or military members found wigs to be the only viable solution to the ban. Some wore them on their bare head after they took off their headscarves while others wore it directly on top of their headscarves. They had to reconcile between how they looked wearing the wig and the psychological implications concomitant to it. One student expressed her frustration over having to wear the wig: "doesn't work! doesn't work! I can't do it! Both ludicrous and horrendous [looking]!"[202] *Başörtülü kadınlar* felt foreignness toward themselves in their transformed appearance with the wig. They were different from who they were when they wore them, but they were certain that they had no other choice.

Wigs served two purposes. They allowed *başörtülü kadınlar* to, in Kandiyoti's term "bargain with the state patriarchy."[203] because the state was the controller, the agenda-setter, and this was what *başörtülü kadınlar* had to come to terms with in order to gain access to public space. Therefore they looked for venues to define themselves in ways that gave them full citizenship rights. In that process, they were ready to sign pacts with the state.[204] By wearing wigs, they complied with the state terms and fit with the definition of the modern Turkish women, at least in appearance. In turn, they were given access to education and workplace. Foucauldian reading of the wigs would bring a different interpretation. Foucault submits that "where there is power, there is resistance."[205] Wigs were instrumental in Lila Abu-Lughod's term, as a "diagnostic of power."[206] That is to say that wearing wigs also represented a form of resistance, not letting go of their identity in its entirety, making a statement while they signed their pact with the regime.[207] Wigs were also symbols of reassertion of the lost power for *başörtülü kadınlar.* They served in "re-inscribing alternative forms of power," through which *başörtülü kadınlar* found access to the public realm under the guise (mask) of modern Turkish women[208] (see Figures 3.4[209] and 3.5[210]).

Figure 3.4 A student adjusting her wig at the school entrance at Çukurova University. Photo by Anadolu Ajansı.

Figure 3.5 Parents who wear wigs over their headscarves at the graduation ceremony at Atatürk University in Erzurum, 2003. Photo by Sabah Gazetesi.

The wig market thrived with the rising demand from *başörtülü kadınlar.* "Wigs for rent" became popular. *Başörtülü kadınlar* who needed them for a limited time—for instance, for the exams—could rent them for a couple of hours.[211] Nonetheless the state did not waste time taking action against wigs. Most universities do not permit wigs today. Some do not even accept students' registration papers if they wear wigs in the photographs that they submit.[212]

CHAPTER 4

SOCIAL AND POLITICAL IMPLICATIONS OF THE BAN ON HEADSCARF

Societal Change

Education for Some

The ban has impacted women's lives to varying degrees and in several ways. By early 2000, the prevalent view was that it affected "directly or indirectly" the majority of the families in the country.[1] In other words, many families were affected either through a close or distant female relative. This view was supported by three facts that will be discussed in this chapter. First, 61.3 percent of Turkish women were in *tesettür.* Second, the headscarf ban emerged as the most important issue that people believed needed to be solved with respect to matters of identity. Finally, it was among the reasons that parents, particularly in the eastern provinces, which are the less-developed regions of the country, did not send their daughters to school. It was a social disaster, a cancerous wound that needed attention without respite.[2] Among the dire implications of the headscarf ban in the educational arena was that girls who were not permitted into *İmam Hatip* schools or universities either discontinued their education or took off their scarves in order to continue. Today, we do not have an exact number of how many students have left educational institutions or taken off their scarves over the years. Only around 30,000 have reported their cases through individual applications to *MAZLUMDER* (the Organization for Human Rights and Solidarity for Oppressed People) during the last decade, in the aftermath of the 1997 coup.[3] This refers to the *başörtülü kadınlar* who experienced the implications of the ban in educational institutions starting in 1997. We do not know an exact number for *başörtülü kadınlar* who have been affected by the ban over the past three decades.

Additional statistics concerning the educational status of women in Turkey can guide us to some extent, for the ban is patently among the deterrents for women to pursue their education. Traditional families, particularly in rural areas, chose not to send their daughters to schools, in part due to the headscarf ban. According to the Turkish Republic Prime Ministry Directorate General on the status of women, the female illiteracy rate by 2000 was 19.4 percent[4] and 32.6 percent in 1990.[5] A research conducted by the Institute of Population Studies of Hacettepe University in 2003 among 8,075 women in 80 cities from 700 residential communities comprising both urban and rural areas depicts that 21.8 percent of women in Turkey have no formal primary education, that is to say that they either have not attended primary school or not completed it. Also, 53.7 percent of females have only five years of primary education. Only 17 percent have completed high school and received a university education.[6] While this study is not indicative of the direct role of the headscarf ban on women's decisions not to pursue education, it points to the fact that there is a problem of women's education in modernizing Turkey. Since religion is an inextricable part of Turkish society and, according to research conducted by *TESEV* in 2006, women in *tesettür* comprise 61.3 percent of the female population it would be a mistake to infer that the ban has no influence on the low rates of female education. On the contrary, the ban impacts the decision of parents not to send their daughters to school. A recent campaign undertaken by Emine Erdoğan, the wife of Prime Minister Erdoğan, named *Haydi Kızlar Okula!* (Come'n girls, you all to school!) vindicates this fact: parents in the eastern and southeastern parts of Turkey stated that they would embrace the campaign if the ban were lifted.[7] Considering the fact that 29 percent of the Turkish population is under the age of fifteen and that only 7 percent of the population is comprised of people aged sixty-five and older, Turkey is a young nation.[8] In a world where education is rendered indispensable for survival and development in general, denying *başörtülü kadınlar* education only hurts the nation in global competition.

The implications of the ban for students with headscarves were immediate throughout the country in the aftermath of the 1997 post-modern coup d'etat (see Figure 4.1[9]). Nonetheless, investigations, suspensions, verbal and physical abuse, and expulsion have been part of their experience since 1981. The official records, however, did not always cite wearing of the headscarf among the reasons for investigations and legal action. What was characteristic of the official investigation/suspension reports was that they included statements to the effect that *başörtülü kadınlar* were disruptive in the classroom and that they were impeding education.[10] Safiye

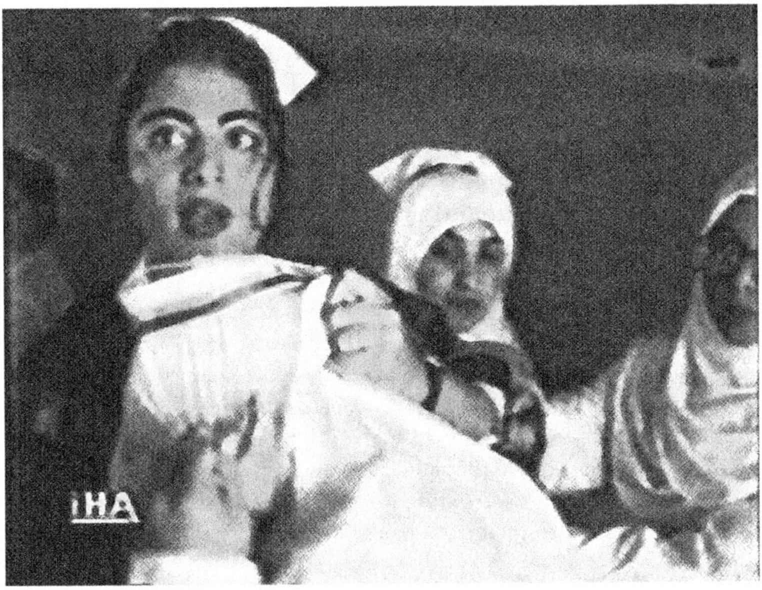

Figure 4.1 The valedictorian of nursing school at Sivas Cumhuriyet University attacked by a classmate, 1990s. Extracted from news clip at Star broadcasting channel.

Dinçer was suspended from the medical school of Hacettepe University in 1981 for a month for "disrespectful demeanor."[11]

Confrontations with professors, classmates, and security forces became part and parcel of the ban experience. A professor intends to belittle the student before her classmates:

> You and I cannot be at the same place! You would want me to go to the mosque and I would want you to take off your scarf, so let us have a contract with you: You wear a bathing suit and come with us to the pool, and I go with you to the mosque.[12]

There were examples of students with headscarves being removed from the examination roster.[13] Also, the presence of *başörtülü kadınlar* in the classroom at times led to the cancellation of classes, public confrontation with the faculty, and physical imprisonment in the classroom overnight. In 1998, three medical school students, one of whom was Reyhan Gök, were held in a classroom overnight by the security personnel of the campus in accordance with the instructions of a professor.[14] In an earlier case that became public and received media attention in 1996, Dr. Şükran

Erdem was kept locked up during work hours in the Medical Museum of the Surgery Department of Cerrahpaşa Medical School where she was on duty as an assistant physician after being ordered to work there for not agreeing to take her headscarf off.[15] Şeyma Aksız Akyürek's picture, which was present in the yearbook of Istanbul University, was removed in 2005.[16] Neslihan Dönmez was a fifteen-year-old junior high student in Karabük who was arraigned and jailed for forty-five days for carrying a picket sign that read: "Religious-less Minister [of Education] get your hands off of the headscarf!"[17]

The implementation of the ban at the outset of the Fall 2002 semester in Istanbul *İmam Hatip* schools, under the order of the Istanbul Governor Erol Çakır, led to an uproar when the students chained themselves to school gates throughout the city.[18] As the chaining protests lasted months, students were forced into the Special Terrorism Forces' vans every day before they were taken to the wilderness and dropped off to prevent their return to the schools[19] (see Figure 4.2[20]). Dozens of students and parents who were present to support their daughters were arrested during year-long protests, were subjected to investigations, and endured beatings and objurgations (Figure 4.3).[21] During one incident, six parents were jailed

Figure 4.2 Junior high school students taken into police custody because they wait at the school gate. Photo by Anadolu Ajansı.

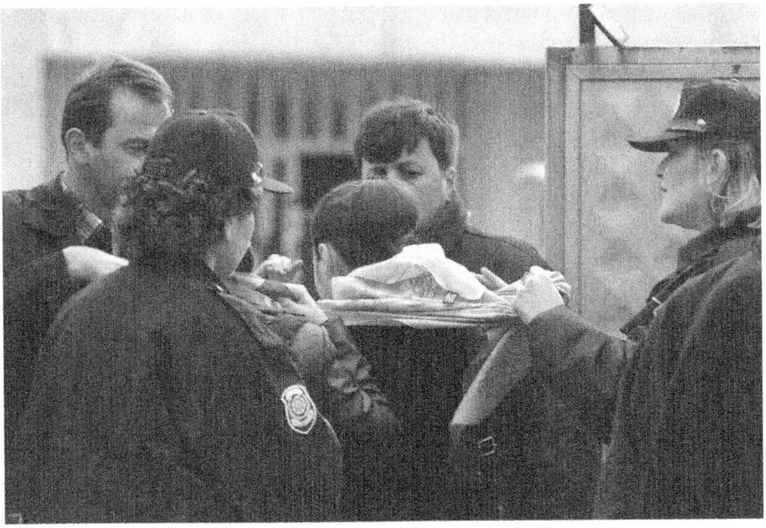

Figure 4.3 A junior high school student amidst male and female police officers (2001). Photo by Ibrahim Usta for Zaman Gazetesi.

for twenty-one days, before they were released by Kadiköy 4. *Asliye Ceza Mahkemesi* (Kadiköy 4. Criminal Court) in Istanbul.[22]

Students were expelled from school without due process.[23] The School of Islamic Studies of Marmara University denied entrance to all *başörtülü kadınlar* in 2001.[24] Throughout the country, teachers with headscarves were forced to resign or were expelled, not only from public schools but also from private institutions.[25] Faculty who chose to publicly support *başörtülü kadınlar* in the classroom or did not implement the ban faced suspensions, removal from departments, investigations, etc.[26] In contrast, enthusiastic implementation of the ban became a mechanism of reward and/or promotion, as well as a shield for covering up corruption schemes within the educational institutions and bureaucracy, as will be discussed later.

Ikna Odalari *or Persuasion Chambers or Gas Chambers for the Soul*

The emotional implications of the ban have not been medically studied. The general view among *başörtüsü mağdurları* is that the ban has affected some of the members of their group more than others, leading some to seek psychological assistance for suffering from ailments such as depression, post-traumatic stress, insomnia, and rapid weight loss.[27] There is inchoate research undertaken by Vienna University of Austria that probes the psychological effects of the ban. This incipient study's focus is on the decision-making process of students who left Turkey to pursue their education. Gülsen Demirkol Özer does an in-depth study of the psychological implications of the ban in *Psikolojik bir Işkence Metodu Olarak İkna Odaları* (*The Persuasion Rooms: As a Psychological Torture Method*), where she analyzes the emotional turmoil students go through as they struggle through life as a result of the ban. Sakine Akça's *Elveda Ankara* (*Farewell to Ankara*), Esra Erol's *Sen Başımın Tacı: Bir Başörtüsü Günlüğü* (*You, the Crown of My Head: A Headscarf Diary*), Sibel Eraslan's *Fil Yazıları* (*Elephant Writings*), and *Yıldız Ramazanoğlu's İkna Odaları* (*Persuasion Rooms*) provide narratives about the inner worlds of *başörtüsü mağdurları* in the form of biographies, diaries, interviews, documentaries, and novels. Emotions such as fear, stress, dread, embarrassment, humiliation, dismay, agitation, and loneliness are attested in the testimonies of *başörtülü kadınlar* in the literature. One of them summarizes her experience:

> It actually takes a toll now [after leaving the school]. While you live through it you cannot quite define it [put your finger on it]. Now, the only thing that the [word] university, which is assumed to be the place to acquire knowledge, resonates with me is "darkness." At this time I do not even want to step in there. For all, the university years are the best years, they would say: "We wish to go back to those years." I remember my university years as years of darkness due to the ban.[28]

This is emblematic for the implications of a systematically orchestrated psychological war carried out against *başörtülü kadınlar* at the universities. Humiliation started at the school gates where they had to uncover at a public site, which they dubbed *türban duvarı* (*türban* wall).[29] One medical school student described her experience at school:

> [The school reminds me of] stress and tension. As if what they were doing was not enough, they were forcing us to uncover before so many people by taking us in from the patients' entrance.[30]

For some, a common emotional implication was a sense of confusion and pressure due to being caught in between their families—who either pushed them away completely because they were insistent on wearing the headscarf or who pressured them to take it off for education—and their desire to reconcile their professional futures and religious convictions.[31] It was particularly hard for younger girls at junior high schools who fell into conflict with their parents over the ban. The younger they were, the harder it was if they failed to garner the support of their families. Some wept when their parents forcefully took them to school.[32] The fact that some of the students submitted to the ban and relinquished their headscarves while others resisted contributed to the pressure on the latter and created friction between the two groups. Özer pinpoints the density of this conflict: one student stated that she felt the need to react when she came to her dorm after being beaten up by the police for not taking her headscarf off, only to find her roommate busy looking for a wig to purchase. This scenario points to the two different reactions put forth against the same ban by two members of *başörtülü kadınlar.* The former finds her attempts to resist the ban to be devalued and even invalidated by the actions of the latter. This leads to building a grudge on the part of the former against the latter. Furthermore, the conflict within one's self exacerbated the emotional instability of the ones who succumbed to the ban. They felt divided against themselves. They invariably recounted the public humiliation of taking off their headscarves at the school gates. The school administrations made the process more difficult to deter students from wearing the headscarf altogether: "At first there was a room for us to uncover, later they locked it up," a student lamented. They all concurred that it never got easier, or that they never got used to the change. The ones who used wigs also stressed the uneasiness they endured. A university student who objected to taking it off likened herself to the street vendors who collect their items while chanting: "They are coming! They are coming!" She submits: "They are running away from the police I am running away from the police too." The emotional roller coaster was not confined to the school premises. One noted her panic attacks, a condition she developed after experiencing the headscarf ordeal at her school.[33]

In the 1990s, the notorious *ikna odaları* (i.e., the persuasion rooms for the *başörtülü kadınlar*) were introduced at the universities. Until then the psychological/emotional impact of the ban was hidden from the public. However, establishment of *ikna odaları* put an institutional face to the sufferings of *başörtülü kadınlar* through a method of psychological torture.[34] Atilla Yayla argues that what took place in *ikna odaları* is criminal.[35] *İkna odaları* were first established at Istanbul University.[36] The mastermind behind it was a group of Kemalists that included the president of Istanbul University, Kemal Alemdaroğlu. His proposal to a very skilled female student at the surgery department of the medical school was to take off her headscarf and wear a miniskirt to be part of the surgery group. The fact that on one occasion he refused to enter a wedding he was invited to after he was informed that most of the guests were *başörtülü kadınlar* was indicative of his stance on *tesettür.*[37]

İkna odaları, in Özer's term, is an "attempt to reign over body and the soul."[38] Foucault would describe this as an attempt at disciplining. Local Orientalists were at work in the treatment of *başörtülü kadınlar* at *ikna odaları*. As much as Turkey sees itself as a role model for the rest of the Muslim world as a westernized state, the local Orientalists within Turkey see themselves as role models for the rest of the nation by imposing discipline. They believed that they had the right to reign over and control *başörtülü kadınlar* at the university. They dealt with them one by one. A student stated that "by taking in one by one, they [were] rendering loneliness first." Through a divide-and-conquer method they were isolating these students from the rest of their group, preventing them from forming any solidarity. Özer also draws attention to the persuaders presenting themselves as the savior of *başörtülü kadınlar,* as the one who knows what is best for them.[39] *Başörtülü kadınlar,* in this context, represent the "Oriental" that needs to be pulled out from the dark to the light, from the backwardness of Islam to the enlightenment of Kemalism. A student recounts a school official's statement that vindicates this very stance:

> We talked to the students. They are uncovered outside as well. We taught them their rights. They are saved off of the pressures upon them. There were some who hugged us and cried for teaching them the truth.[40]

Spillover: Broadening the Scope of the Ban

Over time, the scope of the ban expanded far beyond the original limits of the federal employees and the university students as introduced in 1981. The intensity of the anger toward *başörtülü kadınlar* soared. The university premises became inaccessible for outsider *başörtülü kadınlar* at times. During thunderstorms that occurred in the aftermath of a ceremony, mothers of students at Atatürk University in Erzurum were denied access to a building of the university.[41] The same university did not permit parents who were *başörtülü kadınlar* to attend the graduation ceremonies of their children unless they had worn wigs since 1997 (the university implemented the headscarf ban on and off since 1981. The requirement for parents to wear wigs in lue of the headscarf has been implemented since 1997).[42] If the *başörtülü kadınlar* resisted uncovering or resisted against wearing wigs in lue of the headscarf then, they were coerced to wait outside while their children were conferred their degrees.[43] Then the minister of foreign affairs, Abdullah Gül (who is the current president of Turkey) of *AKP*, renounced the mandate that required that mothers with headscarves wear wigs, in Erzurum in 2005, noting that it divulged the shame of Turkey.[44] The fact that a member of the ruling cabinet who was against the ban was renouncing the treatment of *başörtülü kadınlar* showed that even when the Islamists were in office they were not able to exert power to stop such actions.

The president of another university did not permit a *türbanlı kadin* to attend her child's piano concert on university premises.[45] In another incident, Sivas Cumhuriyet University officials required *başörtülü kadınlar* to get off the public transportation buses that crossed through the campus. At the same university, a valedictorian with a headscarf was denied her diploma at the nursing school graduation ceremony. An award-winning high school student was denied her award at a composition writing competition by university officials.[46]

Wigs are no longer permitted by most of the universities as an option to allow *başörtülü kadınlar* to attend classes. Sütçü İmam University, Süleyman Demirel University, and Atatürk University are among those that deny registration to *başörtülü kadınlar* who wear wigs either in their pictures or on site.[47] In 2006, *YÖK* introduced a new provision requiring students who apply to *ÖSYM* (the University Central Examination) to have their pictures taken by *ÖSYM* officials upon arrival to prevent students from sending images of themselves that downplayed their headscarf. For this purpose *YÖK* bought 5,000 digital cameras.[48] It trained 6,000 officials in two-day workshops and alerted them that students would not be allowed to wear wigs in the school pictures.[49] It was clear that the proponents of the ban put their hearts and minds into thwarting the education of *başörtülü kadınlar* unless they agreed to be transformed into their perception of modern Turkish women.

The ban had its spillover effects in the realm of federal employees as well. The most infamous and recent case, which was discussed earlier, is that of Aytac Kılınç a teacher who was perceived as a bad example for her students by being in *tesettür* outside of the school premise. That is to say it was not sufficient not to wear the headscarf on duty, but one had to become secularized in every facet of her life to be accepted by the system. The headscarf was now a threat on the street.[50] Emine Ergin, a public school teacher for twelve years, was expelled from public service after an investigation about her wearing a wig.[51] The cases of male federal employees whose wives are *başörtülü kadınlar* also expanded the scope of the ban.

A third level of spillover is seen in the treatment of *başörtülü kadınlar*, whom the state recognizes as *türbanlı kadınlar*, who are neither students nor federal employees. Hospitals and departments of motor vehicles are among the public places where *başörtülü kadınlar* face frequent challenges. Sultan Özkan was not permitted to take the driving test in Ankara after being verbally harassed by the officials.[52] Hatice Akçil, a visually impaired *başörtülü kadın* who was the founder and the head of the Organization for Visually Impaired, was first removed from her position and later expelled from the organization.[53] Another case involved Şaziye Gerede, who responded to an urgent blood collection announcement by Hacettepe University, however was told not to dress up in "that manner" again by the attending nurse who argued that this was not a mosque.[54] That is to suggest that the religious attire could only be worn in the religious realm. Another *başörtülü kadın* was denied health care twice by the attending physician at Istanbul University's hospital because she was wearing a headscarf. Due to the delay in her treatment caused by the conflict over her headscarf, her ovaries had to be removed.[55] Her medical report read: "Due to the fact that the patient wears a *türban*, she was denied access to healthcare." Aysu Say, the chief physician of the pediatrics department at Zeynep Kamil Hospital in Istanbul, denied her five-year-old male patient health care due to his mother's *çarşaf*.[56] A complaint was filed by the mother that resulted in a disciplinary action against Say. This is an example of the resistance of *başörtülü kadınlar* against their harassment and discrimination. *Başörtülü kadınlar*, parents of *İmam Hatip* students who were imprisoned in support of their daughters' attempt to wait at school gates, also took their cases to the court and won.[57] Nonetheless, there is a cost for the judges who decide their cases. Five judges who decreed for the plaintiff *başörtülü kadınlar* have been demoted and transferred to various places and three others have faced investigations in the aftermath of their decisions.[58]

These acts of resistance aside, incidents of discrimination and exclusion are ubiquitous. One incident involved a *başörtülü kadın* who was denied her award as first runner-up at a painting competition organized by the Batman Local Educational Directorate under the Ministry of Education.[59] The case of aforementioned Hatice Hasdemir Şahin in 2001 became publicized when she was denied from giving her testimony at a case where she appeared as a defendant.[60] A similar case is that of Naciye Sönmez. She was ousted from the courtroom at Fatih 1st Criminal Court in Istanbul by presiding Judge Ayla Kaya at her alimony hearing because she was wearing a *carsaf*. Scolding Sönmez, Judge Kaya yelled: "Your *Allah* and His laws are not valid here!" She postponed the hearing, pointing to Sönmez's *çarşaf* in the court records as the reason for the delay.[61] Ramazan Acar and his fiancé Cennet Güngör were denied a marriage license by Mehmet Eryılmaz at the municipality of Gürpınar in Civril Denizli due to the fact that Güngör was wearing a headscarf.[62] Journalist *başörtülü kadınlar* faced harassments on a regular basis: Naciye Kaynak was thrown out of Kadir Has University where she was supposed to report on a program.[63] Ayşe Elçi, wife of Dursun Elçi who was going to be presented an award by the bar association in recognition of his 25 years in the profession, was denied entrance to the premise because she wore a headscarf.[64]

Finally, *başörtülü kadınlar* in the political arena paid their dues for wearing the headscarf with the author's experience as an example.[65] The price that I paid was the loss of my seat in the parliament, revocation of my citizenship for treason, a political ban for five years, and a series of prosecutions concomitant with unremitting harassment.[66] Sibel Eraslan sees what was carried out against me as being carried out against all women.[67] Eraslan, a *başörtülü kadın,* uses Arendt's referral to fascism to show that in the Turkish case, people are punished because of what they are, stating that they are ostracized and expelled from the society due to the way they are.[68] I, a democratically elected parliamentarian, was perceived as not worthy of being in the parliament, a place that belonged to the reigning elite and its modern women. Prior to the oath ceremony, the prime minister made a public proposal for me:

> She may enter the Parliament building with her headscarf. She may accept her guests in her room. But in the plenary assembly and the commissions, she must abide by the entrenched rules.[69]

As he stood and made this announcement before the public, he put on the Orientalist's hat. In his eyes, he was the lawmaker and the lawgiver. The laws of the country could be bent or suspended from his perspective when dealing with a *başörtülü kadın.* That is why his reference was not to the rules and regulations of the parliament but rather to the entrenched rules that were "unwritten" codes created by the elite that served their interests in governing modern Turkish society where they dominated the rest. This gave the former the right to make decisions on behalf of the latter, who was perceived to be less human, "antidemocratic, backward, barbaric."[70] The references to the entrenched rules ensured the superiority of one class over the others. Since he saw himself as the master of the "other," it was, in his eyes, his political right to repeal any rule he saw fit, including the rule that governed the dress code of the parliamentarians in the bylaws of the Turkish Grand National Assembly, which was the basis of my "lawful" presence in the parliament with a headscarf.

> Article 56: The President, at the presidential pulpit, wears a white butterfly tie and black vest and a black tuxedo. The reporting members on duty also wear dark colored suit. The parliamentarians, ministers, the employees of Turkish Grand National Assembly and other public personnel at the Plenary Hall are obliged to wear a jacket and a tie. Ladies wear suit. The outfit of the officers is designated by the presidential board.[71]

As the local Orientalist within, Ecevit stood before the people to make his proposal. He knew that he would not be held accountable for his actions, as he had the weight of Kemalist political tradition behind him. He knew that nobody would ridicule him or challenge him, asking "Based on what, do you say that she cannot be in the parliament?" or "How about the parliament's dress code, the Turkish Constitution, the international conventions Turkey is required to observe, the statements of the Founder Atatürk as to who will be in the parliament—do any of those mean anything?" From his perspective, my parliamentary privileges were bestowed upon me by the state, including the parliamentary immunity that he considered non-binding, for I as a *başörtülü kadın* was less than a parliamentarian, less than a human being and incapable of being elected. Turkish law renders one parliamentarian with all privileges once the elected officer receives his/her *mazbata* (i.e., the credential letter) from the state. At this point I was already rendered parliamentarian since I had already been presented with the *mazbata* by the state. Nonetheless that did not matter.

The abridgment of my rights was unlike anything experienced by any other parliamentarian. The process through which I was stripped of my citizenship was not applicable to other citizens who had the same legal status as me. My suffering would not be considered suffering.[72] In Ecevit's eyes, I was a threat to the ruling elite he represented simply by being a *başörtülü kadın* who demanded to be in the public space. I was an Oriental, a "backward" woman, first, then a parliamentarian. No matter how much I would try to "escape the fences placed around [me],"[73] to draw attention to my academic achievements, my skills as a young professional, and the capacity within which I could contribute to the country, I failed. Hence the rules that applied to the rest of the parliamentarians were not applicable to me, such as the responsibility to represent the constituents who sent me there in the first place. The entrenched rules that Ecevit referred to overrode the constitution and the will of the people—in other words, the democratic machinery. The president of Turkey, Süleyman Demirel, argued that I was an "agent provocateur" for wearing the headscarf in parliament. Along the same defensive lines that the less-religious Muslims often feel in the presence of the more-religious Muslims, he argued that I was saying "I am a Muslim because I covered my head, and those who do not cover are not Muslims,"[74] rendering himself the Orientalist who had the right to put himself in the Oriental's shoes, in the Oriental's mind to decipher her thinking system while not vice versa.[75] I, as a *başörtülü kadın,* "could not know [my]self the way that [the] Master knew." Hence I had to be taught what my actions actually meant and what was behind my actions. He acted as the Orientalist social scientist who could get into my head, know what I had in mind, and then "tell me" what I did not know about myself, which was to imply to other women that they were not Muslim but I was.

Demirel followed by declaring my attitude to be the world's biggest sin. With this he was rendering himself the religious authority as well. Although I never made any statement to that effect, I was rendered both discriminating and sinful by the legal and the religious masters. As a consequence of putting words in my mouth, defaming me and my family, and having my children booed at their elementary school, the masters created their own make-believe-Kavakci in the way that Orientalism creates an "Orientalized Oriental" in the "Orientalized" Orient.[76]

The Orientalized Oriental is the creation of the West to carry out its aspirations within the Orient. The Orientalized Oriental is born into Turkish Muslim culture. But either by the virtue of class or political opportunism, he/she alienates himself/herself from the rest of the nation. That is to say that it is not that Orientalized Oriental does not know what his/her culture is, but he/she chooses to distance himself/herself from it as an "other." He/she then imposes his/her westernized ideals that he/she seeks to defend. The process of creation of Orientalized Oriental involves a double alienation. At one level, the nominee is alienated from his/her own culture and people. At another level, from the perspective of Orientalism, he/she is an Oriental, never a Westerner. At the end of the process, in the eyes of the Europeans, he/she is a "good" Oriental, because he/she has been "Orientalized."

What my family, my colleagues, and my friends thought of me had nothing to do with the way I was presented by the state officials and the media, the major servants of the state. The former did not have a public platform, except a few media outlets to speak to, while the latter had the state machinery that created "not only knowledge but also the very reality they appear to describe."[77] According to it, "[I was] not recognized as a woman, an individual, a deputy, and a citizen but [was] rejected and stigmatized as a militant, an Islamist, and an outsider."[78] I symbolized "a devilish power that if left unchecked could bring the Turkish Republic to its knees before an overwhelming wave of Islamism waiting just outside the door."[79]

The symbols of representation employed in narration of stories about me were instrumental in the creation of the "new Kavakci." Esra Doğru Arsan drew attention to the two different pictures revealed by the news media concerning my representation.

> On the one hand, Merve Kavakci who was perceived and presented as a threat to the secular republic and democracy, because of her "*türban*"

> that represented political Islam; On the other hand, Merve Kavakci with "*başörtüsü*" who was presented as contemporary, participatory and the representative of different opinions and convictions in the society.[80]

I was invariably "Merve" in the eyes of the Kemalist media, unlike the Islamist media who referred to me either as "Kavakci" or "Merve Kavakci." In the Turkish culture, to refer to someone by their first name purports disrespect if not used by a family member or close friend. The subliminal message was that I was, "undervalued," was reduced to a "human flatness" divorced from all my "complicating humanity,"[81] hence did not deserve deference. The ultimate goal was to diminish my image before my constituents who sent me to the parliament and insinuate that they must not do this again.

From the Kemalists' perspective, I was challenging the political fetishism that resided within the sacredness of the state.[82] This, in the eyes of the Kemalists, was unforgivable—my example had to be made a lesson for all. Furthermore, in the days following the parliament ordeal, I renounced the Kemalists' actions against me and responded to PM Ecevit's and President Demirel's allegations. The fact that I was speaking, the fact that I was not succumbing to their pressures, agitated the Kemalists further. As an Oriental women, I was expected to keep quiet and appear powerless, corroborating their assumptions about an Oriental woman. They retaliated with even more ire.

In the days following the parliamentary uproar, *başörtülü kadınlar* in various cities were physically or verbally attacked by angered Kemalists. The headscarves of some were pulled by the perpetrators. They were often called "Merve," despite their lack of physical similarity to me. In the eyes of the Orientalized Oriental, all *başörtülü kadınlar*, regardless of their differences, were "Merve" and they all deserved the same treatment—to be put in their places. The ensuing protests received very different reactions from the security forces. People who were against me had the freedom to protest and instigate animosity to others, while my supporters faced arraignments. For instance, one such protest in Malatya resulted in the imprisonment of 500 religious Muslims, among whom were *başörtülü kadınlar,* such as Hüda Kaya, a mother (39), and her three daughters Nurulhak (20), Intisar (18), and Nurcihan (17), who faced the death penalty for attempting to alter the constitutional system by duress from democracy to *Şeriat* (i.e., laws based on Qur'an).[83] The fact that they attended a street protest renouncing the treatment of "Kavakci" by the secular parliamentarians was sufficient for the state to go after them with grave charges such as the destruction of the secular state edifice. The Turkish Criminal Code accommodates such charges to be brought against people whom the state deems a threat. The mother served two years and two months while her daughters served one year, one year and seven months, and eight and half months, respectively.[84]

The Kemalist women took the streets as well, protesting against me. Spaces that were not accessible to the general public, such as the premises of the Turkish Grand National Assembly, were made available to Kemalist women for protests. With the support of the state, they protested at the yard of the parliament.[85] They chanted "Merve out! *Mollas* to Iran!" and "Wake up! Wake up *Ghazi Kemal*! See the plight of this parliament!" calling out to Atatürk for help. Non-Kemalist women's organizations chose to stay out of the discussion. Only religious Muslim women's organizations, such as *Baskent Kadın Platformu* (the Capital Women Platform), publicly supported me. *Kadın Adayları Destekleme Derneği, KADER* (the Organization to Support Female Candidates), an organization that I attended the meetings of, remained silent as well.[86]

With the Islamists in power after the closure of my party, President Sezer introduced a new un-codified practice that denied *başörtülü kadınlar* access to his presidential residence and wherever he was present. This was the most publicized spillover effect of the Kavakci Affair. The fact that the Islamist government failed or chose not to address the matter head on only served to further the restrictions in the political area for *başörtülü kadınlar.* The places that used to be permissible became de facto inaccessible. The danger that this posed was that all of the premises visited by the president were immediately rendered public space. This was particularly pernicious because it would serve as part of the entrenchment of the rules. Once they were put implemented and not resisted they would become part and parcel of the tradition of "political fetishism" to which Kim Shively referred. In a regime where anti-Islamic symbols and habits are embraced unconditionally without delay, it would be hard to change them.

The military was another realm where spillover occurred. Seeing itself as the sole protector of *laiklik*, the military always had its own rules and regulations that were stricter than others. The fact that they did not need to answer to a higher authority allowed them to reign however they felt necessary. To have a wife who wears any kind of *tesettür* in the form of *türban* or *başörtüsü* was perceived as sufficient for discharging one from the military establishment. In the aftermath of the 1997 coup, thousands were expelled by the infamous *Yüksek Askeri Şura, YAŞ* (i.e., the Supreme Military Council) decisions for *irticai faaliyet* (i.e., reactionary activity). This included performing five daily prayers, abstaining from alcoholic beverages, and having *başörtülü kadınlar* as relatives such as wives and daughters. The military's stance introduced a new term, *YAŞ mağdurları* (i.e., the victims of the Supreme Military Council) to the Turkish political vocabulary. *YAŞ mağdurları* were very much germane to *başörtüsü mağdurları*. In the eyes of the public, the former implied the latter. That is to say that when one stated that he was a *YAŞ mağduru*, it would translate as his wife was a *başörtülü kadın* and he was a religious Muslim. In the official records, their discharge would be predicated upon lack of discipline or unbecoming conduct. *Türbanlı kadinlar*, the wives of military officials, were used as the pretext for demotion and denial of promotion.[87] It is noteworthy to pinpoint the enlargement of the range of implications over time. In the past, *başörtülü kadınlar* alone were affected by the ban; now, their male relatives faced the consequences directly. This can be best described by the phrase: burden on one, burden on all.

This created a hierarchy of acceptable religiosity and the punishment of unacceptable religiosity. Accordingly, religiosity was not part of the military man's life in the public or private realm. Moreover, *başörtülü kadınlar*, be they women of the periphery or *türbanlı kadınlar* of the urban areas, were not acceptable as close relatives of military officials. The military members whose wives covered were kept under surveillance in order to collect sufficient evidence to discharge the men from service. Deterrence methods were also used in the process. Then-secretary of the National Security Council General Kılınç went so far as to call upon military officials to "divorce [their] wives who do not take off their *türbans*!"[88] At another occasion, he confronted then-Prime Minister Abdullah Gül about his wife: "If I were you, I would have her uncover her head." When Gül responded, "It is her decision [to cover]," Kılınç castigated: "How could one not control his wife!"[89] Kılınç's stance presents a twofold dilemma with several contradictions. First, Kılınç's demand of Mr. Gül to make his wife take off her scarf reflects an intrinsic belief in men's inherent superiority over women. In the former's eyes, the latter should be able to make her take off her headscarf. Yet Kılınç is a Kemalist who is assumed to believe in women's ability to freely exercise their choices. Kılınç's choice of words vindicates the oxymoron presented in this interpretation and sheds doubt over his commitment to Kemalism if, and only if, Kemalism is truly committed to liberating women. Kılınç starts by: "If I were you ..." that is to say that he puts himself in Gül's shoes. In other words, if this were Kılınç's wife, he would have her take off her headscarf. Kılınç's second confrontation with Mr. Gül, in which he expresses his frustration and disappointment (i.e., "how could one not control his wife") in Gül, invigorates this interpretation further. The subtle message present in this question, that wives are to be controlled by the will of their husbands, is problematic with respect to what Kılınç is assumed to believe versus what he appears to believe.

Secondly, Kılınç is predicating his arguments merely upon the Orientalist assumption that an Oriental man controls the Oriental woman. In other words, in Kılınç's eyes it must be Mr. Gül who is behind the covering of his wife. Accordingly, in the same way that he made her cover, now he must have her uncover. His frustration in the second rhetorical question points to the Orientalist's assumption that the Oriental women are/must be manipulated by the Oriental man in the same way that the Orientalist manipulates the Oriental. Here Kılınç's audacity to confront the prime minister, who is his superior, strengthens this reading. In the former's eye, the latter, albeit superior, is an Oriental who can be ordered around by the former. The Orientalist is expected to reign over the Oriental man, who in return is expected to reign over the Oriental woman. Domestic and personal lives were not immune from the dynamics of power.[90] After Abdullah Gül assumed the presidency, the military looked for ways to avoid First Lady Hayrünisa Gül at the protocol. They simply ignored her and walked away in order to not have to shake her hand or salute her on the red carpet.[91] (See Figure 4.4.[92])

Türbanlı kadınlar are denied entrance to the military complexes as visitors (e.g., weekly ladies' tea parties, social gatherings) as well. This showed the arbitrary nature of the hierarchy and the contradictory

Figure 4.4 Lieutenant General Aslan Güner leaving the protocol to avoid First Lady Gül who wears a headscarf. Photo by Anadolu Ajansı.

nature of the military regulations. One quotidian implication of the strict military tradition was that mothers would be denied attendance to their sons' oath or the ceremony upon completion of their military duty. The coverage of the oath ceremony of the son of the Minister of Culture was in the paper with the title "Minister Koç is in the base, his wife is out!"[93] The application procedure for personnel to train at military academies has recently been amended to require "photographs of the children over the age of twelve and the wife"[94] with the obvious purpose of ensuring that female relatives of the military officers are not in *tesettür*.[95] One of the most recent high-profile cases was that of Emine Erdoğan, the wife of PM Recep Tayyip Erdoğan. In 2007, she attempted to visit a patient at Gülhane Askeri Tıp Akademisi, the military hospital at the capital, but was discouraged from going by the patient's wife, who was simply relaying the message of the military administrators at the hospital.[96]

At social functions, military men would leave receptions celebrating the anniversary of the Turkish Republic's establishment when they realized that *başörtülü kadınlar* were among the guests.[97] At one such occasion, a general made an announcement on the microphone: "*Türbanlı kadınlar* out!"[98] In addition to the military, the National Intelligence Service does not accept either *türbanlı* or *başörtülü kadınlar* on its premises, including the residential complex.[99]

While the rural *başörtülü kadınlar* are not the focus of this book, it is imperative to mention the case of Medine Bircan, which garnered extensive attention and depicted the intensity of the exclusion of this group. Bircan, a seventy-one-year-old woman, was denied health care due to the fact that her identification card had a picture of her with a headscarf. By the time her son got a new identification card with a montaged picture of her uncovered head, Bircan passed away without having received the medical attention she urgently needed.[100] A similar case involved Aynur Tezcan, who sought help at Çapa Medical School's emergency room. She was insulted by the ambulance staff because she was wearing a scarf and her mother wore a çarşaf. She was denied care for six hours, at which point her heart stopped and she was resuscitated and admitted to the ICU in coma. She was subsequently categorized as being in a vegetative state.[101] İlkay Seriner, who wears a headscarf, is the wife of a doorman, Naki Seriner, in Izmir. Figen Tüzün, the apartment manager of the building where Seriner works, fired him due to his wife's headscarf. Tüzün's reason for Seriner's termination reads: "... The wife and daughters cannot wear türban or the like which came to be known a political symbol. They cannot perform their religious prayers in public."[102] Finally, the fact that the summer camps of the State Planning Organization banned *başörtülü kadınlar* from the campsite in 1999, as discussed earlier, showed that the ban's scope included the private realm and family vacation time.

Public Opinion and the Number of *Başörtülü Kadınlar*

Despite the fact that "*türban* has long been among the most important problems of Turkey according to both the laic and the Islamist claims," it is no longer on "the agenda of the Turkish public."[103] *TESEV* field research that was conducted with 1,492 participants in 2006 depicts that among the five most important issues in the eyes of the Turkish people, *türban* ranks fourth with 5.7 percent. The most important issue was unemployment with 70.3 percent, followed by the Kurdish problem with 12.1 percent, and education with 7.9 percent.[104] One of the reasons for the low percentage on the *türban* issue might be because *başörtülü kadınlar* were not well represented in the survey, because it is clear that the issue is a priority for them. Another reason behind the low percentage might be the fact that despite the sensationalization, the views of secular intellectuals who prioritize the problem are a minority.[105] At a more individual level, the reason behind the low prioritization might be the fact that *başörtülü kadınlar* have mostly succumbed to the system, given up hope, and now feel "worn out by the ban."[106] Therefore they do not believe that others see it as a matter of urgency. Another cogent argument that explicates the low percentage might be that the responses to the questionnaires change rapidly depending on the country's current agenda.[107] That is to say that the national issues that were up for debate during the time of the research conducted by *TESEV* might have impacted the findings. It is not accurate to suggest that the *türban/başörtüsü* is not important for the state or *başörtülü kadınlar*. On the contrary, the headscarf ban is the most important issue used to determine matters of identity: the participants give the ban the highest ranking—43 percent—when they were asked about the most important matter "pertinent to identity" that the government is expected to implement as part of its policies.[108] The survey also shows that 71 percent of the participants concurred that not permitting *başörtülü kadınlar* in schools is wrong and that they must be permitted access, while 68 percent agreed that female government officials should be allowed to wear headscarves if they so choose.[109] Finally, the study depicts that despite the ubiquitous public opinion that the number of women in *tesettür* is increasing, it actually decreased from 72.5 percent to 71.2 percent between 1999 and 2006.[110] This 1.3 percent decrease implies that the forceful implementation of the ban is paying off for the proponents of the ban and, through various methods of deterrence used by the state, women are not in *tesettür* as much as they used to be.

Economic Repercussions

In Turkey, 49.8 percent of women work as "unpaid family laborers" and 57.2 percent of women who get paid work in the agrarian field.[111] The assumption is that these women participate in the economy through farm work due to the fact that it is the only way they can contribute to the family economy either through unpaid or paid work. With little or no skills that can open doors for them, they remain stuck in the vicious cycle of no pay or little pay for their labor. Education is therefore a key to women's economic development. The result of a study conducted by Zehra Kasnakoğlu and Meltem Dayıoğlu shows that "schooling is an important determinant of women's market participation" in Turkey.

> An increase in the level of schooling from primary to junior high school increases the probability of participation from 6.18 to 10.75 percent. However, the most drastic change occurs between the high school and university levels, where the probability of participation increases from 28.1 to 67.4 percent.[112]

A study conducted in 2003 by the Institute of Populations Studies at Hacettepe University depicted that 21.8 percent of the female population have little or no education, and that some 53.7 percent have only completed the first five years of their primary education. The fact that women's market participation shows an increase of 39.3 percent from 28.1 percent for those with a high school education to 67.4 percent for those with a university education means that higher education is imperative for women's economic contribution. Economics serves on both sides of the equation as cause and effect: The headscarf ban is a deterrent that contributes to the reasons that girls stay out of school. *Başörtülü kadınlar,* deprived of the opportunity to education (in addition to other factors), would suffer disproportionately from the lack of economic empowerment. Exceptions may be observed among upper-income families, but they are in the minority. Restricting the space in which *başörtülü kadınlar* can move around complicates the problem. *Başörtülü kadınlar* who resist the ban, confined to the private realm, can only contribute to the national economy at reduced capacity. Hence the ban becomes an underlying factor for the lack of economic empowerment. On the other hand, economic necessities force women to be in the public realm, but only in the appearance that the state requires. *Başörtülü kadınlar* who cannot afford not to work must get an education and find jobs to support their families. In these situations, economic needs serve as the driving force behind the decision to relinquish their headscarves. Therefore, lack of economic freedom entails "lack" of the *başörtüsü.*

The 2006 *TESEV* study suggests that the more income increases, the less women tend to cover and for women who are in *tesettür,* there has been a general decline in income over the last decade. The steepest decrease in income is seen in the middle-income groups with 13.2 percent.[113] The opposite also is true: women who are in *tesettür* are less likely to be hired, and even if they find a job or somehow complete their education, they are less likely to pursue their professional careers. For professions that require membership to organizations such as the bar association, or exams such as the Medical Residency Examination, the ban poses an insurmountable challenge for *başörtülü kadınlar.*

The state increased its attacks on religious Muslims in the private sector following the 1997 coup d'etat, leading economic enterprises, including those that belonged to religious Muslims, to be meticulous about who they hired. That is to say that they were fearful of hiring *başörtülü kadınlar* at a time when the military was announcing the names of organizations, plants, stores, and brand names owned by religious Muslims in order to discourage people from consuming their products. To have *başörtülü kadınlar* among their staff would mean that the company was condoning *tesettür* and thus was at risk of being boycotted. Therefore, the organizations felt obliged to put a secular façade on their enterprises. Some of the *başörtülü kadınlar* were demoted to backroom jobs while others were fired. They were paid less than modern Turkish women and men with the same qualifications. They were expected to be content with what they had, and to be thankful to even have a job. This brought with it the exploitation of *başörtülü kadınlar.* That is to say that they were expected to work but not receive any credit for it. Even if their contribution was essential to a project, they would not be permitted to be visible and gain credit for it in the end. At press conferences or photo opportunities, they would not be allowed to attend as a precaution against Kemalist attacks. In their professional relations with their superiors, there was an implied warning not to expect full credit for their work.

These were probably among the hardest adjustments for *başörtülü kadınlar* to adapt to. They saw themselves facing a "double victimization," or if we borrow Leela Gandhi's term "double colonization."[114] The sense of disappointment reigned among them as they found themselves alone in their struggle. This added another layer to their victimization. When *başörtülü kadınlar* looked for jobs, they were often turned down by religious businesses with the advice to go and sit at home. They were also rejected because they were college dropouts or their names were implicated with the headscarf resistance movement.[115] As their own Islamist communities distanced themselves from *başörtülü kadınlar* (to avoid losing customers and being labeled as *yeşil sermaye* which literally means green investment, representing the economies owned by religious Muslims) women realized that their struggle was two-dimensional: one against the Kemalists, secular fundamentalists who did not give them a chance to exist in the public sphere, and the other against their own Islamist communities that marginalized, exploited, and finally forgot them.

The Islamist politicians did not treat them any better. A group of students brought to the attention of religious parliamentarians that starting 1998 their university stopped accepting their headscarved pictures for registration. The parliamentarians downplayed the looming danger and told them: "it would not go further than giving uncovered picture."[116] The greater municipality of Ankara that belonged to *FP* fired a large number of *başörtülü kadınlar* in 1999. In 2007, *başörtüsü mağdurları* who attended a protest in Izmit were beaten up by police forces on *AKP*'s watch while another protest was simultaneously held in Ankara by the Kemalists—all of whom were women against Erdoğan's candidacy for the president—yet the police did not touch them.[117] The irony lay in the fact that on the *AKP*'s watch, *başörtülü kadınlar* were attacked by pepper gas and beaten up for demanding the repeal of the ban while at the same time modern Kemalist women were treated with respect by the security forces for cursing Prime Minister Erdoğan for being a religious Muslim who, in their eyes, did not deserve to become the president. (See Figures 4.5 and 4.6.)

The Fethullah Gülen community, a religious sect known for its educational institutions across the globe, was among the trailblazers in introducing paradoxical changes at its schools. Gülen started off as a follower of the Nursi tradition, a follower of Said-i Nursi. Said-i Nursi, a man of Kurdish origin, was among the dissidents of the regime in the late 1930s to 1940s. He was imprisoned and exiled for his religious activism. One of the characteristics of his movement was to abstain from politics, which promoted an individualistic form of Islam. Gülen's movement, however, diverted from this particular Nursi requirement and became a behind-the-scenes actor in Turkish politics. Gülen did not support Islamist politics in Turkey, but he affiliated himself with other parties. In the 1999 elections, the movement supported the Democratic Leftist Party of Bülent Ecevit. Ecevit returned the favor and enunciated his sympathy for Gülen.[118] On this note, it is important to acknowledge that unlike the prevalent view among Kemalists that religious Muslims comprise a homogeneous group that makes unified decisions, Turkish Islam and religious Muslims are dynamic and heterogeneous, with competing and incessantly changing social and political agendas.

In the post-1997 period, Gülen enforced the headscarf ban immediately at his schools throughout the country to impress upon the state that he was working in accordance with the regime to secure his movement.[119]

Figure 4.5 *İmam Hatip* students breaking under the stress of the ban while hoping to go into their classrooms. Photo by Vakit Gazetesi.

Figure 4.6 Police blockade on the way to school. Photo by ÖNDER.

He described himself as "on the side of the state and military."[120] During the post-modern coup of 1997, he blamed *RP* for creating tension within the society.[121] His community also pulled *başörtülü kadınlar* to the back stage at their various institutions that they established in the United States as a precaution. At the nongovernmental organizations and schools that they founded they placed *başörtülü kadinlar* to the back scenes in order to ensure a secular façade based on modernity and disguised their religiousity. At some instances they turned down applications for teaching because the candidate was a *başörtülü kadın*. At meetings organized within political premises such as the U.S. Congress or the British Parliament, they invariably hid the *başörtülü kadınlar* of their community, presenting "modern" Turkish women as their representative.

Such actions by conservative factions of society strengthened the hand of the state in its hunt for *başörtülü kadınlar*. With the divide and conquer method, the state would distinguish between the pernicious, terrorist, obstinate *başörtülü kadınlar* and the benign, peaceful, obedient Turkish women. This, in turn, would allow the state to continue to discriminate against *başörtülü kadınlar* who chose to remain as *başörtülü/türbanlı kadınlar*. In order to survive in the floundering Turkish economy, religious Muslim men who needed their wives' economic support and men who would like to pursue careers in academia, the military, or public service became more inclined to choose women without headscarves as partners.

The Media and the Representation of "White" and "Black" Turks

Başörtülü kadınlar in the public sphere were perceived as the direct challengers of the modernization project of the republic. The place that the regime appropriated for them was within the confines of the private and the rural realm, as discussed in detail earlier. Now that a new generation of *başörtülü kadınlar* was questioning this spatial division, they would garner more bile from the state than any other group. Hence they were to be pushed back to where they were meant to be. The knowledge about *başörtülü kadınlar* was to be produced, disseminated, and inculcated in the minds of the public via subtle but meticulous messages that would take strength from the Orientalist assumptions.

In the aftermath of the 1997 post-modern coup d'etat, the communities within which *başörtülü kadınlar* emerged started to be recognized as the *zenci Türkler* ("black Turks"). The identification process was a mutually inclusive one. That is to say that the treatment of religious Muslims by the state led them to think of themselves as the underdog and the underprivileged. The ruling elite, perturbed by the rising saliency of these groups, attempted to delegitimize their progression by pointing out the differences between them and others. Hence from their perspective, these groups were the black Turks, not necessarily because they perceived them as the underdog but for the simple fact that if *başörtülü kadınlar* were "black" then they, themselves, were the *beyaz Türkler* ("white Turks"). And they found a pride in that. Çevik Bir, the general known to be the mastermind behind the post-modern coup of 1997, argued: "*Biz beyazız*" (we are white).[122]

Skin color was never part of the equation in the construction of Turkish national identity. Through this dichotomous representation, white and black became affiliated with good/modern vs. bad/Oriental and Western vs. local. This enabled the former to maintain distance from the latter, and to continue to subjugate it. *Başörtülü kadınlar* were the black Turks—in Necip Fazıl's terminology, *oz yurdunda parya* (i.e., outcast in their own land)—and deprived of their educational and professional aspirations.

In the press conference at the parliament after my ordeal, I stated that it was clear that our struggle would be similar to that of the African Americans in the U.S. civil rights movement in the 1950s and 1960s.[123] Recep Tayyip Erdoğan, the current prime minister, made frequent references to the same term, *zenci Türkler*, he himself a member thereof.[124] Erdoğan was imprisoned in 1999, during his term as the mayor of Istanbul, for reading a poem from renowned poet Ziya Gökalp at a public address in the city of Siirt.

> *Minareler süngü,*
> *Kubbeler miğfer,*
> *Camiler kışlamız,*
> *Muminler asker,*
> *Bu ilahi ordu dinimi bekler,*
> *Allahu Ekber Allahu Ekber.*
>
> [The minarets are the bayonet,
> The domes are the helmet,
> The mosques are our garrison,
> The believers are the soldiers,
> This divine military awaits for my religion,
> God is the Greatest, God is the Greatest.][125]

Everything about Erdoğan is a matter for criticism, from the way he dresses and talks to the slippers he wears in his house—which refers to the assumption that he is not westernized and civilized enough to wear shoes inside the house, preferring instead to wear slippers at home since that is where people perform daily prayers, which requires the premise to be spotless. He is belittled for not having any decorum. The fact that a member of the black Turks is ruling over the established political class as the prime minister is a cause of resentment. Erdoğan's constituents are the target for the Orientalized Orientals. The Orientalized Orientals have a condescending attitude toward the black Turks' supporters. They incessantly belittle them—Erdoğan's constituents do not like to read, do not like to watch the news (they only watch "fun and game programs"), they have big bellies that they like to scratch, and "Tayyip Erdoğan trusts" them.[126]

The main goal of Orientalized Oriental's depiction of this constituency is to disparage Erdoğan's opinions and his choices in politics as worthless and invalid. For Orientalized Orientals do not believe in a democracy that would bring the black Turks to power. They do not believe in people's sovereignty; they want selective democracy so that the Orientalized Orientals and people like them can stay in power. Following is a summary of that:

> And when the ballot box is put out there, what the man, who scratches his belly wants, prevails. Because democracy is the system in which man in low-high conscious are equal. If the majority of a society is made up of "man who scratches his belly," in there, there is no democracy, there can not be democracy.[127]

Thus the Orientalized Oriental dread democratic elections with the fear: "what if the 'other' brings one of the 'other' to rule over 'us'?" They do not trust the nation. They want to preserve the status quo where they, as the Orientalized Orientals, decide on behalf of the nation. Hence they are against, for example, the people electing the president of the country. They argue that "that would open a big problem."[128]

The depictions of the prime minister's wife, Mrs. Emine Erdoğan, are similarly harsh. Discussions about Mrs. Erdoğan, and the other *başörtülü kadınlar* who have husbands in the ruling cabinet, center mostly on their headscarves and their subordination. Their belittlement is part of the internalized Orientalist discourse. A sense of shame is invariably voiced due to the way they dress, particularly when Mrs. Erdoğan and other women are on international trips. The same question of dread is consistently expressed: "Are these the women who should be representing us in the international arena, in Europe, in America?" One such commentator describes a function where he watches the first ladies of Syria and Jordan and Emine Erdoğan come in to the hall, and the first two do not cover. He shares his sense of "foreignness for a moment" when he sees that half of the hall is replete with *türbanlı kadınlar.*[129] He feels a mixture of shame and disappointment, so "foreign" and distant from the "other" that he cannot fathom why so many women in Turkey would cover and, more importantly, how on earth he ended up with these *başörtülü kadınlar* representing him in the political sphere. Before he ends, he reiterates his sense of foreignness by screaming out his defiance: "This is not my culture!" His sadness is twofold. First, half of the women in the hall are in *tesettür.* That is to say that they are more visible than they were in the past. Second, one of these *başörtülü kadınlar* is the first lady of his country, representing and ruling over him.

As the Orientalized Oriental, the vicegerent and representative of the European man, he is disturbed by his fellow countrywomen's presumed regression and lack of prudence. In this case, it is particularly hard for the Orientalized Oriental to accept what he sees because the other Muslim women who are in the company of Mrs. Erdoğan (the first ladies of two Arab states) are not wearing headscarves. To see Mrs. Erdoğan, who represents the modernized/westernized Turkish Republic, in the attire that, from his perspective, an "abject" Arab woman is supposed to be in is especially unforgivable. From his perspective, Arabs are the "Orientals" who speak the language of Islam, Arabic. It is the republican spirit and the secular regime that distinguishes the assumed superiority of Turks from the backwardness of the "Muslim" Arabs. Turkish women, in the Orientalized Oriental's eyes, must be a source of pride as the role model for the rest of the Muslim world. Her western appearance, stripped of the trappings of Islam, is to be celebrated. Now that Mrs. Erdoğan is in the Islamic *tesettür* and Mrs. Asad of Syria and Queen Rania of Jordan are "uncovered" in Western outfits, the role-model status of Turkey and its women is challenged.

Albeit not a Kemalist, Taha Akyol relays a similar message: "The wife and the daughter of the Prime Minister of Turkey that will start negotiations with European Union are in *tesettür*... Mrs. [Asad], the woman of an Arab state, is in contemporary attire! I got upset!" Nonetheless Akyol disagrees with the unremitting harsh criticism targeting Mrs. Erdoğan and admires her strength in the face of the attacks.[130] These comments activate the old condescending Ottoman attitude toward Arabs as backward subjects. Hence the old attitude is put to some new use.

Mrs. Erdoğan, a fashionable woman, is never good enough in the Orientalized Oriental's eyes. Even during her *umrah* (a special pilgrimage to the Holy Land in Mecca), she is expected to dress like modern Turkish women in a way that distinguishes her from the rest of the Arab and Muslim women around her. An Orientalized Oriental female commentator castigates her for instead wearing a "black *çarşaf*."[131] Although

Mrs. Erdoğan was in fact wearing not a *çarşaf* but an *abaya* (i.e., a long coat) and a headscarf in accordance with the local culture and the tradition of pilgrimage, the Orientalized Oriental modern Turkish woman is appalled by it: "at this position, I cannot accept this wardrobe... This is a 'different' liking... it is a product of far away times, places, and understandings... [It is] beyond the point of nervousness, it is hurting me."[132] A male Orientalized Oriental concurs and submits that "the more he looks at these pictures the gloomier" he gets.[133]

Essential difference is part of the Orientalist look. Making generalizations and rendering them absolute truths is also a characteristic of this discourse. An Orientalist among "us" just does that with a clear expression.

> Covered spouse tells us a character. Conservative, religious, a person who chose Arab culture and lifestyle is what we have before us. He doesn't like the regulations of the Republican revolutionary reforms. Woman is second class for him. And of course her freedom is limited. He loves men-to-men talks. He does not like woman to speak. He would be disturbed to see her at an environment where she is among men, he wants her as the *harem*.[134]

He then turns to the husband of the *türbanlı kadin* and suggests that he "does not much like civilization" and "he has duplicity." To have a wife with *türban* tells us "a mentality, a stance, a demeanor."[135]

Another case involves a picture of the wife of the president of the Central Bank. She came under an Orientalist's scrutiny, who submits: "I looked at her picture long and hard" and adds that he had to write about it.[136] His main concern is whether the fact that the Central Bank is headed by an "other" indicates that white Turks are leaving the scene But his Orientalist assumptions focus on the woman, Düriye Yılmaz, as a symbol of Islam. He is not focusing on what he would be expected to focus on: the performance of the person who heads the Central Bank. By focusing on the wife he is examining the entire movement—the movement that brought this group of religious Muslims to power to reign over him and other members of the elite. Through scrutiny of the wife, he draws inferences about the larger collectivity.[137] He starts with the way she wears her headscarf in the picture and submits that it is worn in "a way that there is no doubt that it expresses belonging to a certain religious community." Although he has no proof in his hand to support his argument, he presents it so forcefully that he makes new rules. He neither explains what it is that makes him think "there is no doubt" she belongs to a particular religious community, nor provides the name thereof. His subsequent depictions are more than delineations;

they include disparagements of her body and insults such as "[she has] an ordinary posture," "[she wears] flat shoes," and "her gender difference is relegated to the *türban*," meaning that her *türban* is the only thing that differentiates her from a man. The insinuation is her depiction as a manly woman. He goes on to give an account of the surrounding: "muddy shoes outside of the door," "newspapers on the foil," and then concludes: "a surrounding that would make one ask: do not the women of this house ever go out?"

His question involves a typical exercise of Orientalism: one woman's depiction becomes a statement about "women" in general. An Orientalized Oriental is not interested in individuals, but large collectivities.[138] He never explains what it is about the surroundings that prompts him to ask this question. He claims to be foreign to the lifestyle of the "other" to the extent that he does not know that muddy shoes are left outside only because they are muddy and that other shoes belonging to the residing men and women are taken off inside. Nevertheless he makes that leap from the male muddy shoes to the suggestion that religious Muslim women must never go outside. Next, as he turns back to the woman's depiction and submits that he does not catch any sign of fundamentalism or extremism in her, she must be "a Turkish woman busy with her prayers" referring to the Oriental's "regular characteristics" of simplicity, deplorability, and subordination.[139] With this, he explains the "behavior of his Oriental" countrywomen.[140] Then he throws a question to himself: "Then what is it that is disturbing me?" He responds, "a heavy sadness, and worries ..." and finally he drops the bomb: "Are these the women who will be the new role models of the Turkish Republic?" After having created an image of these women into something completely different from reality, he then turns her into a future threat. In this article, he "makes the Orient[al] speak, describes the Orient[al], renders its mysteries plain for and to" the ruling elite.[141] He concludes with a generalization: "I am irked when *türbanism* becomes a revenge mechanism and a password for a Masonic solidarity." The reader is not told how he inferred this final judgment from the description of a single woman whom he felt sorry for. These are examples of how *başörtülü kadınlar* are disparaged based on who they are and what their presence triggers in the public debate.

In the discussion by the Orientalized Oriental, the representation of *başörtülü kadınlar* resorts to untrue or convoluted information to guide or misguide the public through subliminal or overt messages. A headline of "*Tesettür* Disaster"[142] refers to a physician, Kezban Arbağ, who allegedly wears a headscarf (but in reality wears a wig) and refuses to take the ultrasound of a male patient. The subtle message hidden in the fabricated news is that the female doctor is too conservative to examine a male patient and because she allegedly refuses to see him, he is inflicted with a severe medical condition. The ensuing subliminal message is that *başörtülü kadınlar* cannot be physicians and that if they are allowed to become doctors, their patients will suffer hence they must not be permitted. The story appears on prime-time news immediately. Soon thereafter it becomes clear that the story is completely untrue, and Arbağ sues the newspaper and the television producer who implicated her.[143] Judge Abdullah Çoban at the 1st District Court in Konya finds Arbağ's case unsubstantiated hence rejects the case, submitting: "Because the plaintiff, as a doctor who serves as a public servant, in spite of the positive sciences and the rational knowledge, she had acquired, is criticized due of the mentality under the *türban* that she is wearing, even if these are harsh criticisms, she has to bear them. Hence the court decrees to reject the case that cannot be proven."[144]

Another example of misleading anti-*tesettür* "news" is the headline "*Tesettür* makes osteoporosis."[145] The argument is that since *başörtülü kadınlar* cover their whole body they lack vitamin D, which is needed to prevent osteoporosis. The article not only does not acknowledge that there is no direct correlation between full-body covering and osteoporosis but also does not mention any potential benefits of the conservative dress—such as reduced chance of skin cancer. Once the news was aired, the municipality that conducted the research denied that allegation of osteoporosis was among the findings of the study. Another news article that reads "*Türban* pins are scattering horror"[146] points to the women who swallow their pins while putting on their headscarves, and claims that these comprise 23 percent of all cases of foreign elements in the lungs. The article concludes under a subheading: "The Ministry [of Health] must ban [them]." Here the Orientalized Oriental not only informs the public about an issue but imposes what the next action must be as well. It takes on the job of (mis)guiding the Oriental.

Another headline along the same lines reads: "*Türban* separated the engaged couple."[147] According to the story, the couple separate due to the young man's family's insistence on the bride to be in *tesettür,* which she rejects, driving the young man to commit suicide. To what extent the contention over the *türban* contributed to the decision of the suicidal youth, we are not told. However, the goal of sending the subliminal message to "stay away from *türban*" is achieved. Finally in this category is the distorted reporting of the news: "She took off her *türban* because it became politicized,"[148] despite the fact that when asked "Did you take it off because it became politicized?" the interviewee responds "No, I took it off for personal reasons."

The media gives ample space to the statements of people who deride *tesettür*. An example involves an actress who shows up at the premiere of her movie wearing untraditional, designer minishorts. Upon a question about her outfit from the news agencies, she responds, "What should I have done? Wear *türban* and *basma*?"[149] (the latter is a type of cotton material that characteristically the women of rural areas sew their clothes from). It is not what she thinks of *tesettür*, but the way in which it is presented in the news, that underlines its Oriental status. Otherwise, she is simply vindicating the general assumption created by the state and society that *tesettür* is the lifestyle of rural-area women alone. Finally, following a grave earthquake tragedy in Turkey in which 30,000 live were lost, an image of a young *başörtülü kadın* holding a picket sign that reads: "Was 7.4 not enough?" is published. The *başörtüsü mağduru,* with a picket sign in hand, insinuates that this is the wrath of God, for impeding freedom of conscience. A journalist likens her to a prostitute. The Orientalized Oriental, replete with anger, unable to discern the frustration of the girl, backlashes during an interview about the incident.[150] After all, as an Orientalized Oriental he assumes ownership of the religious realm as well. He can have an opinion on religious matters; a *başörtülü kadın,* however, is not entitled to one.

CHAPTER 5

IN SEARCH OF EDUCATION, EMPLOYMENT, AND MORE

Looking for a Solution in Faraway Places

Immigration as a Response to the Ban and Başörtülü Kadınlar *of the Diaspora*

The headscarf ban motivated *başörtülü kadınlar* to look for alternatives for education and work opportunities beyond the borders of Turkey. A cross-generational ban led me to move to the United States in 1988 as a sophomore in medical school, and a few years later my mother, who was teaching German literature at the university, was forced to resign due to her headscarf.[1] Today my daughters (who also wear headscarves) are pursuing their graduate studies in the United States. After years of sporadic individual migrations, the post-modern coup of 1997 was the beginning of a mass migration of some 3,000 *başörtülü kadınlar* to Europe.[2] Austria, in particular, provided hope for them. Vienna University offered transfer opportunities in addition to free education. Some *başörtülü kadınlar* scattered around Europe and the Turkic states of the former Soviet Union. A few migrated to Canada and were granted political asylum due to their suffering in the hands of the Turkish security forces.[3] The United States was a preferred destination for *başörtülü kadınlar* who either had their families' financial backing or received scholarships. The ones who received scholarships or grants from the Ministry of Education were not relieved from the ban's burden. The embassies and local consulates kept students under surveillance and, at times, suspended students' grants for anti-secular activities, such as wearing of the headscarf and attending international conferences with headscarves. Eastern bloc countries and Northern Cyprus became popular destinations for *başörtülü kadınlar* due to their geographic proximity. Education was relatively inexpensive there as well. Nonetheless, the headscarf ban spread to Bulgaria and Cyprus under the sway of the Turkish regime.[4] The Orientalized Orientals paid particular attention to the developments with respect to the headscarf issue in neighboring countries. They expressed their concern and disgruntlement without reservation if they saw neighboring countries allowing *başörtülü kadınlar* into their universities. Cyprus, which was dubbed the "baby of the homeland," quickly caved to the pressures from Turkey. Despite its disadvantages, migration had positive implications for young *başörtülü kadınlar.* There are many undergraduate, graduate, and doctoral students among the *başörtülü kadınlar* of the diaspora. Some students of junior high and high schools also joined with older students in the diaspora. If it had not been for the ban, one could not have fathomed these women leaving their families behind to embark on a new life somewhere else—learning new languages and acquiring knowledge about different peoples and cultures. Most of them did not know the language of their new countries before leaving Turkey. Despite the implications of being away from loved ones and often feeling homesick, this experience helped them become stronger and widely perceptive. In some ways, it was almost a blessing in disguise. It would be an apt conjecture to argue that if and when the ban is repealed, *başörtülü kadınlar,* who are well equipped with the knowledge in their fields of specialization (and maybe even overqualified by Turkish standards), will return home to serve their country with integrity.

Awkward Positionings and Postures

The longer their struggle lasted, the more many *başörtülü kadınlar* learned to become independent. With lack of support from their own communities, they found strength in each other and in the community of *başörtüsü mağdurları.* Years of protests, confrontations, and negotiations taught them how to be stronger advocates of their cause. It also helped them to learn about the democratic machinery and adopt its instruments. They were, in a way, part of a democratizing journey—albeit inadvertently, they contributed to the democratization processes. They were on their own, and they were fighting for themselves alone. In particular, the fact that the private enterprises owned by religious Muslims, as well as their academic and Islamist communities, failed to provide unconditional support for them or remained at a distance played a significant role in this journey.

In this endeavor, they empowered themselves by resisting the ban, becoming politically active, and protesting the ban on campuses.[5] Empowerment within the inner worlds led to an increased yearning for existence in the public sphere. Although they were never allowed to be part of the public sphere on equal terms, they pushed their way into the public sphere through other means, as previously discussed. Some of the *başörtülü kadınlar* who left Turkey for an education came back after pursuing their degrees at American and European universities.

Bumin dubs these women *ultramodern*. As a result of this transformation, the chasm between them and their own communities grew bigger and deeper. Their communities did not know what to do with these women. They failed to integrate them and accommodate their complexities. At the end of the day, like the state, they were used to seeing *başörtülü kadınlar* as their homemakers, wives, daughters, and mothers. Nonetheless these women were now in the public realm. Hence the Islamist community could not figure out how to deal with them either. They were more "modernized," if you will, than the members of their own community. They were ahead of their communities in the "democratization of the minds processes."[6] The lonely fight for their headscarf taught them how to move within the democratic local, national, and international arenas. Hence they became estranged of their own communities. On the other hand, with the headscarf, they were not like the modern Turkish women who fit into the secular communities. Although in most ways they led lives similar to that of modern Turkish women, they were not "civilized enough" (from a *laiklik* perspective) to assume equal membership. They were not welcome there. They found themselves in a bind, caught in between as the women of nowhere.[7]

By 2000, a new transformation was observed among some of the *başörtülü kadınlar* that was not pertinent to their struggle against the ban. It was a "frowned upon" change that young *başörtülü kadınlar* set in the public agenda. Girls with headscarves began wearing excessive makeup, dressing in revealing clothing with a headscarf. , attending public concerts, and dancing in public while their naked bellies were exposed.[8] Smoking and "hanging out" in hookah bars became increasingly popular. This shift in behavior and appearance could be read, in Homi Bhabha's term, as the "mimicry" of the colonized, and in the same way that mimicry "allowed the colonized to try on like a new accessory the colonizer's reflected image in the body/site of the 'native,'" the imitation of the modern attitudes and dress on the part of the *başörtülü kadınlar* were intended for the purpose of acceptance by the Orientalized Oriental, to fit in and prevent becoming outcasts[9] The very young age of these women also pointed to the importance of peer pressure during adolescence.

This development met with opprobrium from the religious Muslims, in general. The Orientalists rose to the occasion to put their researcher hat on again. For some, this change was inevitable, a result of the newly emerging class stratifications among the religious Muslims during the rise of *AKP*.[10] An Orientalized Oriental celebrated the naked-bellied *türbanlı kadınlar* picture he saw on the newspaper and argued that this was a sign of normalization and the vindication of Nilüfer Göle's theory who argued that *türban* was the means of emancipation for girls confined in their households.[11] Göle argued in her *Modern Mahrem* that the headscarf was the password for the religious female to the outside world. So long as she would wear it, the family and the patriarchal world she lived in would not reject the idea that she was in the public arena. Göle's argument has merit to it for the families in the periphery who would perceive the headscarf as a shield that would protect their daughters from evil eyes in the society. Nevertheless, one also has to acknowledge the fact that because the state does not see the headscarf as an acceptable form of attire for women, it becomes a stifler rather than an emancipator for women. The fact that increasing numbers of women are dropping out of school can be used as a counterargument against Göle's argument. Nonetheless, the Orientalized Oriental who is investigating is not interested in this shift. He focuses on the fact that the headscarf is combined with a naked belly. His interpretation is that the girl is leaving the household with the permission of her parents by using the "password," and then she is exposing her belly—a natural development for any female adolescent.

Others saw the naked-bellied women as the "first sign of uprising" against the "abstract generalities,"[12] which presumed that the naked-bellied women were from the Islamist community. In their eyes, *türbanlı kadınlar*, no matter how modernized/westernized they might be, still belonged to a large collectivity of Islamists with a political agenda, and now their youth were defying them. They represented a warning to the Islamists.

> One day you will, too, understand that in this global world you will not be able to keep these girls as the doorkeepers of your politics and as the residents of your backyard.[13]

It was not clear how the naked-bellied woman in the picture was a member of the political Islamist movement. The usage of the "backyard," which is a loaded term in Turkish politics, is an insinuation that has a political history. This term was introduced to Turkish political vernacular by Mesut Yılmaz. During the time that the Islamist movement was on the rise in the 1990s, *ANAP* leader Yılmaz argued that Islamists "see *İmam Hatip* schools as their backyard" (i.e., they get their support from the youth in these religious public schools). "Backyard" also implies underhanded or a hidden agenda where evil and illegal activities take place. Within the convoluted Turkish political realm, credit for coining this term readily stuck to Necmeddin Erbakan, the leader of *RP*. That is to say that Erbakan ended up being the owner of this statement despite his futile attempts to prove otherwise. Since then, the term "backyard" has had negative connotations in Turkish political discourse, implying a resource for political Islam where youngsters are exploited by Islamists for their own political gains. Moreover, these backyards raised many of the future leaders of Turkey, like Erdoğan, the majority of the members of his party, and the majority of the mayors across the country. That poses a threat to the power of the white Turks.

The Orientalized Oriental under our investigation is more interested in the presumed exploitation that takes place at the backyard: He argues that the naked-bellied *başörtülü kadınlar* will not stay forever as supporters of the Islamist movement, enticed by its promises in the backyards. That is to say that their eyes will open, they will realize that they are wronged by the Islamists, and they will run to westernization.

The backyard phenomenon is another construction of the Orientalized Orientals to manipulate the social and political discourse that involve religious Muslims. The Orientalized Orientals conceptualize their own definition of "backyard," link it with the Islamists, and profusely use it in their rhetoric and writings. They solidify a "backyard" as a human resource for the Islamist. Through this, they attempt to discern the increasing support to Islamists and discredit it. They taint this support by loading the term negatively. The main goal here is to discredit the Islamist efforts to expand their bases and label them mischievous and conniving. They also aim to discredit the products of these "backyards," including the Islamist politicians who rule the country. By denigrating the environment that accommodated their emergence, Orientalized Orientals indirectly devalue the Islamist politicians, religious Muslim entrepreneurs, and *başörtülü kadınlar* who are graduates of these schools. By doing so, they send a subliminal message to parents discouraging them from sending their children to *İmam Hatip* schools to avoid the presumed exploitation of their children. Yet these "backyards" (i.e., *İmam Hatip* schools) did not raise anyone involved in corruption schemes, bank embezzlement scandals, or tax fraud, as some Kemalists and many modern Turks are often implicated with. They only raised good citizens with religious and moral values who would abstain from wrongdoing in the name of their religious convictions. Hence this phenomenon has to be read as another implication of the Orientalized Orientals' discourse on the Turkish people.

Political Ramifications

AKP *and New Spaces for the Ban*

The fact that the *AKP* came from a political tradition of *MNP, MSP, RP,* and *FP,* which were all targeted and shut down by the Kemalist establishment, influenced the way it chose to govern by distancing itself from the problems of religious Muslims. The *AKP* positioned itself as an advocate of Turkey's accession process to the EU and a proponent of the U.S. alliance.[14] From the outset, the *AKP* argued that the economy was the priority in its political program. Internationally, it focused on Turkey's long-awaited accession to the European Union. The *AKP* held on tighter than any other government to the Copenhagen criteria to undo the harm inflicted by the coup of 1997. At the end of the day, European Union requirements included an active civil society, separation of powers, transparency, accountability, individual liberties, and an independent government bereft of the clout of the military. For the *AKP,* European Union accession was the panacea for the ills of the Turkish nation. Presenting a pro-EU position would also prove that the *AKP* is not anti-Western and anti-modern. Meeting the Copenhagen criteria and opening the space for liberties would also mean more freedom for religious Muslims. With that in mind, the *AKP* put all its effort into international relations. At the end of its first five-year reign, *AKP* had made more strides toward bringing the Turkish standard of living to a level compatible to that of the Europeans than any other so-called secular government had ever done.

To an extent, the *AKP* also managed to abate the military's influence. The ratio between the civil and military members on the National Security Council was already altered by the previous government just before the *AKP* assumed office. Accordingly, the civil members outnumbered the military members by nine to five at the council. The *AKP* further mandated that the secretary of the council be a civilian rather than a military officer. They amended the civil and criminal code to include more freedom and lesser restrictions—in particular, the freedom of expression. Nonetheless, all of these changes occurred like the *Ottoman Mehter* dance in which the soldiers move two steps forward followed by one step backward. While the government amended Article 312 (the law that had banned freedom of expression so it could be used against intellectuals, activists, journalists, and politicians—including Erbakan, Erdoğan, and myself) and granted amnesty to thousands indicted by it, it introduced further restrictions via other laws such as Article 301 that indicted renowned writers. The *AKP* also mandated the criminal code to enable civilian courts to try military officers.

The Kemalists lamented that the *AKP* was just wielding the European Union card to shield its original intent of changing the system to *Şeriat* (i.e., the Islamic legal code). That did not happen. On the contrary, something unexpected occurred during this time: the country was replete with the spirit of European Union accession, but with people from opposing camps switching sides. The majority of the religious Muslims and Islamists who stood against EU accession initially became pro-EU, realizing that accession might give them a chance to escape from the oppressive dominance of the army and the Kemalists' influence over their lives.[15] *Başörtülü kadınlar* acknowledged that the EU position was very complicated with respect to Turkey, but the prevalent view was that accession could mean repeal of the headscarf ban or relaxation on its implementation. The Kemalists, on the other hand, who were known to be the locomotive of westernization and proponents of Turkey's accession to the European Union, became the major stumbling block to Turkey's democratization and accession process. Islamists, liberals, leftists, democrats, and feminists joined in one camp for a variety of reasons. Kemalist civilians and the Kemalist military remained in the opposing camp. That is to say that Kemalists who were, in the past, vocal proponents of Europeanization became its opponents due to fear of losing power and change of the status quo. Advocacy of westernization was a card of the Orientalized Oriental to exert its power over the *Anatolian* people for a long time. It was a vehicle also to distance itself from the "other." But now that the westernization process had picked up its pace as part of the Turkey's EU accession procedure with the will of the people and the support of the *AKP*, the Orientalized Oriental was left with nothing to support the opposition between them and the "other." On the other hand, the people who suffered from a lack of democratic processes all became proponents of EU accession for the sake of bringing more democracy in order to ameliorate their own particularities.

The EU accession process strengthened the *AKP*'s legitimacy both inside Turkey and abroad. At the national and international level, EU advocacy helped the *AKP* to dissipate the suspicion surrounding the threat of its Islamic identity. Although Erdoğan was incessantly assailed by the Kemalists for his background, he made extra efforts to distance himself from his own religious community. All concurred that *AKP*, during the course of its first five years, met some of the needs of various groups from Kurds, to Alevis, to non-Muslim minorities. It failed, however, to address the two major burning issues for religious Muslims: the headscarf and the *İmam Hatip* schools.[16] That is to say that the naturalization of the Islamist/Muslim democratic movement in the political realm was rendered more important than the agendas of *başörtülü kadınlar* and the religious people.

Very early on, Erdoğan declared that the headscarf was not in his party's agenda.[17] This received a grave reaction from the religious supporters of *AKP*. In response, Bülent Arınç, then the speaker of the parliament and also a member of *AKP*, pointed out that they promised constituents that they would solve the headscarf issue. As a result, Erdoğan changed his position to argue that there needed to be mutual societal agreement before the problem could be solved. The advocates of the repeal of the ban responded again: "The mutual societal consensus is there!" A study conducted by *Milliyet* newspaper showed that 75 percent of the Turkish people concur that the ban must be lifted.[18]

Revisiting its argument one more time, the *AKP* came back with another pretext: "The societal consensus is present in Turkey, now we are looking for institutional consensus."[19] Erdoğan defended his apprehensive stance by suggesting that they were avoiding tension in the society.[20] Nonetheless, the more he shunned the issue, the more his wife's headscarf heeded attention. The media orchestrated public debates on the presidential election of 2007 were reduced to discussion of Mrs. Erdoğan's headscarf.[21] The question was if Turkey was ready to have a president whose wife wore a headscarf. Kemalists were opposed and took to the streets with the chanting of "Mollas to Iran, we don't want *türban*!" The *AKP* had to withdraw its presidential candidate, Abdullah Gül, and declare an early general election in the summer of 2007.

The aforementioned attempt of the speaker of the parliament, Bülent Arınç, to introduce his headscarved wife to the public sphere during his meeting with President Sezer at the airport failed to garner support from within the *AKP*.[22] On the contrary, under pressure from the Kemalists, the *AKP* chose to ignore the matter. The fact that the *AKP* was putting a concerted effort into not speaking about the ban contributed to the rise of new dimensions of the ban. Such a conformist stance was the corroboration of a system that justified "its social order, legitimating a given elite's right to rule."[23] With this attitude, *AKP* contributed to new introductions of the ban and the entrenchment thereof. The fact that under Sezer's presidency the presidential residence was not open to *başörtülü kadınlar* was a direct consequence of *AKP*'s stance. The *AKP*'s calculating attitude to avoid tension clearly legitimized the closure of the presidential premise to *başörtülü kadınlar* starting in 2002.

During the period when the presidential election of 2007 was looming, the *AKP*, by contributing to the entrenchment of the new definition of public sphere, happened to help the political fortunes of its political nemesis. Kemalists challenged the candidacy of *AKP* members based on the fact that their wives were *başörtülü kadınlar*. Erdoğan's candidacy did not come to fruition due to Mrs. Erdoğan's headscarf. Erdoğan caught his opponents off guard when, to the contrary of the prevalent expectation, he pointed to the Secretary of Foreign Affairs, Abdullah Gül, as *AKP*'s presidential candidate rather than assuming the nomination himself. From that moment on, Kemalists went after Mrs. Gül and her headscarf. She became the target of a vicious campaign while her husband's qualifications were not discussed at all. This was a clear shift in the headscarf discourse. Now, the issue was no longer about the headscarf of a female politician or a professional woman who demanded her space in the public realm, as was seen in the Kavakci Affair and many others alluded to earlier in the book. It was rather about the wife of a religious Muslim man who demanded his place in the public sphere. By all accounts, this was a step backwards—first, in the headscarf, second in the religious, third in the democratization discourses overall.

The news media, a majority of which was owned by a few business tycoons, was the public voice of Kemalism during this challenging time. The Doğan Group, which was comprised of many Orientalized Orientals, was a leader in the fight against *başörtülü kadınlar* and a president's election whose wife was a *başörtülü kadın*. Ironically, in the midst of this strife, the *AKP* government lessened the conflict by first canceling half of the debt of Doğan Group to the taxpayers and then reducing the other half dramatically from $735,000,000 to $202,000,000.[24] Rather than holding the tycoons accountable for their actions, accommodating their unjust gains meant strengthening the proponents of the ban with the hand of the religious Muslim politicians. The *AKP* was the sole bearer of that responsibility. In response to the rising visibility of *başörtülü kadınlar* in the public arena and the political success of Islamist politicians, the state continued its political conservatism and increased its restrictions. For instance, a revelation came from President Sezer in 2007, in which he redefined secularism:

> Secularism is not freedom of religion and conscious. Secularism is the security of all freedoms, hence the security of freedom of religion and conscious as well. Secularism is the name of the system where religion could never be conflated in state affairs, politics, and public life, and that the social, economic, political and legal basis of the State, even in part, could not be predicated upon religious rules.[25]

Sezer also brought a new meaning to what the term "public sphere" refers to by arguing that secularism had to be interpreted according to the "societal realities" of each country based on its conditions.[26] That is to say that if Turkey were dealing with this expansive form of secularism, it was because of the conditions it faced (i.e., Islamism); otherwise it could have been a softer kind of secularism. The president was not alone in his view. The Kemalists argued that individual liberties could be compromised in the name of protecting the state. Speaker Arınç, on the other hand, argued that the public good had to expand to benefit the people not to benefit the state, which, rather than securing the practice of religion, on the contrary, constricted freedom of religion and freedom of expression in the public sphere.[27]

The military represented another segment of the state machinery used against the *AKP*. Almost biweekly, sometimes weekly, some of the generals demonstrated their discontent with the government, arguing that reactionary threats were still valid and that Turkey was going to be taken back to the past.[28] *Fişleme,* unfortunately, was still part of the activities of not only the Turkish intelligence service but the military forces as well.[29] The *AKP* government, during its first five years, was not capable of cracking down on the system that kept this machine alive. The military garnered information on religious Muslims, non-Muslim minorities, Satanist groups, ethnic groups, and organizations that were involved in meditation, and defended its position by arguing that the activity merely aimed at being on the safe side.[30] Ironically, the Kemalist military, whose everlasting aspiration was Turkey's westernization, also enunciated that it was using *fişleme* to track down people who were pro-European Union and pro-American.[31] That is to reassert that during the last decade the Kemalists not only moved away from being proponents of westernization and European Union accession but they also became anti-EU and anti-American.

It is noteworthy, at this point, to ponder upon and bring an explication to this shift. The Orientalized Oriental, in his mind, has an image of the Oriental and an image of the Occident that he incessantly employs. Neither of these imageries reflects the reality. The imagery of the former, in the Orientalized Oriental's mind, stands for the deplorable qualities of the Muslim peoples, their territories, and lives while the latter's imagery reflects an image of an Occidental society that the Orientalized Oriental strives to create within the Orient to sustain and protract his hegemony. By fervently adopting the secularizing particularities of the West, employing and re-employing them time and again in his life and renouncing whomever does not do the same, over time he strengthens his "West" as he sees it. In this construction of the Occident, for instance, there is no place for religion. He downplays the role of religion, if not ignores it altogether. Moreover, in this construction, pluralism, diversity, and identity politics are presented as unfathomable in the West. The Orientalized Oriental intentionally undermines aspects that will appear antithetical to, and thus endanger his own construction of, the West. Once the reality of the West is divulged, however, he changes lines and joins the anti-Western camp. Vural Savaş, the chief state prosecutor, in the closure case of the *RP* refers to the example of the United States, arguing that it is forbidden for teachers to wear religious garments at American public schools.[32] While this is not true, it becomes convenient for the Orientalized Oriental to promote such misrepresentations. When what he puts forth as the characteristics of the West do not dovetail with reality, and he can no longer veil what the real West might offer to the oppressed masses of the Orient (which makes the West more appealing to the masses), then the Orientalized Oriental turns against the West.

YÖK also continued to use *fişleme* to determine who was religious in academia. Meanwhile *Diyanet*, the Directorate of Religious Affairs, stated that *tesettür* was a mandate in Islam, adding that the state had the right to make rules to govern lives.[33] As part of the state edifice, *Diyanet* mostly chose to remain passive both on the issue of headscarf ban and the ban on children's Qur'an education for ages twelve and under. *Diyanet* represents a religious authority within the state structure, therefore its stance is invariably congruent with the regime's ideology. In the case of the *tesettür, Diyanet* would lose its legitimacy in the eyes of the people if it argued that *tesettür* was not part of the Islamic credo. To avoid that, it acknowledged it but could not go so far as to suggest that women must be permitted to wear headscarves, which would contradict the state. Hence it put on a Janus-faced act.

The fact that *tesettür* started becoming problematic in other countries (such as Germany, Belgium, Holland, and Switzerland) under the *AKP*'s watch contributed to the change in the nature of the ban's discourse to become an "unsolved global issue" that represents the modern-traditional binary oppositions.[34]

The Kemalists' Corruption and the Ban

One of the most profitable ways to earn easy money in Turkey is through exploitation of Atatürk.[35] Using Atatürk's name and putting on a Kemalist façade would open doors for unaccountability where exploiters could squander taxpayers' money or use it for personal matters, and nobody would dare to question the expenditure.[36] The postmodern coup d'etat period of 1997 "carries corruption, in addition to anti-democratic applications, as its most salient traits."[37] Some see the promotion of the headscarf ban as one of the most fecund cover-up mechanisms for corruption schemes. It diverts attention from more important issues, such as corruption and illegitimate deal-making within the Turkish political class. Several members of the military who were on the front lines of the postmodern coup to defend Kemalism and tamper with the democratic machinery were implicated in corruption scandals, for which they were tried and sentenced.[38] Some of them are currently under investigation while others remain free.[39] In fact, one case that implicated General Yaşar Büyükanıt, a former commander of the Turkish Armed Forces, cost Ferhat Sarıkaya, the prosecutor, not only his position but his profession as well because the bar association disbarred him from the profession and stripped him of his professional entitlements.[40] In the academic world, the mastermind of the *ikna odaları* (the persuasion rooms), Kemal Alemdaroğlu, and president of Istanbul University was convicted for plagiarism. It was covered up by the then-President Demirel.[41] Yücel Aşkın, the president of Yüzüncü Yıl Üniversitesi in Van, was imprisoned for corruption and *fişleme*.[42] On the front lines of the headscarf ban implementation was Bursa's *İmam Hatip* school in the late 1990s, where the governor, Orhan Taşanlar, was prosecuted for corruption.[43] Necla Arat, a fervent Kemalist woman who fights vocally against *başörtülü kadınlar*'s demand to exist in public space, was convicted of plagiarism in the professorial dissertation she had written to become a full professor. She was even banned from the university premise for a period of six months after the investigation committee decreed that 200 pages of her 218-page dissertation were plagiarized from three different books.[44]

Nonetheless, the most recent and novel form of corruption within the Kemalist stratum came in the political realm, from what is now dubbed *Ergenekon Terör Örgütü, ETÖ* (Ergenekon Terror Organization) investigations. An illegal organization, comprised of current and former military members, Kemalist academics, ultranationalist bureaucrats, and journalists, *ETÖ* is now implicated in some of the most heinous crimes perpetrated against Turkey's people over several decades.[45]

Ban in the International Arena

Various groups in Turkey, including *başörtüsü mağdurları,* collaborate with international networks of religious, feminist, and ethnic groups and voice their criticisms in the language of universal rights and freedoms.[46] International recognition of the ban came in the aftermath of my expulsion from parliament. The international media covered the election from the time I was nominated and continued to follow it in the aftermath of the oath ceremony. Prior to the Kavakci Affair, the international community was largely incognizant of the headscarf ban. In 1999, it garnered attention and gained recognition. Unlike the majority of the Turkish media, international media reported on the affair objectively and factually, rather than demogogically and subjectively. Unlike the Turkish media, they did not throw insults or prevarications or carry out character assassinations against me and my family.

The support I garnered in the international realm was noteworthy as well. Neighboring Muslim countries stood on my side, threatening to suspend economic and political relations with Turkey if I was not reinstated in the parliament. Some discussed the matter in their parliamentary sessions. In Jordan, Iran, Qatar, Sudan, and Egypt, women took to the streets in support of my election. In Europe, proponents of human rights and particularly Muslims of Turkish origin expressed full support. In Great Britain, Lord Eric Avebury of the House of Lords brought the ordeal to the attention of the queen. The Interparliamentary Union in Switzerland started an investigation against the Turkish Republic through his initiation. In the United States, an organization called Sisters United for Merve (SUM) organized public protests in support. Prominent American Muslim organizations visited the White House to raise awareness about the issue. Support I garnered in the international realm frustrated the Orientalized Orientals further—they stood their ground mercilessly, and they expected others to do the same.

Once the international community became aware of the headscarf issue in 1999, it was among the items on the list of challenges that Turkey faced in the path to full democratization. The U.S. State Department included the headscarf ban in Turkey among other global human rights violations starting in 2001. The Commission on Security and Cooperation in Europe of the U.S. Congress and the U.S. Commission on International Religious Freedom recognized the ban in their reports stating that it was a violation of basic human rights. The U.S. Congress exhibited the headscarf that I wore to the parliament as a symbol of religious freedom in its rotunda as part of a larger display.[47] It is paramount to reiterate that international recognition is crucial for the solution of the problem. Turkey is part of an interconnected and interdependent global village where it developed important relations with the United States and Europe. It is embarrassing for a country such as Turkey that is striving to become westernized to have its name among violators of democratic rights. That is to say that Turkey cannot afford to be callous to reports that state the headscarf ban is among the violations list. Eventually the Turkish Republic will have to acknowledge the warnings and lift the ban. Nongovernmental organizations such as Freedom House, Becket Fund for Religious Liberty, Human Rights Watch, Amnesty International, and Institute on Religion and Public Policy, which recognized the ban, put pressure on the Turkish government via their reports as well as cooperation with local Turkish organizations to lift the ban.

The European Parliament Resolution on women's role in social, economic, and political life in Turkey included *Şahin v. Turkey* in its 2007 report, while the United Nations' CEDAW urged Turkey to solve the headscarf issue by January 2009.[48] In addition to the European Court of Human Rights, *başörtülü kadınlar* will now be able to take their cases to the U.N. Commission on Human Rights.[49] The European Court of Human Rights decreed against Turkey in 2007, in *Kavakci v. Turkey,* stating that "Turkey has violated Article 3 of Protocol 1 of the European Convention on Human Rights," which guarantees the right to fair election.[50] Nonetheless, ECHR submitted that the state's concern for protecting secular statehood was apt but the state's response was disproportional to my action. That is to say that ECHR acknowledged that the state had the right to react to my parliamentary entrance but exceeded normal limits. Furthermore, the court denied my demand to be compensated for the loss of parliamentary time in form of my parliamentary remuneration. This confirms ECHR's longstanding prejudice against *başörtülü kadınlar.* The court decree, under *AKP*'s rule, fell on deaf ears. The fact that ECHR decisions cannot be retroactive helped *AKP* Government to play down the decision. In other words, the decree did not ignite a public debate about the headscarf ban and its scope in general as it was supposed to.

The increasing number of articles produced suggests that the number of academicians who study the *başörtülü kadınlar* of Turkey is soaring at American and European universities. The attention of the international media in particular is increasing due to the fact that Turkey is no longer alone in its struggle with the headscarf issue. The French law that mandated the prohibition of ostentatious religious symbols and local prohibitions in some parts of Germany, Belgium, and Switzerland proved the headscarf to be on the global agenda. During his visit to the United States in the summer of 2005, Prime Minister Erdoğan was caught off-guard on a live program with CNN's Wolf Blitzer, who asked him if the regulations that ban the headscarf could be reversed. Erdoğan responded, "There must be a consensus between the institutions, and then we can solve this problem," and lamented that his daughters also had to study abroad, in the United States.[51] In 2009, President Obama gave a speech in Cairo that directly targeted the plight of the *başörtülü kadınlar* of Turkey. Albeit without specifically mentioning Turkey, the president renounced the Turkish Republic's stance vis-à-vis *başörtülü kadınlar.* He submitted that "a woman who is denied from education is denied from equality."[52]

CHAPTER 6

CONCLUSION: THE ROAD AHEAD: WHAT'S IN STORE FOR *BAŞÖRTÜLÜ KADINLAR*?

Women's outer appearance did not lose its importance despite the changes that came about throughout the history of Turkish Republic. Some of the introduced changes that were considered to be significant in the modernizing revolutionary movement in the early 1920s became less significant after several decades. Nonetheless, Turkish women's attire and its centrality to the success of the regime's goal of westernizing its people remained as critical as in the early days of the establishment of the republic. The meticulousness that the state depicted in the modern representation of women and their appearance explained the social and political reaction *başörtülü kadınlar* received as they pushed their way into the public sphere. The state perceived these women as a threat to its *laiklik* and a marker of the failure of the westernization project through which modernity was directly linked to women's attire and attitudes. For the Orientalized Oriental that comprised the state and the Kemalist elite, *başörtülü kadınlar* were reminders of the religious past and were identified as internal enemies.

The more *başörtülü kadınlar* foisted themselves as visible forms on various arenas of society, the more they were resented and attacked by the state that strived to purge them from its system, sending *başörtülü kadınlar* back to where it thought they belonged (i.e., the private realm and the periphery). This vicious circle continued to thrive, exacerbating the situation for these women. The result was bleak and cost time, energy, prestige, and most importantly talent and quality of life for all parties involved. The fact that the state channels some of its energy to controlling *başörtülü kadınlar* means stolen time from areas that truly need improvement. The fact that Turkey is often reprimanded by the international community for marginalizing these women creates an image problem for a country that is juggling the East and the West, its Islamic heritage and its westernizing goals. The fact that *başörtülü kadınlar* are prevented from contributing to Turkish society as professionals does not only automatically decrease the quality of life for them as individual citizens, but it also negatively impacts the development effort of the larger society, which is deprived of their services.

Then what does the future hold for them? It is both easy and difficult to conjecture what is in store for *başörtülü kadınlar.* It is easy because, in accordance with the bleak picture presented of the past and present, a premonition of what is yet to come could be offered. The state's desire to create the modern women in its own particular image is unlikely to change after so many decades, hence it would be far-fetched to anticipate that things would alter for the better anytime in the near future for *başörtülü kadınlar.* Yet it is also very difficult to surmise what is next since the past thirty years attest to the dynamism of *başörtülü kadınlar,* which is reflected in their increasing adaptability to changing circumstances and the evolution of the style of their *tesettür.* The following scenarios could be entertained.

Until Further Notice: An Ensuing Fatigue in the Islamist Front

One of the reasons behind the exacerbation of the plight of the *başörtülü kadınlar* over the years was the lack of confidence entrenched in the Islamist community that was supposed to stand by them. As much as these women were pushed around by the state, the Kemalist elite, and a large portion of the mass media, they were also turned away from by the religious group to which they belonged. I recall the starvation protests we held in 1986 as medical school students at the Abdi İpekçi Park in Ankara. Failing to garner support from our own religious community, we were left to our fates. In the political arena, we were told to "wait…and wait…and wait more" through the employment of religious concepts such as *sabır* (patience), which were invariably utilized via religious epics from the historical Islamic past. *Başörtülü kadınlar,* along with the larger female Muslim community, were expected to have full faith in their Muslim brothers and wait until they could take on the state with respect to the headscarf ban. In this line of logic, there existed an implicit underestimation of the dire conditions facing *başörtülü kadınlar.* After all, there was the common perception that these women's primary duty was to be mothers. If they were not permitted into the public realm, they could always go back to their original duties of raising a family. Moreover, there was an intrinsic assumption that things could not get any worse vis-à-vis the treatment of *başörtülü kadınlar*, therefore they should make some concessions and not see these concessions as compromises. Yet things did get worse, and once they did the same Muslim male community that had been advising women to be patient warned that the pressure that *başörtülü kadınlar* were exerting over them could make things worse than they already were.

This explains how the Islamist politicians refused to tackle the headscarf ban for decades, leaving the playing field entirely to the Kemalists and the state to stifle *başörtülü kadınlar*. Finally, when the Islamist politicians stood up against the ban, it was too little too late and they were ousted from the government. This implied that *başörtülü kadınlar* were among the major causes behind the Islamist Welfare Party's closure in 1998 and the marginalization of its leaders, bolstering the argument raised by Islamist men that *başörtülü kadınlar* needed to be more patient. When my attempt to take the oath of office as an MP resulted in the party's closure in 2001, that argument was further augmented.

The new party, *AKP*, has not improved the conditions under which these women operate because its government sacrificed the interests and rights of the *başörtülü kadınlar* in exchange for the larger goal of proving that they were able to work within the system. In this way they managed to persuade the disconcerted Kemalists, to a certain extent, that the *AKP* was not a threat. Most of the cabinet members distanced themselves from the advocates of freedom for the headscarf. They solved the issue at a personal level and sent their daughters to Europe and the United States for education, therefore they eased the pain they felt in their own households. That is to say that, far from their sight, the problem became somewhat far away from their conscience as well. There was always a justification for procrastination. On *AKP*'s watch, the treatment of *başörtülü kadınlar* actually got worse. Unable to appease the bile of the Kemalist military, bureaucracy, and their extremities in the private sector toward *başörtülü kadınlar*, *AKP* stood by while numerous campaigns were launched against these women. In turn, the bashing of *başörtülü kadınlar* was not challenged by the government. The more these actions went unchallenged, the more it became normalized and prevalent. As a result, the headscarf-friendly *AKP* has contributed to the paradoxical narrowing of the political and public space available to *başörtülü kadınlar*.

The final blow to these women came when the *AKP* government, in the aftermath of its second victory in the July 2007 election, attempted to partially lift the ban. The *AKP*, trusting Abdullah Gül as the new president of Turkey who assumed office on *AKP*'s ticket, reached an agreement with the *MHP* to revoke the ban for just one group of *başörtülü kadınlar*, namely the university students. Despite protests from opposing camps—the Kemalists, who argued that this was a blatant attack on *laiklik,* and the Islamists, including the *başörtülü kadınlar,* who argued that rights could not be granted partially—parliament amended the constitution. Nonetheless, *CHP* immediately went to the constitutional court for a reversal of the new amendment while the state prosecutor opened a case against *AKP* asking that it be closed down in the same way that it closed down its predecessors. The court decreed that the new amendment was unconstitutional based on the premise that it promoted anti-secularism, but it decided not to close down the party.

The headscarf issue, once more, was put off for an indefinite period of time, while *AKP* thought that it got a narrow escape. Within this context, it is possible that *AKP* government adheres to the original pretext that women must be more patient until the time comes, pointing out that their party got lucky this time. The fact that *AKP* had attempted to lift the ban, but was just not given the opportunity to revoke it, would strengthen its hand against the castigations of *başörtülü kadınlar* who felt that they were left out of the political machinery.

Eyes quickly turned to other issues waiting to be addressed. The headscarf issue would be forgotten as long as it was deemed necessary and untenable. If and when *başörtülü kadınlar* raise their voices again to demand action from the *AKP*, the response that they get will be: "You know what happens each time we try to lift the ban," insinuating the threat of closure of the party. Their demands will be put off for an indefinite period of time.

For Better or Worse: Women Take the Matter in Their Own Hands

As the democratizing trend sweeps Turkey, including the state's support for a viable civil society, the rigid lines that drive a wedge among various women's groups no longer stand as clear as in the past. This is because today, there are a sizable number of Turkish women from liberal or Marxist schools of thought who believe in women's freedoms, including their right to adopt *tesettür* even if they do not concur that a woman should wear a headscarf. Unlike Kemalist women, these women join hands with *başörtülü kadınlar* in their resistance to the state's restrictive policies. Nonetheless, it is important to note that these purport to be more individual-based actions rather than collective, institutionalized support for *başörtülü kadınlar.* That is to say that the stark ideological divisions among women's organizations continue to exist, however more and more modern Turkish women empathize with *başörtülü kadınlar* and stand by them. Among them are well-recognized secular public figures such as Ümit Cizre, Nuray Mert, Nazlı Ilıcak, and Gülay Göktürk. This is a step forward for the Turkish women's movement. The fact that women from different walks of life are now able to put their differences aside and find a common denominator around which they can organize and act in solidarity against a regime that tampers with women's bodies, attire, and lives simply attests to the strides made in democratization in general and the empowerment of women in particular. It attests to alternative definitions of modernity produced by contemporary *başörtülü kadınlar.* Unlike the attempts to represent them as either backward, subjugated, voiceless, gullible, poor, second-class creatures in the hands of their male relatives or as evil, convoluted, peculiar, mysterious, cold, Janus-faced, terrorist-like foreign agents ready to harm, they have proven that they are no different from other members of society. They already embrace what technology brings their way. A past personal account will help explain. In 1995, as a representative of *RP,* I attended a women's workshop organized by the Middle East Technical University's Women's Studies Department in preparation for the United Nation's upcoming conference on women in Beijing. A graduate student who was among the academics who hosted the program noticed a funky Swatch I was wearing and blurted out in shock: "You are wearing a Swatch watch! I thought you guys are against technology!" As simple and anecdotal as it is, this example reflects on the entrenched dichotomy between the worlds of "us" versus the "other," even among supposedly the most educated. This divide, one can easily argue, is dissipating year after year, as the interactions among women soar.

Today's *başörtülü kadınlar* are increasingly independent, vocal, opinionated, convivial, and ambitious—attributes that were originally ascribed only to modern Turkish women. They keep themselves engaged and aim at excelling in whatever is offered to them in order to sustain their existence and contribute to their personal growth. The fact that they are not granted the same rights and privileges that modern secular women are granted make them value education, knowledge, and participation in public life more and not take them for granted. This leads to a search for betterment on their part. The more education is denied to them, the more precious it becomes for them. This way, the ban becomes a catapult to goad *başörtülü kadınlar* further in their search for ideological and empirical excellence.

Modern Turkish women who are able to see that *başörtülü kadınlar,* in fact, accommodate and therefore embody both religiosity and modernity in their system at the same time support their efforts to lift the ban. A push from the bottom, from the grassroots organizations established by this mixed group of women and their male counterparts, would eventually lead to a change in mentality at the top of the regime. As a country that is striving to democratize itself in order to have access to the European Union, Turkey, inevitably, will have to provide solutions for the disenfranchised groups in the society, such as *başörtülü kadınlar.* The length and duration of this process will be predicated upon the pace of maturation of the women's movements and that of the larger democratization process. While the former will determine how rapidly *başörtülü kadınlar* can garner support among the larger female population, the latter will determine when the state itself will become conducive to change, ready to relinquish the status quo that the ban is part of.

Irreversible Process: Source of the Problem Becomes the Solution

CHP is the political face of the Kemalist ideology that is responsible for the introduction, implementation, and preservation of the headscarf ban. Prior to the ban, *CHP* fought with women who dressed conservatively, accusing them of acting contrary to the revolutionary principles. Following the ban, *CHP* served as the stumbling block for any attempt to repeal it. In December 2008, Deniz Baykal, the leader of *CHP,* had an utterly unexpected epiphany, and, to the shock of the nation, opened his party's doors to women with *çarşaf* as new members. *CHP* immediately became a battle ground between members who supported Baykal and those who opposed his action. Baykal lamented his critics within the Kemalist community: "How could we judge people based on the way they look, the way they dress?" There are two sets of rationale about Baykal's behavioral change. First and foremost, in recent years, *CHP,* which has incessantly been accused of losing touch with the reality of Turkey and neglecting various strata of the society, was now attempting to address some of the underlying reasons behind its many failures. Baykal's new views could be construed as representing the first step toward reconciliation. He was not only testing the waters throughout the country but within his party as well. After all, there would be many in his party who would disapprove of his actions. In particular, female members and some of his constituents were intransigent, dividing the party in two. The embrace of the women in *tesettür* could be seen as an embrace of the Turkish masses that were left out by *CHP*'s elitist politics. Nonetheless it was mind-boggling to note that Baykal did not decide to carry out his experiment by wielding the discussion over *türban* or *başörtüsü,* but rather over *çarşaf*—for many, known to be an extreme form of *tesettür.* It is a conjecture on my part that maybe Baykal knew that if he initiated the discourse on *türban* or *başörtüsü,* women who cover would immediately respond to his call to the affirmative and would demand their public spaces in return for their party loyalty. Not wanting to lift the ban, *CHP* then would be stuck between a rock and a hard place. *Çarşaf,* on the other hand, would not be acceptable in the eyes of his constituents under any circumstances, yet the idea alone would help *CHP* to straighten its back and broaden its base within the religious communities. Knowing that his fellow party men and women would not condone *çarşaf,* Baykal entertained the idea, and posed before cameras with women in *çarşaf* who joined the *CHP* ranks. This takes us to the second rationale. Turkey was getting ready for the municipality elections of March 2009. Local governments, as explained earlier, served as the fortresses, if you will, of Islamist politics. Now *AKP* was planning on winning over the majority of the municipalities. Polls supported this projection hence *CHP* had no time to waste but to reconnect with the people on the ground for mere political gains. Albeit opportunistic, what could have been a bolder step than embracing the extreme form of *tesettür,* the *çarşaf,* to expedite the process? This was a win-win situation that could be summarized as "do not lift the ban, but capitalize on the ban."

Baykal's sincerity was challenged. He was accused of exploiting religion, an accusation he resorted to quite often to bash *AKP* and the Islamists. Upon receiving questions about the headscarf ban, he stood firm, arguing that to be a member of a party was different than to be a professional or a student, hence there was no change in *CHP*'s views with respect to the ban. Although Baykal's stance attests to the limits of his pragmatist politics, he still positions himself as a proponent of the ban. That is to say, after embracing *çarşaf* publicly and denouncing prejudices based on appearance and belief, the discourse on the ban might change for good. *CHP* very well may become, in the future, the party that lifts the ban. There are two factors behind this reasoning: One is that *CHP*'s new move will eventually sway the inner discourse about the shortcomings of the party, giving the upper hand to the reformist wing of the party, which is ready to learn from past mistakes and move forward for change. The reformist wing will argue that marginalization of the majority of female population is not something that any party can afford to ignore. That is to say that *CHP* will experience an internal overhaul that is long overdue, bringing the party up-to-date vis-à-vis the demands of the Turkish people, leaving *CHP,* in the end, not a proponent of the ban but an opponent thereof.

Secondly, it is very much in *CHP*'s interest, as well as the Kemalists', to be the mover and shaker in the political system. At this point, a *CHP* that proved to be doomed to lose election after election, only helping its opponents to further increase their votes as a backlash to its negative campaigns, might happen to realize that it cannot fight with *başörtülü kadınlar* any longer. On the contrary, it is imperative that it includes them in its target of mass constituencies. In other words, rather than allowing *AKP* to collect the fruits of the headscarf issue by lifting the ban, *CHP* may plan to be the one who is to revoke the ban, hence becoming the hero garnering support of *başörtülü kadınlar.* Ironically, this would bring *CHP* full circle: the *CHP* that fought against the *çarşaf* in the early ages of the republic can become the *CHP* that embraces the *çarşaf* and lifts the headscarf ban.

One other scenario for the *CHP*'s future lay in an obstinate *CHP* that does not budge in the headscarf discourse, losing further credit in the eyes of the Turkish people who demand a solution. It may also become disconnected with some of its hard-core constituents who fervently disagree with Baykal's recent embrace of the *çarşaf.* They would accuse him of being unprincipled and punish him by disassociating themselves from the party.

An Islamist Principled Position

Another scenario would involve Islamists' or former Islamist *AKP*'s acting with audacity to respond to their constituents of *başörtülü kadınlar* immediately without waiting for any further pressure from them. The *AKP* can get rid of the ban through various channels. One of them would involve the previous process of amending the constitution, coupled with another constitutional amendment to prevent the constitutional court from interfering as it did previously. This time, in addition to the *MHP*, the *AKP* can also seek support from the opposition party, the *CHP,* which is already changing its discourse because of its recent *çarşaf* embrace.

A second option would involve introducing a referendum concerning the ban. If the nation is given a chance to opine on the headscarf issue, polls suggest they would decide to revoke the ban in all public spaces. This option would probably be the least messy and easiest way of lifting the ban. The caveat, however would involve any impediment *CHP* might use to block the process. The *CHP* has never been a fan of referendums, acknowledging that if the nation speaks out, it might speak out in a way that benefits the Islamists. The *AKP* can encourage *CHP* to be open with the nation as to where it stands: for or against personal freedoms? The *AKP* can also demand from *CHP* an explanation as to why it embraces women in *tesettür* as its constituents but rejects their opportunity to have education and to work. A *CHP* under pressure from the ballot box might turn around and support *AKP* on this issue in order to share the credit of revoking the ban.

Guess Who Is Calling? The International Community

Another scenario might involve an intervention by an active international community. A country like Turkey that is striving to strengthen its niche in the international arena while presenting itself as an indispensable actor that can bridge gaps and take part in negotiation and reconciliation processes to mediate between conflicting regions pays excessive attention to its image around the world. This image is directly linked to the international reports on a wide spectrum of issues from economics and social development to political welfare. Turkey has shown in the past that, in its dealings with a particular group, it generally takes the necessary legal steps to ameliorate the plight of that group when external pressure is exerted, particularly if this pressure comes around the time of an election. If the international community applied serious pressure, it would not fall on deaf ears in the Turkish government.

Here I concede that it might be, currently, too optimistic to anticipate international actors to emerge as blatant supporters of the *başörtülü kadınlar.* The Turkish regime has sustained its repressiveness and justified crimes perpetrated against different facets of Turkish society through the long-term support of Western democracies like the United States, which, due to their deliberate ignorance, became its accomplices.[1] If and when the members of the international community decide to stand up for what is morally right, rather than what is convenient for them and expedient for their national interests, and confirm that the headscarf issue must be rendered an indispensable component of Turkey's acceptance by the industrialized Western community as a full-fledged democratic and developed partner, or for Turkey's accession process to the EU, then the reverberation within would be formidable enough to challenge the ban and revoke it for any party that is in office.

REVISITING MY ORIGINAL EXTRAPOLATION: IN LOOKING BACK AT A DISTANCE

Since this book was first produced four years ago, there have been some remarkable changes with respect to the basortulu kadinlar. To a large extent, history attests to the veracity of the conjectures put forth in the conclusion section of this book. It appears that a little bit of all possibilities articulated in the concluding remarks were somehow entertained during the last four years, since the book was produced.

Reluctance to resolve the problem basortulu kadinlar were facing led the Islamists to continue beating around the bush via polemical and apologetic rhetoric. This purported to the ensuing fatigue in the Islamist front. Pretenses disguised behind statements embroidered with Islamic motifs such as the following were commonly recounted: "It is just not the time!" or "Patience is a precious virtue of all" from an all-male Islamist political space. Then the prime minister, now the recently elected president of Turkey, Tayyip Erdoğan even went to the extent to offer an uncanny analogy that coalesced the struggle of basortulu kadinlar and the divine revelation. He submitted that "even it took twenty three years for the Qur'an to be revealed," adumbrating the need for the society to internalize the demands of basortulu kadinlar and to stress the role patience plays in the process.[1] Only hours after prime minister's remarks, I challenged his take on national state channel TRT asking the prime minister to divulge the reasons behind his reluctance to revoke the headscarf ban, knowing that he personally would want to see the ban lifted. The nation deserved to know the "invisible hand" that forced the elected authority to be callous toward basortulu kadinlar. While a wave of series of democratizing reforms, one after another, swept across the country for all disenfranchised groups, one was left out: basortulu kadinlar. The response to my critique was immediate.[2] Prime Minister Erdoğan and Deputy Prime Minister Bekir Bozdağ announced in tandem that basortulu kadinlar could run for office in the upcoming general and local elections.[3]

Women continued to put effort in raising awareness with respect to the ban. Primarily, before anybody else, they acknowledged that this was "their" problem. If only one group was to contribute to the solution of this problematic, who would it be, if not women. Protests ensued as usual. Women utilized the democratic packages introduced by the AKP government to their advantage by being vocal about human, but in particular women's, rights. This indeed hastened the process of change. Yet one other factor catapulted change in the months to come. Year 2011 became the marker of Turkey facing its authoritarian past, namely its infamous coup d'états. To account for the military interventions of Turkish history, people such as General Evren and Tahsin Sahinkaya, the masterminds behind the 1980 coup, were brought to justice. Postmodern coup of February 28, 1997, also found its niche within the pre-reconciliation process. As an undisputable symbol of the coup, the headscarf ban was tabled at various platforms as a violation of basic human rights. Under unequivocal pressure from the religious parts of the society, CHP, the major opposition party and the promoter of the headscarf ban for decades, turned around to suggest that all deserved citizenship rights independent of their religious identity. The head of CHP, Kemal Kilicdaroglu, stated that he "would not have ousted Merve Kavakci."[4] Hence, the source of the problem, namely the Kemalist ideology, was short of breath to continue fight against basortulu kadinlar. Smelling the changing atmosphere sagaciously, the AKP government wielded its power to lift the headscarf ban for students attending higher education.[5] This was groundbreaking. It was revolutionary. Starting in fall 2012, students covered their heads if they chose to. A few of the administrative position holders and professors attempted to take action against girls' right to cover their heads. The authorities opened investigations against them resulting in penalizing disciplinary action against the former. Turkey was, finally in a track of normalization—more importantly, democratization. In line with that process, lifting of the headscarf ban for middle and high school students came in late 2014.[6]

On my personal front, albeit slow and gradual, there were some reverberations of the positive changes. First, after the lifting of the headscarf ban at the universities, I had a chance to pick up my papers from Ankara University Medical School. It was an emotional experience. After 25 years, 6 months, and 2 days, I was back where I had abandoned my dreams of becoming a physician for good.[7] By 2014, as a political figure, I was no longer harassed by the media that carried out a political lynching campaign against me as well as my immediate and extended family. I was now considered the face of the postmodern coup. Turkish Parliament invited me to address its committee on investigation of military interventions, which I did. After 13 years, I was back at the very Parliament from where I was ousted. Head of the committee, Ms. Nimet Bas, welcomed me. My testimony lasted uninterrupted for a little over two and a half hours.

I also became a party on the postmodern coup d'état trial that began through the aforementioned process of reckoning with our past. The trial is still in progress.

My appeal to the Turkish Parliament to grant back my usurped parliamentary privileges was, though, rejected. Despite my attempt to receive one, I still do not hold a Turkish passport. On AKP's watch, I was not treated much differently than the previous government that stripped me off my citizenship. My former colleagues who established AKP chose to let the request for revisiting the repercussions of Kavakci Affair fall on deaf ears. On the campaign trail, however, they did utilize my story to unite voters against secular fundamentalist front.

In contrast, while I was honored to be recognized among the World's 500 Most Influential Muslims, I could not be more delighted to see my own story being told through the authorship of an American academic, Richard Peres, in his *Headscarf: The Day Turkey Stood Still*. He eloquently told how I was persecuted and prosecuted as a result of defending the right to cover.[8] Furthermore, I compiled an overhauled version of my own *Basortusuz Demokrasi: Tarih Icinde Tarih* (Scarf-less Democracy: History within History) under a new title *Basortusuz Demokrasi'de Adi Konmamis Darbe* (Un-dubbed coup at Scarf-less Democracy) where I unveiled new and updated information pertinent to Kavakci affair after 15 years. There, I referred to what occurred then on May 2, 1999, as a coup against national will.[9]

The following expansion of the public space for basortulu kadinlar came within the judiciary body. Lawyers were permitted to cover at the courtroom through a decree from council of state that would set precedence on the personal case of FigenŞaştım, a female lawyer with *hijab*.[10] Finally, AKP government lifted the 30-year-old headscarf ban for public servants in October 2013.[11] This was the second wave of revolutionizing change that ushered Turkey into a new era in human and women's rights discourse. The democratization package introduced by Erdoğan's government had provision for four exceptional areas that did not permit head covering. This was within the judiciary, security, and military bodies. According to this, basortulu kadinlar would not be permitted to be a prosecutor, a judge, a police officer, or a soldier. The underlying premise that, so to speak, justifies this ban in the eyes of its proponents was orientalist in nature and hence, deserved a postcolonial critique. They argued that prosecutors, judges, police officers, and soldiers had to be impartial and basortulu kadinlar, inherently lacked impartiality. While the overall lifting of the ban for public servants could not be taken for granted, to have an Islamically sensitive AKP government to preserve the ban in these four professions translated into a huge step backward in the struggle of basortulu kadinlar. Albeit in a limited sense, this was a clear entrenchment to further and reify the ban. Moreover, this would be taken as a clear concession on part of the state that basortulu kadinlar were not trustworthy and thus were rendered "lesser" of a citizen in comparison to women who do not wear basortusu. This kind of second classification was precisely what basortulu kadinlar were suffering from for decades under discriminatory secular fundamentalism. Now to have AKP to concur with such positioning of basortulu kadinlar was a setback to their efforts.

Finally, a few weeks after the lifting of the ban for public officers in October 2013, AKP decided to support five of its female parliamentarians who donned the Islamic headscarf after conducting their pilgrimage ritual. They walked into the Turkish Parliament with their headscarves. Some members of the CHP were not content to see them. Yet, no one dared to carry out a protest similar to that of 1999. Through this, some argued, CHP helped end the ban. International community covered the story in the way it did 14 years ago, only with much cheers supplanted with trepidation.

Now that the ban is largely lifted, there is no doubt that we, basortulu kadinlar, wake up every day to a better Turkey. Someday, our own stories will fade away into the oblivion, only to be considered unfathomable to a mind of its time. That day is worth longing for.

AFTERWORD

Lord Eric Avebury

I first met the feisty Merve Kavakci in November 2000 when I chaired a meeting for her in the House of Lords to explain how she had been wrongfully prevented from taking her oath as an elected member of the Turkish Grand National Assembly, purely because she insisted on wearing the Islamic headscarf.

It reminded me of an episode in the history of our own parliament when Charles Bradlaugh, a famous atheist, was prevented from taking his seat in the House of Commons for refusing to take a religious oath of loyalty. That barrier was removed in 1883, and it would be unthinkable that an MP would nowadays be denied entry for reasons connected with religious belief.

The Inter-Parliamentary Union (IPU) took up Ms. Kavakci's case on my request, and I asked them also to write to the European Union's Enlargement Commissioner, then Mr. Gunter Verheugen, so that it could be taken into account as one factor in the determination of Turkey's application to join the EU.

Five years on, Turkey had ignored the IPU, but in the meanwhile Ms. Kavakci had applied to the European Court of Human Rights. After another two years, the court ruled that there had been a violation of the right to free elections, and that the sanctions imposed on Ms. Kavakci and two of her colleagues were not proportionate to the aims pursued.

In this book, Merve Kavakci deals with the "modernization" of Turkey following the Atatürk revolution, and its insistence on the secularisation of women. There was no room in that ideology for the *başörtülü kadınlar*, the emancipated women who consciously decided to wear the headscarf, and until the advent of religious parties there was hardly any challenge to Atatürk's secularist legacy. Not only was Kavakci herself banned; her party was closed down, a frequent event in Turkey's politics. Yet if Turkey wants to become part of Europe, it will have to allow women the freedom to make these decisions for themselves. Here is a paradox that has yet to be resolved.

NOTES

1 Introduction

1. Yeşim Arat, "From Emancipation to Liberation: The Changing Role of Women in Turkey's Public Realm," *Journal of International Affairs*, vol. 54 (2000): 107–23.
2. Nikki Keddie and Lois Beck, "Introduction," in *Women in the Muslim World*, Nikki Keddie and Lois Beck eds. (Boston: Harvard University Press, 1978), 14.
3. Vamik D. Volkan and Norman Itzkowitz, *The Immortal Atatürk: A Psychobiography* (Chicago: University of Chicago Press, 1984), 352.
4. Edward W. Said, *Orientalism* (New York: Vintage Books, 1978), 7.
5. Robert Young, *Postcolonialism: An Historical Introduction* (Malden, MA: Blackwell, 2001), 59.
6. Bart Moore-Gilbert, *Postcolonial Theory: Context, Practices, Politics* (London: Verso, 1997), 9.
7. Geeta Chowdhry and Sheila Nair, "Power in a Postcolonial World: Race, Gender, and Class in International Relations," in *Power, Postcolonialism and International Relations: Reading Race, Gender and Class*, Geeta Chowdhry and Sheila Nair eds. (London: Routledge, 2004), 13.
8. Robert J.C. Young, *Postcolonialism: A Very Short Introduction* (Oxford: Oxford University Press, 2003), 146.
9. Ibid., 2.
10. Said, *Orientalism*, 121.
11. Ibid., 102.
12. Wendy Brown, *States of Injury: Power and Freedom in Late Modernity* (Princeton, NJ: Princeton University Press, 1995), 97.
13. Michael Goodhart, "Human Rights and Non-State Actors: Theoretical Puzzles," in *Non-State Actors in the Human Rights Universe*, George Andreopoulos, Zehra F. Kabasakal Arat, and Peter Juviler eds. (West Hartford, CT: Kumarian Press Inc., 2006), 25.
14. Joan Wallach Scott, *Only Paradoxes to Offer: French Feminists and the Rights of Men* (Cambridge: Harvard University Press, 1996), 6.
15. Ibid., 5.
16. Hannah Arendt, *The Origins of Totalitarianism* (London: Andre Deutsch, 1967), 291.

17. Amy Gutmann, "Communitarian Critics of Liberalism," *Philosophy and Public Affairs*, vol. 14, no. 3 (Summer 1985): 308–22.
18. Jane Flax, "Beyond Equality: Gender, Justice and Difference," in *Beyond Equality and Difference: Citizenship, Feminist Politics and Female Subjectivity*, Gisela Bock and Susan James eds. (London: Routledge, 1992), 193.
19. Arendt, *The Origins of Totalitarianism*, 41.
20. Gisela Bock and Susan James, "Introduction: Contextualizing equality and difference," in *Beyond Equality and Difference: Citizenship, Feminist Politics and Female Subjectivity*, Gisela Bock and Susan James eds. (London: Routledge, 1992), 10.
21. Michel Foucault, "The Subject and Power," in *Michel Foucault: Beyond Structuralism and Hermeneutics*, Herbert L. Dreyfus and Paul Rabinow eds. (Chicago: University of Chicago Press, 1983), 216.
22. Karen Zivi, "Feminism and the Politics of Rights: A Qualified Defense of Identity-Based Rights Claiming," *Politics and Gender*, vol. 1, no. 3 (September 2005): 377–97.

2 Women in Nation-Building

1. Ayşe Afetinan, *Tarih Boyunca Türk Kadınının Hak ve Görevleri* (Istanbul: Milli Eğitim Basımevi, 1968), 108–28.
2. Deniz Kandiyoti, "Women and the Turkish State: Political Actors or Symbolic Pawns?" in *Women, Nation and State,* Nira Yuval-Davis and Floya Anthias eds. (New York: St. Martin's Press, 1989), 135–38.
3. Sonia Alverez, "Women's Movement and Gender Politics in the Brazilian Transition," in *The Women's Movement in Latin America: Feminism and the Transition to Democracy,* Jane S. Jaquette ed. (Boulder, CO: Westview Press, 1994), 22.
4. Kumar Jayawedana, *Feminism and Nationalism in the Third World* (London: Zed Books, 1986), 35–36.
5. Ibid.
6. İlbeyi Özer, *Avrupa Yolunda Batılaşma yada Batılılaşma: Istanbul'da Sosyal Değişimler* (Istanbul: Truva Yayınları, 2005), 238.
7. Umut Özkırımlı, *Theories of Nationalism: A Critical Introduction* (New York: St. Martin's Press, 2000), 67–68.
8. *Atatürk'ün Söylev ve Demecleri* (Istanbul: 1945–1952).
9. Ziya Gökalp, *Turkish Nationalism and Western Civilization*, translated by Niyazi Berkes (Westport, CT: Greenwood Press, 1981), 289.
10. Taha Parla and Andrew Davison, *Corporatist Ideology in Kemalist Turkey* (Syracuse, NY: Syracuse University Press, 2004), 37.
11. Yücel Bozdağlıoğlu, *Turkish Foreign Policy and Turkish Identity: A Constructivist Approach* (New York: Routledge, 2003), 46.
12. Yael Navaro-Yashin, *Faces of the State: Secularism and Public Life in Turkey* (Princeton, NJ: Princeton University Press, 2002), 6.
13. Binnaz Toprak, "Islam and the Secular State in Turkey," in *Turkey: Political, Social and Economic Challenges in the 1990s*, Cigdem Balim, Ersin

Kalaycıoğlu, Cevat Karataş, Gareth Winrow, and Feroz Yasamee eds. (Leiden: E.J. Brill, 1995), 91.

14. Ahmet Kuru, "Reinterpretation of Secularism in Turkey: The Case of Justice and Development Party," in *The Emergence of New Turkey: Democracy and the AK Parti*, M. Hakan Yavuz ed. (Salt Lake City: The University of Utah Press, 2006), 137–38.
15. Niyazi Berkes, *The Development of Secularism in Turkey* (Montreal: McGill Press, 1964), 463–664.
16. Osman Okyar, "Atatürk's quest for Modernism," in *Atatürk and the Modernization of Turkey*, Jacob Landau ed. (Boulder, CO: Westview Press, 1984), 53.
17. Max Weber, *Economy and Society: An Outline of Interpretive Sociology*, volume I, Guenther Roth and Claus Wittich eds. (New York: Bedminster Press, 1968), 215.
18. Valentine M. Moghadam, "Gender and Revolutions," in *Theorizing Revolutions*, John Foran ed. (London: Routledge, 1997), 154.
19. Joanna De Groot, "Gender, Discourse and Ideology," in *Gendering the Middle East*, Deniz Kandiyoti ed. (Syracuse, NY: Syracuse University Press, 1996), 42.
20. Yeşim Arat, *The Patriarchal Paradox: Women Politicians in Turkey* (Cranbury, NJ: Associated University Presses, 1989), 28.
21. Nermin Abadan-Unat, "Social Change and Turkish Women," in *Women in Turkish Society*, Nermin Abadan-Unat ed. (Leiden: E.J. Brill, 1981), 12–13.
22. Ayşegül Baykan, "Women Between Fundamentalism and Modernity," in *Theories of Modernity and Postmodernity*, Bryan S. Turner ed. (London: Sage, 1990), 143.
23. Bozdağlıoğlu, *Turkish Foreign Policy and Turkish Identity*, 50.
24. Ibid.
25. Mahmut Göloğlu, *Devrimler ve Tepkileri 1924–1930* (Ankara: Basnur Matbaası, 1972), 138.
26. Fahri N. Taş, *Atatürk Ilkeleri ve Inkilaplari Tarihi II* (Istanbul: Sahhaflar Kitap Sarayı, 1995), 202.
27. Halide Edip Adıvar, "Dictatorship and Reforms in Turkey," *The Yale Review*, vol. 19 (September 1929): 27–44.
28. Andrew Mango, *Atatürk: The Biography of the Founder of Modern Turkey* (New York: Overlook Press, 1999), 433.
29. Cihan Aktaş, *Tanzimattan Günümüze Kılık Kyafet ve İktidar* (Istanbul: Nehir Yayınları, 1991), 150.
30. Ziya E. Karal, *Atatürk'ten Düşünceler* (Istanbul: Milli Eğitim Bakanlığı, 1981), 70.
31. Rıfat N. Bali, "Atatürk'ün Dine Bakışı," *Toplumsal Tarih Dergisi*, No: 153 (Eylül: 2006) (In this article Balı translated a report (no. 423, date: March 17, 1933) prepared by Charles H. Sherrill, U.S. ambassador to Turkey in 1932–1933).
32. Şevket Süreyya Aydemir, *Tek Adam Mustafa Kemal* (Istanbul: Remzi Kitabevi, 1988), 260.

33. Bernard Caporal, *Kemalizm ve Kemalizm Sonrasında Türk Kadını* (Ankara: Iş Bankası Kültür Yayınları, 1982), 651.
34. Baykan, "Women Between Fundamentalism and Modernity," 143.
35. İpek Çalışlar, *Latife Hanım* (Istanbul: Doğan Kitap, 2006), 198.
36. Özer, Avrupa Yolunda Batılaşma yada Batılılaşma: Istanbul'da Sosyal Değişimler, 238.
37. Caparol, *Kemalizm ve Kemalizm Sonrasında Türk Kadını,* 651.
38. Özer, *Avrupa Yolunda Batılaşma yada Batılılaşma: Istanbul'da Sosyal Değişimler,* 256.
39. Ali Çarkoğlu and Binnaz Toprak, *Değişen Türkiye'de Din, Toplum ve Siyaset* (Istanbul: TESEV Yayınları, 2006), 24.
40. Nüket Kardam, *Turkey's Engagement with Global Women's Human Rights* (Hants: Ashgate, 2005), 46.
41. Çarkoğlu and Toprak, *Değişen Türkiye'de Din,* 62–64.
42. *Milliyet,* May 28, 2003.
43. Murat Aksoy, *Başörtüsü-Türban: Batılılaşma—Modernleşme, Laiklik ve Örtünme* (Istanbul: Kitap Yayınevi, 2005), 16.
44. Cihan Aktaş, *Türbanın Yeniden İcadı* (Istanbul: Kapı Yayınları, 2006), xv.
45. *Milliyet,* October 26, 2005.
46. *Yenişafak,* October 26, 2005.
47. Ayşe Kadıoğlu, "Civil Society, Islam and Democracy in Turkey: A Study of Three Islamic Non-Governmental Organizations," *The Muslim World,* vol. 95, (January 2005): 23–41.
48. Neşe Düzel, "Türbanlı Kızlar Ultramodern!" *Radikal,* December 29, 2003.
49. James C. Scott, *Weapons of the Weak: Everyday Forms of Peasant Resistance* (New Haven, CT: Yale University Press, 1985), 304.
50. Chandra Talpade Mohanty, "Under Western Eye: Feminist Scholarship and Colonial Discourses," in *Third World Women and the Politics of Feminism,* Chandra Talpade Mohanty, Ann Russo and Lourdes Torres eds. (Bloomington, IN: Indiana University Press, 1991), 74.
51. Hanna Fenichel Pitkin, *The Concept of Representation* (Berkeley, CA: University of Berkeley Press, 1967), 99.
52. Kardam, *Turkey's Engagement with Global Women's Human Rights,* 37.
53. Carol Delaney, "Untangling the Meanings of Hair in Turkish Society," *Anthropological Quarterly,* vol. 67, no. 4 (October 1994): 159–72.
54. Mervat F. Hatem, "Egyptian Discourses on Gender and Political Liberalization: Do Secularist and Islamist Views Really Differ?" *The Middle East Journal,* vol. 48, no. 4 (Autumn 1994): 661–76.
55. *Holy Qur'an,* (24:31).
56. Ibid., (33:59).
57. Lamia Ben Youssef Zayzafoon, *The Production of the Muslim Women: Negotiating Text, History, and Ideology* (Lanham, MD: Lexington Books, 2005), 127.
58. Meral Akkent and Gaby Franger, *Başörtüsü* (Frankfurt: Dağyeli Yayınları, 1987), 105.

59. Aksoy, *Başörtüsü-Türban,* 41.
60. Aktaş, *Tanzimattan Günümüze Kılık Kıyafet ve İktidar 1,* 118.
61. Ekrem Işın, "Tanzimat, Kadın ve Gündelik Hayat," *Tarih ve Toplum* (Mart 1988): 22–24.
62. Aksoy, *Başörtüsü-Türban,* 62–78.
63. Halide Edip Adıvar, *Yeni Turan* (Istanbul: Atlas Kitabevi, 1982), 78.
64. Mahmut Göloğlu, *Türkiye Cumhuriyeti 1923* (Ankara: Başnur Matbaası, 1971), 85.
65. *Atatürk'ün Söylev ve Demeçleri II* (Ankara: Türk Inkilap Tarihi Enstitüsü, 1989), 155.
66. Akkent and Franger, *Başörtüsü,* 192–93.
67. Göloğlu, *Türkiye Cumhuriyeti 1923,* 84–85.
68. Göloğlu, *Devrimler ve Tepkileri 1924–1930,* 140.
69. Aksoy, *Başörtüsü-Türban,* 116.
70. Aktaş, *Tanzimattan Günümüze Kılık Kıyafet ve İktidar 1,* 168.
71. Caparol, *Kemalizm ve Kemalizm Sonrasında Türk Kadını,* 648.
72. Aktaş, *Tanzimattan Günümüze Kılık Kıyafet ve İktidar 1,* 194.
73. Jenny White, *Islamist Mobilization in Turkey: A Study in Vernacular Politics* (Seattle: University of Washington Press, 2002), 104.
74. Mehmet Yaşar Geyikdağı, *Political Parties in Turkey: The Role of Islam* (New York: Praeger, 1984), 88.
75. Ben Lombardi, "Turkey—The Return of the Reluctant Generals?" *Political Science Quarterly,* vol. 112, no. 2 (1997): 191–215.
76. Aktaş, *Tanzimattan Günümüze Kılık Kıyafet ve İktidar 1,* 172.
77. Cihan Aktaş, *Bacı'dan Bayan'a: Islamcı Kadınların Kamusal Alan Tecrübesi* (Istanbul: Kapı Yayınları, 2005), 50–51.
78. Aktaş, *Bacı'dan Bayan'a: Islamcı Kadınların Kamusal Alan Tecrübesi,* 207.
79. Aktaş, *Türbanın Yeniden İcadı,* 2.
80. Ibid.
81. Ibid., 246.
82. Susan Starr Sered, " 'Woman' as Symbols and Women as Agents: Gendered Religious Discourse and Practices," in *Revisioning Gender,* Myra Marx Ferree, Judith Lorber, and Beth B. Hess eds. (Walnut Creek, CA: Alta Mira Press, 2000), 206.
83. Iris Marion Young, "The Logic of Masculinist Protection: Reflections on the Current Security State," in *Women and Citizenship,* Marilyn Friedman ed. (Oxford: Oxford University Press, 2005), 21.
84. Aktaş, *Bacı'dan Bayan'a: Islamcı Kadınların Kamusal Alan Tecrübesi,* 205.
85. DPT Genelgesi # B.02.1.DPT. 070.73 (May 20, 2000).
86. Jeanne Morgan, "More on Cosmetics," in *Cosmetics, Fashions and the Exploitation of Women,* Joseph Hansen and Evelyn Reed eds. (New York: Pathfinder Press, 1986), 53.
87. Maxine Molyneux, "Mobilization Without Emancipation? Women's Interests, State, and Revolution," in *Transition and Development: Problems of Third World Socialism,* Richard R. Fagen, Carmen Diana

Deere, and Jose Luis Coraggio eds. (New York: Monthly Review Press, 1986), 285.

88. Aktaş, *Tanzimattan Günümüze Kılık Kıyafet ve İktidar 1,* 181.
89. Hakan Yavuz, "Cleansing Islam from the Public Sphere," *Journal of International Affairs*, 54 (2000): 20–42.
90. Zehra Arat, "Politics of Representation and Identity," in *Deconstructing Images of The Turkish Woman,* Zehra Arat ed. (New York: Saint Martin Press, 1998), 10.
91. Kardam, *Turkey's Engagement with Global Women's Human Rights,* 40.
92. Fatmagül Berktay, *Tarihin Cinsiyeti* (Istanbul: Metis Yayınları, 2003), 106.
93. Arat, "Politics of Representation and Identity," 16.
94. Ayşe Durakbaşa, "Kemalism as Identity Politics In Turkey," in *Deconstructing Images of The Turkish Woman,* Zehra Arat ed. (New York: St. Martin's Press, 1998), 140.
95. Hatem, "Egyptian Discourses on Gender and Political Liberalization: Do Secularist and Islamist Views Really Differ?" 661–76.
96. Arat, "Politics of Representation and Identity," 23.
97. Deniz Kandiyoti, "The End of Empire: Islam, Nationalism, and Women in Turkey," in *Women, Islam, and the State.* Deniz Kandiyoti ed. (Philadelphia: Temple University Press, 1991), 42.
98. Kumari Jayawedana, *Feminism and Nationalism in the Third World* (London: Zed Books, 1986), 36.
99. Arat, "Politics of Representation and Identity," 23, 24.
100. Said, *Orientalism*, 239.

3 Politics of Religion (1938–2000s)

1. Ayşe Saktanber, *Living Islam: Women, Religion and the Politicization of Culture in Turkey* (London: I.B. Tauris, 2002), 18.
2. Abdurrahman Dilipak, *İnönü Dönemi,* 2. Baskı (Istanbul: Beyan Yayınları, 1989), 47.
3. Ali Fuat Başgil, *27 Mayis Ihtilali ve Sebepleri* (Istanbul: Yağmur Yayınları, 1966), 49.
4. Geyikdağı, *Political Parties in Turkey,* 65.
5. Aktaş, *Tanzimattan Günümüze Kılık, Kıyafet ve İktidar 1,* 195.
6. Metin Heper, *İsmet İnönü: The Making of a Turkish Statesman* (Leiden: E.J. Brill, 1998), 100.
7. Hugh Poulton, *Top Hat, Grey Wolf and Crescent: Turkish Nationalism and the Turkish Republic* (New York: New York University Press, 1997), 117.
8. Faik Ökte, *The Tragedy of Turkish Capital Tax* (London: Croom Helm, 1964), xi.
9. Geyikdağı, *Political Parties in Turkey,* 66–67.
10. Baykan, "Women Between Fundamentalism and Modernity," 142.

11. Geyikdağı, *Political Parties in Turkey,* 66–67.
12. Ibid., 68.
13. Feroz Ahmad, *The Turkish Experiment in Democracy: 1950–1975* (London: C. Hurst, 1977), 364–65.
14. Geyikdağı, *Political Parties in Turkey,* 74.
15. Ibid., 69.
16. Geyikdağı, *Political Parties in Turkey,* 75.
17. Ibid., 77.
18. Aksoy, *Başörtüsü-Türban,* 135.
19. Aktaş, *Tanzimattan Günümüze Kılık Kıyafet ve İktidar,* 219.
20. William Hale, *Turkish Politics and the Military* (London: Routledge, 1994), 106.
21. Geyikdağı, *Political Parties in Turkey,* 88–89.
22. Aktaş, *Tanzimattan Günümüze Kılık Kıyafet ve İktidar 1,* 228.
23. Geyikdağı, *Political Parties in Turkey,* 101.
24. Feroz Ahmad, "Politics and Islam in Modern Turkey," *Middle Eastern Studies* vol. 27, no. 1 (January 1991): 3–21.
25. Necmeddin Erbakan, "Mukaddesatçı Türk'e Beyanname," in *Salname 1390* (Istanbul: 1970), 196.
26. Geyikdağı, *Political Parties in Turkey,* 122.
27. Araştırma ve Kültür Vakfı, *Albüm: Şule Yüksel Şenler* (Istanbul: AKVAKFI), 10.
28. Demet Tezcan, *Bir Çığır Öyküsü: Şule Yüksel Şenler* (Istanbul: Timaş Yayınları, 2007), 13.
29. Aktaş, *Tanzimattan Günümüze Kılık, Kıyafet ve İktidar 1,* 256.
30. Istanbul *İmam Hatip* Okulu Yıllık Komitesi, *Istanbul İmam Hatip Okulu Yıllığı: 1971–1972* (Istanbul: 1972), 22.
31. *Yargıtay Cumhuriyet Başsavcılığınca Fazilet Partisi'nin Kapatılması İstemiyle Açılan Davanın İddianamesi,* No. SP.95 Hz.1999/116 (Ankara: TC. Yargıtay Cumhuriyet Başsavcılığı, May 7, 1999).
32. Aktaş, *Tanzimattan Günümüze Kılık, Kıyafet ve İktidar 1,* 241.
33. Ibid., 242.
34. Aksoy, *Başörtüsü-Türban,* 158.
35. Aktaş, *Tanzimattan Günümüze Kılık, Kıyafet ve İktidar 1,* 238.
36. Ibid., 247.
37. Aksoy, *Başörtüsü-Türban,* 144.
38. Aktaş, *Tanzimattan Günümüze Kılık, Kıyafet ve İktidar 1,* 234.
39. Aktaş, *Türbanin Yeniden Icadi,* 14.
40. Aksoy, *Başörtüsü-Türban,* 151.
41. Aktaş, *Tanzimattan Günümüze Kılık, Kıyafet ve İktidar 1,* 245–46.
42. Aksoy, *Başörtüsü-Türban,* 152.
43. Ibid., 153.
44. Aktaş, *Tanzimattan Günümüze Kılık, Kıyafet ve İktidar 1,* 253.
45. Geyikdağı, *Political Parties in Turkey,* 106.

46. Şerif Mardin, "Religion in Modern Turkey," *International Social Science Journal* vol. 29, no. 2 (1977): 279–97.
47. Geyikdağı, *Political Parties in Turkey,* 107.
48. Ibid., 108–09.
49. Ibid., 133.
50. Ersin Kalaycıoğlu, "The Turkish Grand National Assembly: A Brief Inquiry into the Politics of Representation in Turkey," in *Turkey: Political, Social and Economic Challenges in the 1990s*, Çiğdem Balım, Ersin Kalaycıoğlu, Cevat Karataş, Gareth Winrow, and Feroz Yasamee eds. (Leiden: E.J. Brill, 1995), 43.
51. Aksoy, *Başörtüsü-Türban,* 158.
52. "Sağdan bir tane, soldan bir tane asalım dedik!" *Vatan,* September 13, 2005. Also see: Television special "12 Eylül Türkiye'nin Miladı" Special aired on September 12, 2005 on TV8.
53. Arda Uskan, "Asmayalım da besleyelim mi," *Takvim*, January 25, 2010.
54. Hakan Yavuz, *Islamic Political Identity in Turkey* (New York: Oxford University Press, 2003), 70.
55. Ibid.
56. Geyikdağı, *Political Parties in Turkey,* 141.
57. Nilüfer Göle, *The Forbidden Mahrem: Civilization and Veiling* (Ann Arbor: University of Michigan Press, 1996), 84–85.
58. Aksoy, *Başörtüsü-Türban,* 155.
59. Yavuz, *Islamic Political Identity in Turkey*, 74.
60. M. Bülent Çaparoğlu, *Meclis'te Başörtüsü Mücadelesi* (Istanbul: Şule Yayınları, 1998), 47.
61. Aksoy, *Başörtüsü-Türban,* 163.
62. *Resmi Gazete*, no.17537, December 7, 1981 (*Milli Eğitim Bakanlığı Ile Diğer Bakanlıklara Bağlı Okullardaki Görevliler İle Ögrencilerin Kılık ve Kıyafetlerine Dair Yönetmelik*).
63. *Resmi Gazete*, no. 17849, October 25, 1982 (*Devlet Memurları Kanunu*, no. 657, Kamu Kurum ve Kuruluşlarda Çalışan Personelin Kılık ve Kıyafetine Dair Yönetmelik no. 8/5105, Madde 5).
64. Nilüfer Göle, "Toward and Autonomization of Politics and Civil Society in Turkey," in *Politics in the Third Turkish Republic*, Metin Heper and Ahmet Evin eds. (Boulder, CO: Westview Press, 1994), 84–85.
65. *Sabah*, June 4, 2007.
66. Çaparoğlu, *Meclis'te Başörtüsü Mucadelesi,* 36.
67. Göle, "Toward and Autonomization of Politics and Civil Society in Turkey," 221–22.
68. Ümit Cizre, "From Ruler to Pariah: The Life and Times of the True Path Party," *Turkish Studies,* Special Edition, Metin Heper and Barry Rubin eds. vol 3, no. 1 (Spring 2002): 82–101.
69. Huri Tursan, *Democratization in Turkey: The Role of Political Parties* (Brussels: P.I.E-Peter Lang, 2004), 228.
70. *YÖK Decision*, no. 84.35.527, May 10, 1984.

71. Aksoy, *Başörtüsü-Türban,* 168.
72. *Danıştay. 8. Daire kararı*, Esas no: 1983/207 Karar 1984 no:330 (See also no. 1984/1574, 12/13/1984, Esas no: 1987/178 Karar no: 1988/512 and Esas no: 1987/128 Karar no: 1987/486).
73. Çaparoğlu, *Meclis'te Başörtüsü Mücadelesi,* 45.
74. *Resmi Gazette*, January 8, 1987.
75. Çaparoğlu, *Meclis'te Başörtüsü Mücadelesi,* 52.
76. *Yenişafak*, February 10, 2006.
77. Ibid.
78. *Resmi Gazete*, December 4, 1988.
79. *Resmi Gazete*, December 27, 1988.
80. Çaparoğlu, *Meclis'te Başörtüsü Mücadelesi,* 71–78.
81. *Resmi Gazete*, no. 20216, July 5, 1989.
82. *Milli Gazete*, October 13, 1989.
83. *Milliyet*, October 27, 1990.
84. *Resmi Gazete*, no. 20679, October 28, 1990.
85. Constitutional Court Decree, Esas no: 1990/36, Karar no: 1991/8, 4/9/1991.
86. Council of State Decree, Esas no: 609 Karar no: 2809, November 13, 1992.
87. http://www.anayasa.gov.tr/general/icerikler.asp?contID=363&curID=98&menuID=58 retrieved on April 21, 2007.
88. Merve Kavakcı, "Put This Woman in Her Place!," *QNEWS*, 353 (January 2004): 30–32.
89. Zeki Ünal, *Anarşi: Kainat Nizamı Anarşiyi Reddeder* (Ankara, 1992), 177.
90. Hasan Karakaya, "MHP güme gitmiş, Bay Osman Durmuş!" *Vakit,* February 4, 2010.
91. İlhami Bekir, "İlk Adam," *Hava Kuvvetleri Dergisi*, no. 301 (November 1988): 55.
92. Ünal, *Anarşi,* 179.
93. http://www.anayasa.gen.tr/1961ay.htm retrieved on April 21, 2007.
94. Faruk Bildirici, *Maskeli Leydi: Tekmili Birden Tansu Çiller* (Ankara: Ümit Yayıncılık, 1998), 203.
95. Ibid., 144–45.
96. Cizre, "From Ruler to Pariah: The Life and Times of the True Path Party," 82–101.
97. White, *Islamist Mobilization in Turkey*, 119.
98. Cizre, "From Ruler to Pariah: The Life and Times of the True Path Party," 82–101. Also see: Ümit Cizre, "Lusting for Power and Undermining Democracy," in *Political Leaders and Democracy in Turkey*, Metin Heper and Sabri Sayari eds. (Lanham: Lexington Books, 2002), 203.
99. Cizre, "Lusting for Power and Undermining Democracy," 206.
100. Ibid.
101. Ibid.
102. Yavuz, *Islamic Political Identity in Turkey*, 214.

103. Aydin Gönel, *Araştırma Raporu: Önde gelen STK'lar* (Istanbul: Tarih Vakfı Yurt Yayınları, 1998), 21.
104. Fuat E. Keyman and Ahmet İçduygu, "Globalization, Civil Society and Citizenship in Turkey: Actors, Boundaries and Discourses," *Citizenship Studies*, vol. 7, no. 2 (2003): 219–34.
105. Keyman and İçduygu, "Globalization, Civil Society and Citizenship in Turkey."
106. Kadıoğlu, "Civil Society, Islam and Democracy in Turkey," 23–41.
107. Rubin, "Introduction-Turkey's Political Parties," 1.
108. White, *Islamist Mobilization in Turkey*, 205.
109. Ibid.
110. Jenny White, "The Islamist Paradox," in *Fragments of Culture: The Everyday of Modern Turkey*, Deniz Kandiyoti and Ayşe Saktenber eds. (Piscataway, NJ: Rutgers University Press, 2002), 210.
111. Yavuz, *Islamic Political Identity in Turkey*, 241.
112. White, *Islamist Mobilization in Turkey*, 122.
113. Ibid., 224.
114. T.C. Cumhuriyet Başsavcılığı, "Refah Partisinin Kapatılması İstemiyle Yargıtay Cumhuriyet Başsavcılığı'nca Anayasa Mahkemesi'ne Açılan Davanın Iddianamesi," May 21, 1997.
115. T.C. Cumhuriyet Başsavcılığı, "Refah Partisinin Kapatılması İstemiyle Yargıtay Cumhuriyet Başsavcılığı'nca Anayasa Mahkemesi'ne Açılan Davanın Iddianamesine RP'nin Cevabı," Esas no: 1997/1, October 6, 1997.
116. Özlem Albayrak, "28 Subat'tan gelecek hayır," *Yenişafak,* February 27, 2007.
117. Ümit Cizre and Menderes Çınar, "Turkey 2002: Kemalism, Islamism, and Politics in the Light of the February 28 Process," *The South Atlantic Quarterly* 102:2/3 (Spring/Summer 2003): 309–32.
118. Ronald Inglehart and Christian Welzel, *Modernization, Cultural Change, and Democracy: The Human Development Sequence* (Cambridge: Cambridge University Press, 2005), 218.
119. Nazlı Ilıcak, "Beyaz Turkler," *Takvim*, March 1, 2007.
120. Esra Özyürek, "Public Memory as Political Battleground: Islamist Subversions of Republican Nostalgia," in *The Politics of Public Memory in Turkey,* Esra Özyürek ed. (Syracuse, NY: Syracuse University Press, 2007), 120.
121. Esra Özyürek, *Nostalgia for the Modern: State Secularism and Everyday Politics in Turkey* (Durham, NC: Duke University Press, 2006), 99.
122. *Tempo Dergisi*, August 17, 2006.
123. Nazlı Ilıcak, "Dün de fişleniyordu, bugün de," *Bugün*, December 1, 2005.
124. Burton Bollag, "A Ban on Islamic Head Scarves Unsettles Turkey's Universities," *The Chronicle of Higher Education,* vol. 44, no. 33 (April 24, 1998): 59–60.
125. *Akit,* January 5, 2000.

126. *Vatan*, November 20, 2006.
127. Yavuz, *Islamic Political Identity in Turkey*, 244.
128. *Zaman*, March 23, 2007.
129. White, *Islamist Mobilization in Turkey*, 206.
130. Letter dated July 14, 1998 (no. 010306) sent from T.C. Genelkurmay Başkanlığı to Yüksek Ögretim Kurumu Başkanlığı, signed by Çevik Bir. Also see: *Bugün*, December 3, 2009 and *Star*, January 14, 2009.
131. *Yenişafak*, July 21, 2006. Also see *Zaman*, August 24, 2006, *Vakit*, July 20, 2006.
132. *Resmi Gazete*, "Diyanet Işleri Başkanlığı Kur-an Kursları ile Öğrenci Yurt ve Pansiyonlari Yönetmeliği," no. 23982, March 3, 2000. Also see: Serdar Arseven, "12 yaş' meselesi!" *Vakit*, March 30, 2007.
133. *Sabah*, December 8, 2005.
134. *Wall Street Journal*, June 13, 1997.
135. A. Turan Alkan, "Arabistan'a gidin Arabistan'a," *Zaman*, November 15, 2006.
136. Amikam Nachmani, *Turkey: Facing a New Millenium: Coping with Intertwined Conflicts* (Manchester: Manchester University Press, 2003), 116.
137. R. Quinn Mecham, "From the Ashes of Virtue, A Promise of Light: The Transformation of Political Islam in Turkey," *Third World Quarterly*, vol. 25, no. 2 (2004): 339–58.
138. Ümit Cizre and Menderes Çınar, "Turkey 2002: Kemalism, Islamism, and Politics in the Light of the February 28 Process," 309–32.
139. Ibid.
140. Yavuz, *Islamic Political Identity in Turkey*, 251.
141. Robert Olson, *Turkey-Iran Relations, 1979–2004: Revolution, Ideology, War, Coups and Geopolitics* (Costa Mesa, CA: Mazda, 2004), 48.
142. Fatma Müge Göçek, "To Veil or Not to Veil," *Interventions*, vol. 1, no. 4 (1999): 521–35.
143. Murat Çemrek, "How Could the Rights to Education and Representation Challenge National Security? The Headscarf Conflict in Turkey Revisited," *Human Security Perspectives*, vol. 1, no. 2 (2004): 52–58.
144. Yavuz, *Islamic Political Identity in Turkey*, 249.
145. Frank Tachau, "From Idealist to Pragmatist," in *Political Leaders and Democracy in Turkey*, Metin Heper and Sabri Sayari eds. (Lanham, MD: Lexington Books, 2002), 118.
146. Gülşen Demirkol Özer, *Psikolojik Bir Işkence Metodu Olarak Ikna Odaları* (Istanbul: Beyan Yayınları, 2005), 25.
147. Yavuz, *Islamic Political Identity in Turkey*, 249.
148. This picture is used with the permission of *Anadolu Ajansı*.
149. Gül Aldıkaçtı Marshall, "Ideology, Progress, and Dialogue: A Comparison of Feminist and Islamist Women's Approaches to the Issues of Head Covering and Work in Turkey," *Gender and Society*, vol. 19 (February 2005): 104–20.

150. T.C. Cumhuriyet Başsavcılığı, "Fazilet Partisinin Kapatılması İstemiyle Yargıtay Cumhuriyet Başsavcılığı'nca Anayasa Mahkemesi'ne Açılan Davanın İddianamesi," July 5, 1999.
151. European Court of Human Rights Decree on *Kavakcı v. Turkey*: Application no. 71907/01.
152. Tachau, "From Idealist to Pragmatist," 121.
153. *Devlet Planlama Teşkilati Genelgesi*, # B.02.1.DPT.070.73.
154. Şakir Süter, "Demirel konuşunca," *Akşam Gazetesi*, May 2, 2006.
155. Gareth Jenkins, *Political Islam in Turkey: Running West, Heading East?* (New York: Palgrave, 2008), 170.
156. *The Economist*, November 18, 2000.
157. Hasan Kösebalaban, "Party with Islamist Roots Set to Modernize Turkey," *Yale Global*, August 28, 2007.
158. White, *Islamist Mobilization in Turkey*, 273.
159. William Hale and Ergun Özbudun, *Islamism, Democracy and Liberalism in Turkey: The Case of the AKP* (Abingdon: Routledge, 2010), 5.
160. Jenkins, *Political Islam in Turkey,* 181. Also see: Serdar Turgut, "Türban meselesi konusunda ilk kez açıklıkla konuştu," *Akşam,* December 7, 2005.
161. Ibid., 167.
162. Hale and Özbudun, *Islamism, Democracy and Liberalism in Turkey,* 184.
163. Jenkins, *Political Islam in Turkey,* 173.
164. *Danıştay 2. Dairesi, no. 3366/2005 K, 2004/4051 E*, October 26, 2005.
165. Nazlı Ilıcak, "Başörtüsü," *Yenişafak,* November 26, 2002.
166. ECHR, Application No: 42393/98, ECHR 2001-V.
167. ECHR, Application No: 44774, Judgment: Strasbourg, November 10, 2005.
168. Fatma Benli, *Legal Evaluation of the Ban Imposed on the University Students Who Wear Headscarf Subsequent to the ECHR's Ruling in Leyla Sahin v. Turkey* (Istanbul: AKDER, 2005), 1–2.
169. http://cmiskp.echr.coe.int/tkp197/view.asp?item=2&portal=hbkm&action=html&highlight=sahin%20%7C%20turkey%20%7C%2044774/98&sessionid=9971709&skin=hudoc-pr-en retrieved on May 1, 2007.
170. Ibid.
171. Hikmet Kırık, *Kamusal Alan ve Demokrasi: Örtünme Sorununu Yeniden Düşünmek* (İstanbul: Salyangoz Yayınları, 2005), 126.
172. Baykan, "Women Between Fundamentalism and Modernity," 136.
173. Neşe Düzel, "Türbanlı Kizlar Ultramodern!" *Radikal,* December 29, 2003.
174. Kırık, 125.
175. Ibid.
176. Etyen Mahçupyan, "Osmanlı'dan Günümüze Parçalı Kamusal Alan ve Siyaset," *Doğu Batı,* 5 (Nov–Jan 1998–1999): 22–48.
177. *Milliyet,* October 22, 2003.
178. *Milliyet,* November 24, 2002. Also see: Ali Bayramoğlu, "Başörtüsü sorunu dedikleri. . .," *Yenişafak,* November 23, 2002.

179. *Milliyet,* October 22, 2003.
180. Mustafa Karaalioğlu, "Sezer'in affedilmez unutkanlığı!" *Yenişafak,* October 29, 2003.
181. *Yenişafak,* June 29, 2004.
182. *Yenişafak,* January 7, 2006.
183. *Yenişafak,* April 23, 2003.
184. Volkan Aytar, "Monthly Monitoring Report," *TESEV* (February 2006): 4–5.
185. Aksoy, *Başörtüsü-Türban,* 202.
186. E. Fuat Keyman, "Türban-demokrasi ilişkisi," *Radikal2,* November 16, 2003.
187. *Yenişafak,* November 7, 2003.
188. Yeşim Arat, *Political Islam in Turkey and Women's Organizations* (Istanbul: The Turkish Economic and Social Studies Foundation, 1999), 36–39.
189. Neşe Düzel, "Türban ikinci sınıflığın kabulüdür," *Radikal,* November 17, 2003.
190. Çemrek, "How Could the Rights to Education and Representation Challenge National Security? The Headscarf Conflict in Turkey Revisited," 52–58.
191. Constitutional Court's Decree on the Closure of Fazilet Party, date: June 22, 2001.
192. Ali Ihsan Yıldız, "Postmodern Türban," *Radikal2,* July 2, 2006.
193. David L. Rousseau, *Identifying Threats and Threatening Identities: The Social Construction of Realism and Liberalism* (Palo Alto, CA: Stanford University Press, 2006), 4.
194. Murat Yetkin, "Siyasette türban açmazı," *Radikal,* June 22, 2005.
195. Cüneyt Ülsever, "Türban meselesiyle ilgili somut bir öneri," *Hürriyet,* June 22, 2005.
196. Flax, "Race/Gender and the Ethics of Difference: A Reply to Okin's 'Gender Inequality and Cultural Differences,'" 500–10.
197. Ibid.
198. This picture is used with the permission of *Anadolu Ajansı.*
199. This picture is used with the permission of *Vakit.*
200. AKDER, *"baş" üstüne: Fotoğraflarla Başörtüsü Yasağının Yakın Tarihi, "with" pleasure: Near History of the Scarf Ban by Photographs* (Istanbul: Kırkambar Yayınları, 1999), 100.
201. Göle, "Toward and Autonomization of Politics and Civil Society in Turkey," 84.
202. Esra Erol, *Sen Başımın Tacı: Bir Başörtüsü Günlüğü* (Istanbul: Birun Kültür Sanat Yayıncılık, 2001), 93.
203. Deniz Kandiyoti, "Bargaining with Patriarchy," in *The Social Construction of Gender,* Judith Lorber and Susan A. Farrell eds. (Newbury Park, CA: Sage, 1991), 104–18.
204. Sibel Eraslan, "Uğultular...Siluetler," in *90larda Türkiye'de Feminism,* Aksu Bora and Asena Günal eds (Istanbul: Iletişim Yayınları, 2002), 242.

205. Michel Foucault, *The History of Sexuality: An Introduction Volume 1* (New York: Random House, 1978), 95–96.
206. Lila Abu-Lughod, "The Romance of Resistance: Tracing Transformation of Power Through Bedouin Women," *American Ethnologist*, vol. 17, no. 1 (February 1990): 41–55.
207. Özer, *Psikolojik Bir Işkence Metodu Olarak Ikna Odaları*, 258.
208. Saba Mahmood, *Politics of Piety: The Islamic Revival and the Feminist Subject* (Princeton, NJ: Princeton University Press, 2005), 9.
209. This picture is used with the permission of *Anadolu Ajansı*.
210. This picture is used with the permission of *Sabah*, June 19, 2003.
211. *Akşam*, June 16, 2006.
212. Mehmet Kara, "Başörtüsü ve 'irtica,'" *Yeni Asya*, September 10, 2006.

4 Social and Political Implications of the Ban on Headscarf

1. Merve Kavakcı, *Başörtüsüz Demokrasi* (Istanbul: Timaş Yayınları, 2004), 267.
2. Ibid.
3. http://www.mazlumder.org/ana.php?konu=duyuru&id=25&lang=tr retrieved on March 21, 2007.
4. http://www.die.gov.tr/tkba/t098.xls retrieved on March 21, 2007.
5. http://nkg.die.gov.tr/1990.asp?gosterge=16&Submit=G%F6r%FCnt%FCle retrieved on May 29, 2007.
6. Nüfus Etütleri Enstitüsü, *Turkiye Nüfus ve Sağlik Arastırması 2003* (Ankara: Hacettepe Üniversitesi Nüfus Etütleri Enstitüsü, 2004), 34.
7. *Yenişafak*, December 25, 2005.
8. Nüfus Etütleri Enstitüsü, *Turkiye Nüfus ve Sağlik Arastırması 2003*, xv.
9. The picture is extracted from *Ihlas Haber Ajansı* news broadcasting.
10. Nevzat Tarhan, *Psikolojik Savas: Gri Propaganda* (Istanbul: Timaş Yayınları, 2006), 239.
11. Sakine Akça, *Elveda Ankara* (Istanbul: Beyan Yayınları, 2005), 193.
12. Serdar Arseven, "Bazı kızlar okula!" *Vakit*, March 8, 2007.
13. Fatma Benli, *Başörtüsü ile Ilgili Hukuka Aykırılıkta Sınır Yok* (Istanbul: AKDER Yayınları, 2004), 199.
14. Ibid., 11.
15. TBMM Insan Haklarını Inceleme Komisyonu, *Cerrahpaşa Tıp Fakültesinde Dr. Şükran Erdem'le Ilgili Iddiaların Incelenmesine Dair Alt Komisyon Raporu,* 1/Nisan/1997, http://www.tbmm.gov.tr/komisyon/insanhaklari/belge/kr_20sukranerdem.pdf, retrieved on February 16, 2010. Also see: *Akit*, December 1, 1996.
16. *Zaman*, December 5, 2005.
17. *Akit*, September 5, 2000.
18. *Zaman*, October 4, 2002.

19. ÖNDER, *İmam-Hatip Liseleri'nde Insan Hakları Ihlalleri* (Istanbul: ÖNDER, 2002), 43.
20. This picture is used with the permission of *Anadolu Ajansı*.
21. *Vakit*, October 5, 2002.
22. *Vakit*, October 25, 2002.
23. *Vakit*, October 10, 2002.
24. *Yenişafak*, January 11, 2001.
25. Gülay Göktürk, "SMS'LERE SIĞMAZ," *Tercüman*, November 28, 2004.
26. *Akit*, January 5, 2000.
27. Özer, *Psikolojik Bir Işkence Methodu Olarak Ikna Odaları*, 237.
28. Ibid., 218.
29. *Sabah*, June 4, 2007.
30. Özer, *Psikolojik Bir Işkence Methodu Olarak Ikna Odaları*, 218.
31. Akça, 176. See also: Gülşen Demirkol Özer's *Psikolojik Bir Işkence Methodu Olarak Ikna Odaları* and ÖNDER's *İmam-Hatip Liseleri'nde Insan Hakları Ihlalleri* for student testimonies.
32. Erol, *Sen Başımın Tacı*, 84.
33. Özer, *Psikolojik Bir Işkence Methodu Olarak Ikna Odaları*, 210–28.
34. Ibid., 271.
35. Atilla Yayla, "Ahlak, Hukuk ve Başörtüsü Yasagı," *Liberal Düşünce Topluluğu*, December 14, 2004 (retrieved from http://www.liberal-dt.org.tr/index.php?lang=tr&message=article&art=162 on March 24, 2007).
36. Özer, *Psikolojik Bir Işkence Methodu Olarak Ikna Odaları*, 52.
37. *Sabah*, October 18, 2004.
38. Özer, *Psikolojik Bir Işkence Methodu Olarak Ikna Odaları*, 271.
39. Ibid., 104–06.
40. Ibid., 108.
41. *Zaman*, May 27, 2005.
42. *Sabah*, June 19, 2003.
43. *Sabah*, June 14, 2005. Also see: *Yenişafak*, June 14, 2005.
44. *Milliyet*, June 14, 2005.
45. Can Dündar, "Karşi manifesto," *Milliyet*, June 27, 2006.
46. *Vakit*, March 23, 2006.
47. *Yenişafak*, September 18, 2006.
48. *Yenişafak*, December 3, 2005.
49. *Yenişafak*, January 27, 2006.
50. Nazlı Ilicak, "Sokaktaki Tehlike: Başörtüsü," *Bugün*, February 11, 2006.
51. Benli, *Başörtüsü ile Ilgili Hukuka Aykırılıkta Sınır Yok* , 107.
52. *Milli Gazete*, August 28, 2005. Also see: *Vakit*, August 28, 2005.
53. Sibel Eraslan, "Hatice Akçil'in suçu," *Vakit*, March 8, 2005.
54. *Yenişafak*, October 22, 2006.
55. Ertuğrul Özkök, "Yumurtalıkları alınan türbanlı," *Hürriyet*, December 21, 2006.

56. *Aksiyon*, January 15, 2007. Also see: *Zaman*, July 13, 2005.
57. *Vakit*, March 27, 2006.
58. Benli, *Başörtüsü ile Ilgili Hukuka Aykırılıkta Sınır Yok*, 231.
59. *Dünden Bugüne Tercuman*, June 16, 2005.
60. *Yenişafak*, November 7, 2003.
61. *Zaman*, May 23, 2009.
62. *T.C. Denizli/Çivril Gürpınar Belediye Baskanligi*, Sayi: M.20.8.GUP.0.10.0. 0.0.0.1_/_218.
63. Sibel Eraslan, " Küçük dağlar, büyük dağlar," *Vakit*, June 7, 2005.
64. *Zaman*, June 6, 2005.
65. Kim Shively, "Religious Bodies and the Secular State: The Merve Kavakcı Affair," *Journal of Middle East Women's Studies*, vol. 1, no. 3 (Fall 2005): 47–72.
66. Mehmet Sılay, *Mecliste Merve Kavakcı Olayı* (Istanbul: Birey, 2000), 62.
67. Fadime Özkan, *Yemenimde Hare Var: Dünden Yarına Başörtüsü* (Istanbul: Elest Yayınları, 2005), 126.
68. Ibid.
69. *Hürriyet*, May 1, 1999.
70. Said, *Orientalism*, 150.
71. *Resmi Gazete*, no. 14506, April 13, 1973 (also available at http://www.tbmm.gov.tr/ictuzuk/ictuzuk.htm retrieved on May 2, 2007).
72. Ibid., 155.
73. Ibid., 102.
74. *Cumhuriyet*, May 3, 1999.
75. Said, *Orientalism*, 160.
76. Ibid., 104.
77. Ibid., 94.
78. Nilüfer Göle, "Islam in Public: New Visibilities and New Imaginaries," 173–90.
79. Shively, "Religious Bodies and the Secular State: The Merve Kavakcı Affair," 47–72.
80. Esra Doğru Arsan, "Medya-Güç Ideoloji Ekseninde Merve Kavakcı Haberlerinin Iki Farkli Sunumu," in *Haber Hakikat ve Iktidar Ilişkisi*, Çiler Dursun ed. (Ankara: Elips Kitap-Kesit Tanıtım, 2004), 152.
81. Said, *Orientalism*, 150.
82. Shively, "Religious Bodies and the Secular State: The Merve Kavakcı Affair," 47–72.
83. *Yenişafak*, May 8, 1999. Also see: *Zaman* April 25, 2004.
84. Özkan, *Yemenimde Hare Var*, 37.
85. *Hürriyet*, May 4, 1999.
86. Gülay Göktürk, "KADER siyaset üstü mü?" *Bugün*, April 4, 2007.
87. *Yenişafak*, January 19, 2006.
88. *Akşam*, January 19, 2006.
89. http://www.haber7.com/haber/20100205/Gulun-karinin-ortusunu-cikar-cevabi.php, retrieved on February 5, 2010.

90. Susan Moller Okin, "The Public/Private Dichotomy," in *Contemporary Political Theory*, Colin Farrelly ed. (London: Sage, 2004), 188.
91. *Radikal*, September 20, 2007.
92. This picture is used with the permission of Anadolu Ajansı.
93. *Milliyet*, July 7, 2006.
94. http://www.ahmettasgetiren.com.tr/gunluk.php retrieved on February 2, 2006.
95. Erhan Başyurt, "Tel örgüler neyi ayırıyor?" *Bugün*, November 9, 2008. Also see: *Milli Gazete*, November 9, 2008, *Zaman*, November 7, 2008, and *Vakit*, November 8, 2008.
96. *Today's Zaman*, February 3, 2010.
97. Tamer Korkmaz, "Şehit Anaları icin de Ikna Odaları Kurulmalı!," *Zaman*, November 3, 2006.
98. Nuh Gönültaş, "Guncelleyelim dostlar, irticayı surekli guncelleyerek ancak varolabiliriz," *Bugün*, November 28, 2006.
99. Serdar Arseven, "Vakit okuyucusu da işte budur!" *Vakit*, February 3, 2007.
100. *Zaman*, June 29, 2002.
101. Sibel Eraslan, "Başbakanım, bizim mayın tarlasına sıra ne zaman gelecek?" *Vakit*, June 5, 2009.
102. http://www.ak-der.org/tr/gundem/guncel-haberler/1207-basortusu-yasag.html retrieved on February 9, 2010.
103. Çarkoğlu and Toprak, *Değişen Türkiye'de Din*, 23.
104. Ibid.
105. Ibid.
106. Ülkü Özel Akagündüz, "Başörtülü Kızlar Yasak Yorgunu," *Aksiyon*, no. 524 (December 2004).
107. Çarkoğlu and Toprak, *Değişen Türkiye'de Din*, 23.
108. Ibid., 24.
109. Ibid., 71.
110. Ibid., 24.
111. *Radikal*, February 11, 2007.
112. Zehra Kasnakoğlu and Meltem Dayıoğlu, "Female Labor Force Participation and Earnings Differentials between Genders in Turkey," in *Economic Dimensions of Gender Inequality: A Global Perspective*, Janet M. Rives and Mahmood Yousefi eds. (Westport, CT: Praeger, 1997), 116.
113. Çarkoğlu and Toprak, *Değişen Türkiye'de Din*, 25.
114. Leela Gandhi, *Postcolonial Theory* (New York: Columbia University Press, 1998), 83.
115. Özer, *Psikolojik Bir Işkence Methodu Olarak Ikna Odaları*, 207–8.
116. Ayşe Kandırmaz, "Başörtüsü Yasağına Maruz Kalanların Dilinden Yasak Uygulamaları," in *Dünü, Bugünü ve Yarınıyla Başörtüsü*. Başörtüsüne Özgürlük Girişim Grubu ed. (Istanbul: Pınar Yayınları , 2005), 189.
117. *Yenişafak*, April 15, 2007.

118. Suat Kınıklıoğlu, "The Democratic Left Party: Kapikulu Politics Par Excellence," in *Political Parties in Turkey*, Metin Heper and Barry Rubin eds. (Abington: Routledge, 2002), 17.
119. Yavuz, *Islamic Political Identity in Turkey*, 199.
120. *Sabah*, January 27, 1995.
121. Yasin Aktay, "Diaspora and Stability: Constitutive Elements in a Body of Knowledge," in *Turkish Islam and the Secular State: The Gulen Movement*, M. Hakan Yavuz and John L. Esposito eds. (Syracuse, NY: Syracuse University Press, 2003), 146.
122. Nazlı Ilicak, "Beyaz Türkler," *Takvim*, March 1, 2007.
123. Kavakcı, *Başörtüsüz Demokrasi*, 110.
124. Perihan Mağden, "Zencileme," *Radikal*, May 15, 2003.
125. http://tr.wikipedia.org/wiki/Asker_Duas%C4%B1 retrieved on May 29, 2007.
126. Bekir Coşkun, "Göbeğini kaşıyan adam...," *Hürriyet*, May 3, 2007.
127. Ibid.
128. *Vakit*, 5/12/2007. Also see: *Radikal*, January 29, 2010, Davut Dursun, "Cumhurbaskanının halk tarafından secilmesi..." *Yenişafak*, January 18, 2007.
129. Yalçin Doğan, "Bu kültür benim kültürüm değil," *Hürriyet*, November 22, 2006.
130. Taha Akyol, "Tesettür, Suriye, Türkiye," *Milliyet*, December 28, 2004.
131. Nur Çintay, "Emine Erdoğan'ın kara çarşafı," *Radikal*, February 26, 2007.
132. Ibid.
133. Hıncal Uluç, "Kiyafetler!" *Sabah*, February 28, 2007.
134. Bekir Coşkun, "Türbanin dili vardir," *Hürriyet*, March 21, 2006.
135. Ibid.
136. Ertuğrul Özkök, "Beyaz Turklerin tasfiyesi mi," *Hürriyet*, April 21, 2006.
137. Said, *Orientalism*, 154.
138. Ibid.
139. Ibid., 42.
140. Ibid.
141. Ibid., 20–21.
142. Ahmet Kekeç, "Tesettür faciasi değil, Ertuğrul faciası," *Star*, December 21, 2006. Also see: *Hürriyet*, December 17, 2006, and *Sabah*, December 21, 2006.
143. *Vakit*, March 22, 2007. Also see: *Zaman*, June 7, 2009 and Reşat Petek, "Okuduğu müspet ilmin ve akılcı bilimin aksine taktıgı 'türban' altindaki zihni," *Zaman*, June 10, 2009.
144. Konya 1st District Court Decree, Esas no: 2007/40, Karar no: 2008/159.
145. *Sabah*, November 27, 2005. Also see: *Radikal*, October 3, 2005.

146. *Takvim*, November 20, 2004.
147. *Akşam*, March 20, 2007.
148. *Hürriyet*, November 12, 2005.
149. *Milliyet*, March 1, 2007.
150. Nuriye Akman, "Fatih Altaylı: Aydın Doğan'a ucuza mal oluyorum," *Zaman*, August 11, 2002.

5 In Search of Education, Employment, and More

1. Özkan, *Yemenimde Hare Var*, 38.
2. Ayşe Böhürler, "28 Subat en cok kadınları vurdu," *Yenişafak*, March 3, 2007.
3. Sibel Eraslan, *Fil Yazıları* (Istanbul: Birun Kültür Sanat Yayıncılık, 2002), 15.
4. Tamer Korkmaz, "Tabusal Alandan Enstantaneler," *Zaman*, September 1, 2006. Also see: *Milliyet*, August 30, 2006.
5. Kardam, *Turkey's Engagement with Global Women's Human Rights*, 46.
6. Merve Kavakcı, "Turkey's Test with Its Deep State," *Mediterranean Quarterly* vol. 20, no. 4 (Fall 2009): 83–97.
7. Kardam, *Turkey's Engagement with Global Women's Human Rights*, 73.
8. *Hürriyet*, July 27, 2005.
9. I.H.M. Ling, "Cultural Chauvinism and the Liberal International Order: "West versus Rest," in Asia's financial crisis," in *Power, Postcolonialism and International Relations: Reading Race, Gender and Class*, Geeta Chowdhry and Sheila Nair eds. (London: Routledge, 2004), 116.
10. Özlem Albayrak, "Göbeği açık türbanlı!" *Yenişafak*, August 25, 2005.
11. Ertuğrul Özkök, "Modern mahrem mi demiştiniz?" *Hürriyet*, August 6, 2005.
12. Said, *Orientalism*, 154.
13. Ertuğrul Özkök, "Modern mahrem mi demiştiniz?" *Hürriyet*, August 6, 2005.
14. Özyürek, "Public Memory as Political Battleground," 137.
15. Olivier Roy, "Introduction: Turkey on the Road to Europe," in *Turkey Today: A European Country?*, Olivier Roy ed. (London: Anthem Press, 2004), 2.
16. Kazım Güleçyüz, "Başörtüsü ve Çankaya," *Yeni Asya*, March 10, 2007.
17. Resul Tosun, "Toplumsal mutabakat," *Yenişafak*, June 22, 2005.
18. *Milliyet*, May 30, 2003.
19. *Radikal*, November 14, 2005.
20. *Sabah*, December 7, 2005.
21. Kazim Güleçyüz, "Başörtüsü ve Çankaya," *Yeni Asya*, March 10, 2007.
22. Edibe Sözen, "Gender Politics of the JDP," in *The Emergence of a New Turkey: Democracy and the AK Parti*, Hakan Yavuz ed. (Salt Lake City: The University of Utah Press, 2006), 270.

23. Ronald Inglehart, *Modernization and Postmodernization: Cultural, Economic, and Political Change in 43 Societies* (Princeton, NJ: Princeton University Press, 1997), 53.
24. *Sabah*, May 12, 2007.
25. *Yenişafak*, February 7, 2007.
26. *Milliyet*, October 2, 2006.
27. *Yenişafak*, April 23, 2006.
28. *Vatan*, September 30, 2006.
29. Tarhan, 270.
30. Nazlı Ilicak, "Dün de fişleniyordu, bugün de," *Bugün*, December 1, 2005.
31. *Hürriyet*, March 10, 2004.
32. *Constitutional Court decree on the closure of RP*: Esas no: 1997/1 Karar no: 1998/1, January 16, 1998.
33. *Yenişafak*, May 6, 2006.
34. Sözen, "Gender Politics of the JDP," 271.
35. Taceddin Ural, *Ankara Dükalığı* (Istanbul: Etkin Kitaplar, 2005), 231.
36. Ibid.
37. Ibid., 360.
38. *Zaman*, July 28, 2005.
39. *Milliyet*, January 24, 2005.
40. *Turkish Daily News*, July 19, 2006.
41. Neşe Düzel, "Hırsızlıgı Cumhurbaşkanı biliyor," *Radikal*, August 2, 2004.
42. *Milliyet*, December 9, 2005.
43. Adem Yavuz Arslan, "Yasak'çı yolsuzlar," *Aksiyon*, no. 255, October 23, 1999.
44. Mehmet Kenan Kaya, "Laikçi Hoca'nın fikrine güvenmeyin: Çalıntı cıkabilir!," *Akşam*, December 8, 2008.
45. Merve Kavakcı, "Turkey's Test with Its Deep State." *Mediterranean Quarterly*, vol. 20, no. 4 (Fall 2009): 83–97.
46. Chris Rumford, "Placing Democratization within the Global Frame," *The Sociological Review*, vol. 50, no. 2 (May 2002): 258–77.
47. *Yenişafak*, October 26, 2005.
48. http://www.europarl.europa.eu/sides/getDoc.do?Type=TA&Reference=P6-TA-2007-0031&language=EN retrieved on April 8, 2007.
49. *Yenişafak*, March 4, 2006.
50. ECHR Decree on *Kavakcı v. Turkey* (application no. 71907/01).
51. Wolf Blitzer, "Erdogan Interview," in *Wolf Blitzer Reports*, June 7, 2005 (http://transcripts.cnn.com/TRANSCRIPTS/0506/07/wbr.01.html retrieved on June 10, 2005).
52. White House, "*President Obama's Speech in Cairo*," June 4, 2009 (http://www.nytimes.com/2009/06/04/us/politics/04obama.text.html retrieved on February 7, 2010).

6 Conclusion: The Road Ahead: What's in Store for *Başörtülü Kadınlar*?

1. Noam Chomsky, *Hegemony Or Survival: America's Quest For Global Dominance* (New York: Henry Holt, 2003), 49.

Revisiting My Original Extrapolation: In Looking Back at a Distance

1. "Erdogan: Alevilik din degil; Ali ile alakalari yok," *Radikal*, February 22, 2013.
2 Merve Kavakci-Islam, *Basortusuz Demokrasi'de Adi Konmamis Darbe* (Istanbul: Timas Yayinlari, 2014), 335.
3. "Bekir Bozdag: Basortusu yasagi yok!," *Yenisafak*, March 1, 2013.
4. "Kilicdaroglu'ndan Sarigul aciklamasi," *Hurriyet*, September 8, 2013.
5. " Universitede artik turbana engel yok!," *Radikal*, February 2, 2011.
6. "Ortaogretimde basortu ozgurlugu," *Yeni Akit*, September 23, 2014.
7. Merve Kavakci, "25 sene 6 ay 2 gun," *Yeni Akit*, January 10, 2014.
8. Richard Peres, *Headscarf: The Day Turkey Stood Still* (London: Ithaca, 2012), 213.
9. Kavakci-Islam, *Basortusuz Demokrasi'de Adi Konmamis Darbe*, 11.
10. "Basortusuyle avukatlik yapilir," *Sabah*, January 25, 2013.
11. Merve Kavakci, "32 yildir bugunu bekledim," *Yeni Akit*, October 4, 2013.

BIBLIOGRAPHY

Abadan-Unat, Nermin. "Social Change and Turkish Women." In *Women in Turkish Society*. Nermin Abadan-Unat ed. Leiden: E.J. Brill, 1981.

Abu-Lughod, Lila. "The Romance of Resistance: Tracing Transformation of Power Through Bedouin Women." *American Ethnologist*, Vol. 17, no. 1 (February 1990): 41–55.

Adıvar, Halide Edip. "Dictatorship and Reforms in Turkey." *The Yale Review*, Vol. 19 (September 1929): 27–44.

———. *Yeni Turan*. Istanbul: Atlas Kitabevi, 1982.

Afetinan, Ayşe. *Tarih Boyunca Türk Kadınının Hak ve Görevleri*. Istanbul: Milli Eğitim Basımevi, 1968.

Ahmad, Feroz. "Politics and Islam in Modern Turkey." *Middle Eastern Studies*, Vol. 27, no. 1 (January 1991): 3–21.

———. *The Turkish Experiment in Democracy: 1950–1975*. London: C. Hurst, 1977.

Akagündüz, Özel Ülkü. "Başörtülü Kızlar Yasak Yorgunu." *Aksiyon*, no. 524 (December 2004).

Akça, Sakine. *Elveda Ankara*. Istanbul: Beyan Yayınları, 2005.

AKDER. *'baş' üstüne: Fotoğraflarla Başörtüsü Yasağının Yakın Tarihi, 'with' pleasure: Near History of the Scarf Ban by Photographs*. Istanbul: Kırkambar Yayınları, 1999.

Akit, September 5, 2000, January 5, 2000, December 1, 1996.

Akkent, Meral and Gaby Franger. *Başörtüsü*. Frankfurt: Dağyeli Yayınları, 1987.

Akman Nuriye. "Fatih Altaylı: Aydın Doğan'a ucuza mal oluyorum," *Zaman*, August 11, 2002.

Aksam. January 19, 2006, June 16, 2006, March 20, 2007.

Aksiyon. January 15, 2007.

Aksoy, Murat. *Başörtüsü-Türban: Batılılaşma-Modernleşme, Laiklik ve Örtünme*. Istanbul: Kitap Yayınevi, 2005.

Aktaş, Cihan. *Bacı'dan Bayan'a: Islamcı Kadınların Kamusal Alan Tecrübesi*. Istanbul: Kapı Yayınları, 2005.

———. *Tanzimattan Günümüze Kılık Kıyafet ve Iktidar1*. Istanbul: Nehir Yayınları, 1991.

———. *Türbanın Yeniden Icadı*. Istanbul: Kapı Yayınları, 2006.

Aktay, Yasin. "Diaspora and Stability: Constitutive Elements in a Body of Knowledge." In *Turkish Islam and the Secular State: The Gulen Movement*. M. Hakan Yavuz and John L. Esposito eds. New York: Syracuse University Press, 2003.

Akyol Taha. "Tesettür, Suriye, Türkiye," *Milliyet*, December 28, 2004.

Albayrak Özlem. "28 Subat'tan gelecek hayir," *Yenişafak*, February 27, 2007.

———. "Göbeği açik türbanlı!" *Yenişafak*, August 25, 2005.

Alkan Turan A. "Arabistan'a gidin Arabistan'a," *Zaman*, November 15, 2006.

Alverez, Sonia. "Women's Movement and Gender Politics in the Brazilian Transition." In *The Women's Movement in Latin America: Feminism and the Transition to Democracy*, Jane S. Jaquette ed. Boulder: Westview Press, 1994.

Araştırma ve Kültür Vakfı. *Albüm: Şule Yüksel Şenler*. Istanbul: AKVAKFI.

Arat, Yeşim. "From Emancipation to Liberation: The Changing Role of Women in Turkey's Public Realm." *Journal of International Affairs*, 54 (2000): 107–123.

———. *Political Islam in Turkey and Women's Organizations*. Istanbul: The Turkish Economic and Social Studies Foundation, 1999.

———. *The Patriarchal Paradox: Women Politicians in Turkey*. Cranbury, NJ: Associated University Presses, 1989.

Arat, Zehra. "Politics of Representation and Identity." In *Deconstructing Images of The Turkish Woman*. Zehra Arat ed. New York: Saint Martin Press, 1998.

Arendt, Hannah. *The Origins of Totalitarianism*. London: Andre Deutsch, 1967.

Arsan, Esra Doğru. "Medya-Güç Ideoloji Ekseninde Merve Kavakcı Haberlerinin Iki Farklı Sunumu." In *Haber Hakikat ve Iktidar Ilişkisi*. Çiler Dursun ed. Ankara: Elips Kitap-Kesit Tanıtım, 2004.

Arseven Serdar. "'12 yaş' meselesi!" *Vakit*, March 30, 2007.

———. "Bazı kızlar okula!" *Vakit*, March 8, 2007.

———. "Vakit okuyucusu da işte budur!" *Vakit*, February 3, 2007.

Arslan, Adem Yavuz. "Yasak'çı yolsuzlar." *Aksiyon*, no. 255, October 23, 1999.

Atatürk'ün Söylev ve Demeçleri II. Ankara: Türk Inkilap Tarihi Enstitüsü, 1989.

Atatürk'ün Söylev ve Demecleri (Istanbul: 1945–1952).

Aydemir, Sevket Süreyya. *Tek Adam Mustafa Kemal*. Istanbul: Remzi Kitabevi, 1988.

Aytar Volkan. "Monthly Monitoring Report," *TESEV* (February 2006): 4–5.

Bali, Rıfat N. "Atatürk'ün Dine Bakişi." *Toplumsal Tarih Dergisi*, no: 153 (Eylul: 2006).

Başgil, Ali Fuat. *27 Mayis Ihtilali ve Sebepleri*. Istanbul: Yağmur Yayınları, 1966.

Başyurt, Erhan. "Tel örgüler neyi ayırıyor?" *Bugün*, November 9, 2008.

Baykan, Ayşegül. "The Turkish Women: An Adventure in History." *Gender and History*, Vol. 6, no. 1 (April 1994): 101–116.

———. "Women between Fundamentalism and Modernity." In *Theories of Modernity and Postmodernity*. Bryan S. Turner ed. London: Sage, 1990.

Bayramoğlu Ali. "Başörtüsü sorunu dedikleri...," *Yenişafak*, November 23, 2002.

Bekir, Ilhami. "Ilk Adam." *Hava Kuvvetleri Dergisi*, No. 301 (November 1988): 55.

Benli, Fatma. *Legal Evaluation of the Ban Imposed on the University Students Who Wear Headscarf Subsequent to the ECHR's Ruling in Leyla Sahin v. Turkey*. Istanbul: AKDER, 2005.

———. *Başörtüsü ile Ilgili Hukuka Aykırılıkta Sınır Yok*. Istanbul: AKDER Yayınları, 2004.

Berkes Niyazi. *The Development of Secularism in Turkey*. Montreal: McGill Press, 1964.

Berktay, Fatmagül. *Tarihin Cinsiyeti*. Istanbul: Metis Yayınları, 2003.

Bildirici, Faruk. *Maskeli Leydi: Tekmili Birden Tansu Çiller*. Ankara: Ümit Yayıncılık, 1998.

Bock, Gisela and Susan James. "Introduction: Contextualizing equality and difference." In *Beyond Equality and Difference: Citizenship, Feminist Politics and Female Subjectivity*. Gisela Bock and Susan James eds. London: Routledge, 1992.

Böhürler Ayşe, "28 Subat en cok kadınları vurdu," *Yenişafak*, March 3, 2007.

Bollag, Burton. "A Ban on Islamic Head Scarves Unsettles Turkey's Universities." *The Chronicle of Higher Education*, Vol. 44, no. 33 (April 24, 1998): 59–60.

Bozdağlıoğlu, Yücel. *Turkish Foreign Policy and Turkish Identity: A Constructivist Approach*. New York: Routledge, 2003.

Brown, Wendy. *States of Injury: Power and Freedom in Late Modernity*. NJ: Princeton University Press, 1995.

Bugün. December 3, 2009.

Çalışlar, Ipek. *Latife Hanım*. Istanbul: Doğan Kitap, 2006.

Çaparoğlu, M. Bülent. *Meclis'te Başörtüsü Mücadelesi*. Istanbul: Şule Yayınları, 1998.

Caporal, Bernard. *Kemalizm ve Kemalizm Sonrasında Türk Kadını*. Ankara: Iş Bankası Kültür Yayınları, 1982.

Çarkoğlu, Ali and Binnaz Toprak. *Değişen Turkiye'de Din, Toplum ve Siyaset*. Istanbul: TESEV Yayınları, 2006.

Çemrek, Murat. "How Could the Rights to Education and Representation Challenge National Security? The Headscarf Conflict in Turkey Revisited." *Human Security Perspectives*, Vol. 1, no. 2 (2004): 52–58.

Chomsky, Noam. *Hegemony or Survival: America's Quest for Global Dominance*. New York: Henry Holt, 2003.

Chowdhry Geeta and Sheila Nair. "Power in a Postcolonial World: Race, Gender, and Class in International Relations." In *Power, Postcolonialism and International Relations: Reading race, gender and class*. Geeta Chowdhry and Sheila Nair eds. London: Routledge, 2004.

Çintay Nur. "Emine Erdoğan'ın kara çarşafı," *Radikal*, February 26, 2007.

Cizre, Ümit. "Lusting for Power and Undermining Democracy." In *Political Leaders and Democracy in Turkey*. Metin Heper, Sabri Sayari eds. Lanham: Lexington Books, 2002.

———. "From Ruler to Pariah: The Life and Times of the True Path Party." *Turkish Studies*, Special Edition, Metin Heper and Barry Rubin eds. Vol. 3, no. 1 (Spring 2002): 82–101.

Cizre, Ümit and Menderes Çınar. "Turkey 2002: Kemalism, Islamism, and Politics in the Light of the February 28 Process." *The South Atlantic Quarterly*, Vol. 102, nos. 2/3 (Spring/Summer 2003): 309–332.

Constitutional Court's Decree on the Closure of Fazilet Party, June 22, 2001.

Constitutional Court Decree on the closure of RP: Esas no: 1997/1 Karar no: 1998/1, January 16, 1998.

Constitutional Court Decree. Esas no: 1990/36, Karar no: 1991/8, April 9, 1991.

Council of State Decree. Esas no: 609 Karar no: 2809, November 13, 1992.

Coşkun Bekir. "Gobeğini kaşıyan adam...," *Hürriyet*, May 3, 2007.

———. "Türbanın dili vardir," *Hürriyet*, March 21, 2006.

Cumhuriyet. May 3, 1999.

Danıştay. 2. Dairesi, no. 3366/2005 K, 2004/4051 E, October 26, 2005.

———. *6. Daire kararı, no. 2001/1604, K, 2002/239*, March 22, 2002.

———. *8. Daire kararı*, Esas no: 1987/178 Karar no: 1988/512.

———. *8. Daire kararı*, Esas no: 1987/128 Karar no: 1987/486.

———. *8. Daire kararı, no. 1984/1574*, December 13, 1984.

———. *8. Daire kararı*, Esas no: 1983/207 Karar 1984 no: 330.

Delaney, Carol. "Untangling the Meanings of Hair in Turkish Society." *Anthropological Quarterly*, Vol. 67, no. 4 (October 1994): 159–172.

De Groot, Joanna. "Gender, Discourse and Ideology." In *Gendering the Middle East*, Deniz Kandiyoti ed. New York: Syracuse University Press, 1996.

Doğan Yalçın. "Bu kültür benim kültürüm değil," *Hürriyet*, November 22, 2006.

Devlet Planlama Teşkilatı Genelgesi # B.02.1.DPT. 070.73 (May 20, 2000).

Dilipak, Abdurrahman. *Inönü Dönemi*, 2. Baskı. Istanbul: Beyan Yayınları, 1989.

Dünden Bugüne Tercüman, April 16, 2005.

Dündar Can. "Karşi manifesto," *Milliyet*, April 27, 2006.

Durakbaşa, Ayşe. "Kemalism as Identity Politics in Turkey." In *Deconstructing Images of The Turkish Woman*. Zehra Arat ed. New York: Saint Martin Press, 1998.

Dursun, Davut. "Cumhurbaskanının halk tarafından secilmesi..." *Yenişafak*, January 18, 2007.

Düzel Neşe. "Hırsızlıgı Cumhurbaşkanı biliyor," *Radikal*, August 2, 2004.

———. "Türbanlı Kızlar Ultramodern!" *Radikal*, December 29,2003.

———. "Türban ikinci sinifligin kabulüdür," *Radikal*, November 17, 2003.

Eraslan, Sibel. "Başbakanım, bizim mayın tarlasına sıra ne zaman gelecek?" *Vakit*, June 5, 2009.

———. "Küçük dağlar, büyük dağlar," *Vakit*, April 7, 2005.

———. "Hatice Akçil'in suçu," *Vakit*, March 8, 2005.

Eraslan, Sibel. "Uğultular...Siluetler." In *90larda Turkiye'de Feminism*. Aksu Bora and Asena Gunal eds. Istanbul: Iletisim Yayınları, 2002.

———. *Fil Yazıları*. Istanbul: Birun Kültür Sanat Yayıncılık, 2002.

Erbakan, Necmeddin. "Mukaddesatçı Türk'e Beyanname." In *Salname 1390*. Istanbul: 1970.

Erol, Esra. *Sen Başımın Tacı: Bir Başörtüsü Günlüğü*. Istanbul: Birun Kültür Sanat Yayıncılık, 2001.

European Court of Human Rights. Decree on *Kavakcı v. Turkey*: Application no. 71907/01.

European Court of Human Rights. Application No: 42393/98, ECHR 2001-V.

———. Application No: 44774, Judgment: Strasbourg, November 10, 2005.

Flax, Jane. "Race/Gender and the Ethics of Difference: A Reply to Okin's 'Gender Inequality and Cultural Differences'." *Political Theory*, Vol. 23, no. 3 (Aug. 1995): 500–510.

———. "Beyond Equality: Gender, Justice and Difference." In *Beyond Equality and Difference: Citizenship, Feminist Politics and Female Subjectivity*. Gisela Bock and Susan James eds. London: Routledge, 1992.

Foucault, Michel. "The Subject and Power" In *Michel Foucault: Beyond Structuralism and Hermeneutics*. Herbert L. Dreyfus and Paul Rabinow eds. Chicago: University of Chicago Press, 1983.

———. *The History of Sexuality Vol. 1*. Robert Hurley trans. Harmondsworth: Penguin, 1981.

———. *The History of Sexuality: An Introduction Volume 1*. New York: Random House, 1978.

Gandhi, Leela. *Postcolonial Theory*. New York: Columbia University Press, 1998.

Geyikdağı, Mehmet Yaşar. *Political Parties in Turkey: The Role of Islam*. New York: Praeger, 1984.

Göçek, Fatma Müge. "To Veil or Not to Veil." *Interventions*, Vol. 1, no. 4 (1999): 521–535.

Göktürk Gülay. "KADER siyaset üstü mü?" *Bugün*, April 4, 2007.

———. "SMS'LERE SIĞMAZ," *Tercuman*, November 28, 2004.

Gökalp, Ziya. *Turkish Nationalism and Western Civilization*. Niyazi Berkes trans. Westport: Greenwood Press, 1981.

Göle, Nilüfer. "Islam in Public: New Visibilities and New Imaginaries." *Public Culture*, Vol. 14, no. 1 (2002): 173–190.

———. *The Forbidden Mahrem: Civilization and Veiling*. Ann Arbor: University of Michigan Press, 1996.

———. "Toward and Autonomization of Politics and Civil Society in Turkey." In *Politics in the Third Turkish Republic*. Metin Heper, Ahmet Evin eds. Boulder: Westview Press, 1994.

Göloğlu, Mahmut. *Devrimler ve Tepkileri 1924–1930*. Ankara: Basnur Matbaası, 1972.

———. *Turkiye Cumhuriyeti 1923*. Ankara: Basnur Matbaası, 1971.

Gönel, Aydın. *Araştırma Raporu: Önde gelen STK'lar*. Istanbul: Tarih Vakfı Yurt Yayınları, 1998.

Gönültaş Nuh. "Guncelleyelim dostlar, irticayı surekli guncelleyerek ancak varolabiliriz," *Bugün*, November 28, 2006.

Goodhart, Michael. "Human Rights and Non-State Actors: Theoretical Puzzles." In *Non-State Actors in the Human Rights Universe*. George Andreopoulos, Zehra F. Kabasakal Arat, Peter Juviler eds. CT: Kumarian Press, 2006.

Güleçyüz Kazım. "Başörtüsü ve Çankaya," *Yeni Asya*, March 10, 2007.

Gutmann, Amy. "Communitarian Critics of Liberalism." *Philosophy and Public Affairs*, Vol. 14, no. 3 (Summer 1985): 308–322.

Hale, William. Turkish Politics and the Military. London: Routledge, 1994.

Hale, William and Ergun Özbudun. *Islamism, Democracy and Liberalism in Turkey: The Case of the AKP.* Abingdon: Routledge, 2010.

Hatem, Mervat F. "Egyptian Discourses on Gender and Political Liberalization: Do Secularist and Islamist Views Really Differ?" *The Middle East Journal*, Vol. 48, no. 4 (Autumn 1994): 661–676.

Heper, Metin. *Ismet Inönü: The Making of a Turkish Statesman.* Leiden: Brill, 1998.

Holy Qur'an

Hürriyet. May 1, 1999, May 4, 1999, March 10, 2004, July 27, 2005, November 12, 2005, December 17, 2006.

Ilıcak Nazlı. "Beyaz Türkler," *Takvim*, March 1, 2007.

———. "Sokaktaki Tehlike: Başörtüsü," *Bugün*, February 11, 2006.

———. "Dün de fişleniyordu, bugün de," *Bugün*, December 1, 2005.

———. "Başörtüsü," *Yenişafak*, November 26, 2002.

Inglehart, Ronald. *Modernization and Postmodernization: Cultural, Economic, and Political Change in 43 Societies.* Princeton: Princeton University Press, 1997.

Inglehart, Ronald and Christian Welzel. *Modernization, Cultural Change, and Democracy: The Human Development Sequence.* Cambridge: Cambridge University Press, 2005.

Işın, Ekrem. "Tanzimat, Kadin ve Gundelik Hayat." *Tarih ve Toplum* (Mart: 1988): 22–24.

Istanbul Imam Hatip Okulu Yıllık Komitesi. *Istanbul Imam Hatip Okulu Yıllığı: 1971–1972.* Istanbul: 1972.

Jayawedana, Kumari. *Feminism and Nationalism in the Third World.* London: Zed Books, 1986.

Jenkins, Gareth. *Political Islam in Turkey: Running West, Heading East?* New York: Palgrave Macmillan, 2008.

Kadıoğlu, Ayşe. "Civil Society, Islam and Democracy in Turkey: A Study of Three Islamic Non-Governmental Organizations." *The Muslim World*, Vol. 95 (January 2005): 23–41.

Kalaycıoğlu, Ersin. "The Turkish Grand National Assembly: A Brief Inquiry into The Politics of Representation in Turkey." In *Turkey: Political, Social and Economic Challenges in the 1990s.* Ciğdem Balım, Ersin Kalaycıoğlu, Cevat Karataş, Gareth Winrow, and Feroz Yasamee eds. Leiden: E.J. Brill, 1995.

Kandırmaz, Ayşe. "Başörtüsü Yasağına Maruz Kalanların Dilinden Yasak Uygulamaları." In *Dünü, Bugünü ve Yarınıyla Başörtüsü.* Başörtüsüne Özgürlük Girişim Grubu ed. Istanbul: Pınar Yayınları, 2005.

Kandiyoti, Deniz. "Bargaining with Patriarchy." In *The Social Construction of Gender.* Judith Lorber and Susan A. Farrell eds. CA: Sage, 1991.

———. "Women and the Turkish State: Political Actors or Symbolic Pawns?" In *Women, Nation and State.* Nira Yuval-Davis and Floya Anthias eds. New York: St. Martin's Press, 1989.

Kara Mehmet. "Başörtüsü ve 'irtica'." *Yeni Asya*, September 10, 2006.

Karaalioğlu Mustafa. "Sezer'in affedilmez unutkanlıgı!" *Yenişafak*, October 29, 2003.

Karakaya, Hasan. "MHP güme gitmiş, Bay Osman Durmuş!" *Vakit*, February 4, 2010.

Karal, Ziya E. *Atatürk'ten Düşünceler*. Istanbul: Milli Eğitim Bakanlığı, 1981.

Kardam, Nüket. *Turkey's Engagement with Global Women's Human Rights*. Hants: Ashgate, 2005.

Kasnakoğlu, Zehra, Meltem Dayıoğlu. "Female Labor Force Participation and Earnings Differentials between Genders in Turkey." In *Economic Dimensions of Gender Inequality: A Global Perspective*. Janet M. Rives and Mahmood Yousefi eds. CT: Praeger, 1997.

Kavakcı, Merve. "Turkey's Test with Its Deep State." *Mediterranean Quarterly*, Vol. 20, no. 4 (Fall 2009): 83–97.

———. *Başörtüsüz Demokrasi*. Istanbul: Timaş Yayınları, 2004.

———. "Put This Woman in Her Place." *QNews*, no. 353 (January 2004): 30–32.

Kaya, Mehmet Kenan. "Laikçi Hoca'nın fikrine güvenmeyin: Çalıntı cıkabilir!," *Akşam*, December 8, 2008.

Keddie, Nikki and Lois Beck. "Introduction." In *Women in the Muslim World*. Nikki Keddie and Lois Beck eds. Cambridge, MA: Harvard University Press, 1978.

Kekeç, Ahmet. "Tesettür faciasi değil, Ertuğrul faciası," *Star*, December 21, 2006.

Keyman, Fuat E. "Türban-demokrasi ilişkisi," *Radikal2*, November 16, 2003.

Keyman, Fuat E. and Ahmet Içduygu. "Globalization, Civil Society and Citizenship in Turkey: Actors, Boundaries and Discourses." *Citizenship Studies*, Vol. 7, no. 2 (2003): 219–234.

Kınıklıoğlu, Suat. "The Democratic Left Party: Kapıkulu Politics Par Excellence." In *Political Parties in Turkey*. Metin Heper and Barry Rubin eds. Abington: Routledge, 2002.

Kırık, Hikmet. *Kamusal Alan ve Demokrasi: Örtünme Sorununu Yeniden Düşünmek*. Istanbul: Salyangoz Yayınları, 2005.

Konya 1st District Court Decree, Esas no: 2007/40, Karar no: 2008/159

Korkmaz, Tamer. "Şehit AnalarI icin de Ikna OdalarI Kurulmalı!" *Zaman*, November 3, 2006.

———. "Tabusal Alandan Enstantaneler," *Zaman*, September 1, 2006.

Kösebalaban, Hasan. "Party with Islamist Roots Set to Modernize Turkey." *Yale Global*, August 28, 2007.

Kuru, Ahmet. "Reinterpretation of Secularism in Turkey: The Case of Justice and Development Party." In *The Emergence of New Turkey: Democracy and the Ak Parti*. M. Hakan Yavuz ed. Salt Lake City: University of Utah Press, 2006.

Ling, I.H.M. "Cultural Chauvinism and the Liberal International Order: 'West versus Rest' in Asia's Financial Crisis." In *Power, Postcolonialism and International Relations: Reading race, gender and class*. Geeta Chowdhry and Sheila Nair eds. London: Routledge, 2004.

Lombardi, Ben. "Turkey—The Return of the Reluctant Generals?" *Political Science Quarterly*, Vol. 112, no. 2 (1997): 191–215.

Mağden Perihan. "Zencileme," *Radikal*, May 15, 2003.

Mahçupyan, Etyen. "Osmanlı'dan Günümüze Parçalı Kamusal Alan ve Siyaset." *Doğu Batı*, 5 (November–January 1998–1999): 22–48.

Mahmood, Saba. *Politics of Piety: The Islamic Revival and the Feminist Subject.* Princeton: Princeton University Press, 2005.

Mango, Andrew. *Atatürk: The Biography of the Founder of Modern Turkey.* New York: Overlook Press, 1999.

Mardin, Şerif. "Religion in Modern Turkey." *International Social Science Journal*, Vol. 29, no. 2 (1977): 279–297.

Marshall, Gül Aldikaçtı. "Ideology, Progress, and Dialogue: A Comparison of Feminist and Islamist Women's Approaches to the Issues of Head Covering and Work in Turkey." *Gender and Society*, Vol. 19 (February 2005): 104–120.

Mecham, R. Quinn. "From the Ashes of Virtue, A Promise of Light: The Transformation of Political Islam in Turkey." *Third World Quarterly*, Vol. 25, no. 2 (2004): 339–358.

Moghadam, Valentine M. "Gender and Revolutions." In *Theorizing Revolutions*, John Foran ed. London: Routledge, 1997.

Milli Gazete. November 9, 2008, August 28, 2005, October 13, 1989.

Milliyet. March 1, 2007, October 2, 2006, August 30, 2006, July 7, 2006, December 9, 2005, October 26, 2005, June 14, 2005, January 24, 2005, October 22, 2003, May 30, 2003, May 28, 2003, November 24, 2002, October 27, 1990.

Mohanty, Chandra Talpade. "Under Western Eye: Feminist Scholarship and Colonial Discourses." In *Third World Women and the Politics of Feminism*. Chandra Talpade Mohanty, Ann Russo, and Lourdes Torres eds. Indianapolis: Indiana University Press, 1991.

Molyneux, Maxine. "Mobilization Without Emancipation? Women's Interests, State, and Revolution." In *Transition and Development: Problems of Third World Socialism*. Richard R. Fagen, Carmen Diana Deere, and Jose Luis Coraggio eds. New York: Monthly Review Press, 1986.

Moore-Gilbert, Bart. *Postcolonial Theory: Context, Practices, Politics*. London: Verso, 1997.

Morgan, Jeanne. "More on Cosmetics." In *Cosmetics, Fashions and the Exploitation of Women*. Joseph Hansen and Evelyn Reed eds. New York: Pathfinder Press, 1986.

Nachmani, Amikam. *Turkey: Facing a New Millenium: Coping with Intertwined Conflicts*. Manchester: Manchester University Press, 2003.

Navaro-Yashin, Yael. *Faces of the State: Secularism and Public Life in Turkey*. Princeton: Princeton University Press, 2002.

Nüfus Etütleri Enstitüsü. *Turkiye Nüfus ve Sağlik Arastırması 2003*. Ankara: Hacettepe Üniversitesi Nüfus Etütleri Enstitüsü, 2004.

Okin, Susan Moller. "The Public/Private Dichotomy." In *Contemporary Political Theory*. Colin Farrelly ed. London: Sage, 2004.

Ökte, Faik. *The Tragedy of Turkish Capital Tax*. London: Croom Helm, 1964.

Olson, Robert. *Turkey-Iran Relations, 1979–2004: Revolution, Ideology, War, Coups and Geopolitics*. CA: Mazda, 2004.

Okyar, Osman. "Atatürk's quest for Modernism." In *Atatürk and the Modernization of Turkey*. Jacob Landau ed. Colorado: Westview Press, 1984.

ÖNDER. *İmam-Hatip Liseleri'nde Insan Hakları Ihlalleri*. Istanbul: ÖNDER, 2002.

"Ortaogretimde basortu ozgurlugu," *Yeni Akit*, September 23, 2014.

Özer, Demirkol Gulşen. *Psikolojik Bir Işkence Metodu Olarak Ikna Odaları*. Istanbul: Beyan Yayınları, 2005.

Özer, Ilbeyi. *Avrupa Yolunda Batılaşma ya da Batılılaşma: Istanbul'da Sosyal Değisimler*. Istanbul: Truva Yayınları, 2005.

Özkan, Fadime. *Yemenimde Hare Var: Dünden Yarına Başörtüsü*. Istanbul: Elest Yayınları, 2005.

Özkırımlı, Umut. *Theories of Nationalism: A Critical Introduction*. New York: Saint Martin's Press, 2000.

Özkök Ertuğrul. "Beyaz Türklerin tasfiyesi mi," *Hürriyet*, April 21, 2006.

———. "Yumurtalıkları alınan türbanlı," *Hürriyet*, December 21, 2006.

———. "Modern mahrem mi demiştiniz?" *Hürriyet*, August 6, 2005.

Özyürek, Esra. "Public Memory as Political Battleground: Islamist Subversions of Republican Nostalgia." In *The Politics of Public Memory in Turkey*. Esra Özyürek ed. New York: Syracuse University Press, 2007.

———. *Nostalgia for the Modern: State Secularism and Everyday Politics in Turkey*. NC: Duke University Press, 2006.

Parla Taha and Andrew Davison. *Corporatist Ideology in Kemalist Turkey*. New York: Syracuse University Press, 2004.

Petek, Reşat. "Okudugu müspet ilmin ve akılcı bilimin aksine taktıgı 'türban' altindaki zihni," *Zaman*, June 10, 2009.

Pitkin, Hanna Fenichel. *The Concept of Representation*. CA: University of Berkley Press, 1967.

Poulton, Hugh. *Top Hat, Grey Wolf and Crescent: Turkish Nationalism and the Turkish*

Republic. New York: New York University Press, 1997.

Radikal. January 29, 2010, September 20, 2007, February 11, 2007, November 14, 2005, October 3, 2005.

Resmi Gazete. No. 23982, March 3, 2000, no. 20679, October 28, 1990, no. 20216, June 5, 1989, no. 17849, October 25, 1982, no. 17537, December 7, 1981, no. 14506, April 13, 1973.

Resmi Gazete. December 27, 1988, December 4, 1988, January 8, 1987.

Rousseau, David L. *Identifying Threats and Threatening Identities: The Social Construction of Realism and Liberalism*. CA: Stanford University Press, 2006.

Roy, Olivier. "Introduction: Turkey on the Road to Europe." In *Turkey Today: A European Country?* Olivier Roy ed. London: Anthem Press, 2004.

Rubin, Barry. "Introduction-Turkey's Political Parties: A Remarkably Important Issue." In *Political Parties in Turkey*. Metin Heper and Barry Rubin eds. Abingdon: Routledge, 2002.

Rumford, Chris. "Placing Democratization within the Global Frame." *The Sociological Review*, Vol. 50, no. 2 (May 2002): 258–277.

Sabah. June 4, 2007, May 12, 2007, December 21, 2006, December 8, 2005, December 7, 2005, November 27, 2005, June 14, 2005, October 18, 2004, June 19, 2003, January 27, 1995.

Said, Edward W. *Orientalism*. New York: Vintage Books, 1978.

Saktanber, Ayse. *Living Islam: Women, Religion and the Politicization of Culture in Turkey*. London: I.B. Tauris, 2002.

Scott, James C. *Weapons of the Weak: Everyday Forms of Peasant Resistance*. New Haven: Yale University Press, 1985.

Scott, Joan Wallach. *Only Paradoxes to Offer: French Feminists and the Rights of Men*. Cambridge, MA: Harvard University Press, 1996.

Sered, Susan Starr. "'Woman' as Symbols and Women as Agents: Gendered Religious Discourse and Practices." In *Revisioning Gender*. Myra Marx Ferree, Judith Lorber, and Beth B. Hess eds. CA: Alta Mira Press, 2000.

Shively, Kim. "Religious Bodies And The Secular State: The Merve Kavakcı Affair." *Journal of Middle East Women's Studies*, Vol. 1, no. 3 (Fall 2005): 47–72.

Sılay, Mehmet. *Mecliste Merve Kavakcı Olayı*. Istanbul: Birey, 2000.

Sözen, Edibe. "Gender Politics of the JDP." In *The Emergence of A New Turkey: Democracy and the AK Parti*. Hakan Yavuz ed. Utah: University of Utah Press, 2006.

Star. January 14, 2009.

Süter Şakir. "Demirel konusunca," *Aksam*, May 2, 2006.

Tachau, Frank. "From Idealist to Pragmatist." In *Political Leaders and Democracy in Turkey*. Metin Heper and Sabri Sayari eds. Lenham: Lexington Books, 2002.

Takvim. November 20, 2004.

Tarhan, Nevzat. *Psikolojik Savaş: Gri Propaganda*. Istanbul: Timas Yayınları, 2006.

Taş, Fahri N. *Atatürk Ilkeleri ve Inkılapları Tarihi II*. Istanbul: Sahhaflar Kitap Sarayi, 1995.

TBMM Insan Haklarını Inceleme Komisyonu, *Cerrahpaşa Tıp Fakültesinde Dr. Şükran Erdem'le Ilgili Iddiaların Incelenmesine Dair Alt Komisyon Raporu*, 1/ Nisan/ 1997.

T.C. Cumhuriyet Başsavcılığı. *Fazilet Partisinin Kapatılması Istemiyle Yargıtay Cumhuriyet Başsavcılığı'nca Anayasa Mahkemesi'ne Açılan Davanın Iddianamesi*. July 5, 1999.

———. *Fazilet Partisi'nin Kapatılması Istemiyle Açılan Davanın Iddianamesi, No. SP.95 Hz.1999/116*. Ankara: TC. Yargitay Cumhuriyet Başsavcılığı, May 7, 1999.

———. *Refah Partisinin Kapatılması Istemiyle Yargitay Cumhuriyet Başsavcılığı'nca Anayasa Mahkemesi'ne Açılan Davanın Iddianamesi*. May 21, 1997.

———. "Refah Partisinin Kapatılması Istemiyle Yargitay Cumhuriyet Başsavcılığı'nca Anayasa Mahkemesi'ne Açılan Davanın Iddianamesi RP'nin Cevabı," Esas no: 1997/1, October 6, 1997.

T.C. Genelkurmay Başkanlığı. Letter to Yüksek Öğretim Kurumu Başkanlığı, no: 010306 signed by Çevik Bir, July 14, 1998.

T.C. Denizli/Çivril Gürpınar Belediye Başkanlığı, Sayı:M.20.8.GUP.0.10.0.0.0.0.1_/_218

Tempo Dergisi. August 17, 2006.

Tezcan, Demet. *Bir Çığır Öyküsü: Şule Yüksel Şenler.* Istanbul: Timas Yayınları, 2007.

The Economist. June 24, 2006.

The Economist. November 18, 2000.

Today's Zaman. February 3, 2010.

Toprak, Binnaz. "Islam and the Secular State in Turkey." In *Turkey: Political, Social and Economic Challenges in the 1990s.* Cigdem Balim, Ersin Kalaycıoğlu, Cevat Karataş, Gareth Winrow, and Feroz Yasamee eds. Leiden: E.J. Brill, 1995.

Tosun Resul. "Toplumsal mutabakat," *Yenişafak,* June 22, 2005.

Turgut Serdar. "Türban meselesi konusunda ilk kez açıklıkla konuştu," *Akşam,* December 7, 2005

Turkish Daily News. July 19, 2006.

Tursan, Huri. *Democratization in Turkey: The Role of Political Parties.* Brussels: P.I.E-Peter Lang, 2004.

Ülsever Cüneyt. "Türban meselesiyle ilgili somut bir öneri," *Hürriyet,* June 22, 2005.

Uluç Hıncal. "Kıyafetler!" *Sabah,* February 28, 2007.

Ünal, Zeki. *Anarşi: Kainat Nizami Anarşiyi Reddeder.* Ankara, 1992.

Ural, Taceddin. *Ankara Dukalığı.* Istanbul: Etkin Kitaplar, 2005.

Uskan Arda. "Asmayalım da besleyelim mi," *Takvim,* January 25, 2010.

Vakit. November 8, 2008, May 12, 2007, March 22, 2007, July 20, 2006, March 27, 2006, March 23, 2006, August 28, 2005, October 25, 2002, October 10, 2002, October 5, 2002.

Volkan D., Vamik and Norman Itzkowitz. *The Immortal Atatürk: A Psychobiography.* Chicago: University of Chicago Press, 1984.

Vatan. September 13, 2005, November 20, 2006, September 30, 2006.

Wall Street Journal. June 13, 1997.

Weber, Max. *Economy and Society: An Outline of Interpretive Sociology.* Edited by Guenther Roth and Claus Wittich, Vol. 1. New York: Bedminster Press, 1968.

White House. "*President Obama's Speech in Cairo,*" June 4, 2009.

White, Jenny. "The Islamist Paradox." In *Fragments of Culture: The Everyday of Modern Turkey.* Deniz Kandiyoti and Ayşe Saktenber eds. New Brunswick, NJ: Rutgers University Press, 2002.

———. *Islamist Mobilization in Turkey: A Study in Vernacular Politics.* Seattle: University of Washington Press, 2002.

Yargıtay Cumhuriyet Başsavcılığınca Fazilet Partisi'nin Kapatılması Istemiyle Açılan Davanın Iddianamesi. No. SP.95 Hz.1999/116 (Ankara: TC. Yargıtay Cumhuriyet Başsavcılığı, May 7, 1999).

Yavuz, Hakan. *Islamic Political Identity in Turkey.* New York: Oxford University Press, 2003.

Yavuz, Hakan. "Cleansing Islam from the Public Sphere." *Journal of International Affairs*, 54 (2000): 20–42.

Yayla, Atilla. "Ahlak, Hukuk ve Başörtüsü Yasağı." *Liberal Düşünce Topluluğu*, December 14, 2004.

Yenişafak. April 15, 2007, February 7, 2007, August 18, 2006, July 21, 2006, May 6, 2006, March 23, 2006, March 4, 2006, February 10, 2006, January 27, 2006, January 19, 2006, January 7, 2006, December 25, 2005, December 3, 2005, October 26, 2005, June 14, 2005, June 29, 2004, April 23, 2003, January 11, 2001.

Yetkin Murat. "Siyasette türban açmazı," *Radikal*, June 22, 2005.

Yıldız Ali Ihsan. "Postmodern Türban," *Radikal2*, July 2, 2006.

YOK Decision. No. 84.35.527, May 10, 1984.

Young, Iris Marion. "The Logic of Masculinist Protection: Reflections on the Current Security State." In *Women and Citizenship*. Marilyn Friedman ed. Oxford: Oxford University Press, 2005.

Young, Robert. *Postcolonialism: An Historical Introduction*. Boston, MA: Blackwell, 2001.

Young, Robert J.C. *Postcolonialism: A Very Short Introduction*. Oxford: Oxford University Press, 2003.

Zaman. June 7, 2009, May 23, 2009, November 7, 2008, March 23, 2007, August 24, 2006, July 28, 2005, July 13, 2005, May 27, 2005, April 6, 2005, April 25, 2004, October 4, 2002, June 29, 2002.

Zayzafoon, Lamia Ben Youssef. *The Production of the Muslim Women: Negotiating Text, History, and Ideology*. Baltimore, MD: Lexington Books, 2005.

Zivi, Karen. "Feminism and the Politics of Rights: A Qualified Defense of Identity-Based Rights Claiming." *Politics and Gender*, Vol. 1, no. 3 (September 2005): 377–397.

Internet Sources

http://cmiskp.echr.coe.int/tkp197/view.asp?item=2&portal=hbkm&action=html&highlight=sahin%20%7C%20turkey%20%7C%2044774/98&sessionid=9971709&skin=hudoc-pr-en, retrieved on May 1, 2007.

http://nkg.die.gov.tr/1990.asp?gosterge=16&Submit=G%F6r%FCnt%FCle, retrieved on May 29, 2007.

http://transcripts.cnn.com/TRANSCRIPTS/0506/07/wbr.01.html, retrieved on June 10, 2005.

http://tr.wikipedia.org/wiki/Atat%C3%BCrk%27%C3%BCn_T%C3%BCrk_Gen%C3%A7li%C4%9Fine_Hitabesi, retrieved on May 22, 2007

http://www.ahmettasgetiren.com.tr/gunluk.php, retrieved on February 2, 2006.

http://www.anayasa.gen.tr/1961ay.htm, retrieved on April 21, 2007.

http://www.anayasa.gov.tr/general/icerikler.asp?contID=363&curID=98&menuID=58, retrieved on April 21, 2007.

http://www.die.gov.tr/tkba/t098.xls, retrieved on March 21, 2007 http://www.europarl.europa.eu/sides/getDoc.do?Type=TA&Reference=P6-TA-2007-0031&language=EN, retrieved on April 8, 2007.

http://www.mazlumder.org/ana.php?konu=duyuru&id=25&lang=tr, retrieved on March 21, 2007.

http://www.nytimes.com/2009/06/04/us/politics/04obama.text.html, retrieved on February 7, 2010.

http://www.ak-der.org/tr/gundem/guncel-haberler/1207-basortusu-yasag.html, retrieved on February 9, 2010.

http://www.tbmm.gov.tr/komisyon/insanhaklari/belge/kr_20sukranerdem.pdf, retrieved on February 16, 2010.

INDEX

CPSIA information can be obtained at www.ICGtesting.com
Printed in the USA
LVOW04s1922040315

429282LV00012B/259/P

9 781137 484734